A Goodly Heritage

The lines are fallen unto me in pleasant places; yea, I have a goodly heritage.

Psalm 16.6

One of a list of books in the cultural history
of Western Pennsylvania—made possible
through a grant-in-aid from
The Buhl Foundation of Pittsburgh.

Frontispiece

" . . . if I should die or be killed by the Indians before I come back . . . . "
The Will of John Bredy, first will recorded in Allegheny County, 1789.

In the Name of god Amen I John Brady of
one thousand eleven hundred and Eighty Eight St John Brady
of franklin County and State of pennsylvania Lay man being now
on the Living from the mouth of yough River to not kindness of
the health of mine and Getting to mind the mortally of my body &
knowing that it is apointed to all men once to dy, It maid
this my Last Wile and testament, that is to say first of all
I do bequeath my soul to god who give it Not Inedoting but at
the General Resurection I shal Receive the Same again by
the mighty power of god I say tacking my Wourtly Estate
which it hath pleased god to bless me with I do by these
presents apoint John Smith my Whole and Sole Executor
to Give him all my Wourtly Estate Real & personal
and to his own and to be at his own Disposal for Every I
do die or be killed by the providions before I come
that he is to pay this my Just Debts give under
my hand this day and year above Written

                                                    John Brady

                                                    George Armstrong

                                                    John McLaughlin

A Goodly Heritage

Earliest Wills on an American Frontier

Ella Chalfant

UNIVERSITY OF PITTSBURGH PRESS

Library of Congress Catalog Card Number: 55-6875

Copyright, 1955
First Printing, June 1955
Second Printing, November 1955
University of Pittsburgh Press
Printed in U.S.A.

For my brothers, Charles and Frank

Acknowledgments

Many people have been kind and encouraging as I worked on this book—too many to name them all. I thank here only a few, hoping that their names may stand for themselves and for others.

First of all I thank Mr. Gwilym A. Price, whose original suggestion has been the basis of this study. At the time I started my work he was the president of the Peoples-Pittsburgh Trust Co., where I was the librarian.

For their interest and encouragement I am grateful to Mr. Robert C. Downie, chairman of the Board, and Mr. John H. Lucas, who is now president of Peoples First National Bank and Trust Co.; Mr. Robert D. Ferguson, vice president in charge of the Trust Department; and Mr. Malcolm E. Lambing, vice president in charge of the Trust Investment Department.

I am indebted, too, to the Purse Company of Chattanooga, Tennessee, whose staff artists made our fine illustrations from my notes at a time when the bank was having brochures made to advertise Trust Department services.

For help in writing and research I wish to thank the following: Mr. Percival Hunt, Mr. Henry C. Fisher, and Mr. Charles R. Crow of the Department of English; Mrs. Lois Mulkearn of the Darlington Library, University of Pittsburgh; Miss Rose Demorest and the staff of the Pennsylvania Room, Carnegie Library of Pittsburgh; Mr. Franklin Holbrook, Historical Society of Western Pennsylvania; Mr. Raymond Cristina; Mr. Oscar Emrick, Allegheny County Law Library; and Mr. William H. Mitchell, verger of Trinity Cathedral.

A special thank you goes from me to Mr. and Mrs. Wm. Graham Heiner, who have made available photostats of old maps to clarify wills.

Finally, for their generous assistance in providing photostats of original documents and numerous old wills which I examined at first hand, I owe a debt of gratitude to the late Mr. John M.

Huston, register of wills in Allegheny County; Mr. Bernard Goodwin, the present register of wills; Mr. William Shaffer, deputy register of wills; Mr. Fred Rockman, probate clerk; and other members of the staff in the Register's Office.

Mr. J. P. Russell, Jr., of the Russell Index Company, kindly gave us permission to reproduce the *Master Russell Index*.

Mr. Theodore Bowman's maps, his lettering on the dust jacket, and his drawing of the head piece for the final chapter have helped beautify the format beyond the matching with any words of gratitude.

ELLA CHALFANT

Introduction

In the files of the Office of the Register of Wills, City-County Building, each in its individual numbered envelope, are the wills made by men and women in the late eighteenth and early nineteenth centuries, when Allegheny County, Pennsylvania, was an American frontier. This book is concerned with these wills.

The very earliest of them were written when Pittsburgh was little more than a clearing in the wilderness. They are the wishes of people who hoped the land which they had carved out of the wilderness would be home for their children's children.

The names of those who signed and those who witnessed them sometimes are names familiar on city and county landmarks —streets and buildings and businesses. None of the will-makers are storybook people; they lived and worked and planned right here, where we live and work and plan, at the Point, in the Diamond, in Old Allegheny, on farms and in villages nearby—and they are vital still. Casual references to everyday matters illumine the thinking and the values which stirred their generation, faraway, yet close.

As you read their formal or their homely phrasing you are reading more than a cold legal document. You are reading the meaning of a life.

Often there is even a kind of perfection in the words. What matters most gets into a will—what the man truly believes, what he counts precious enough to want continued in the lives of his children or grandchildren. To bequeath pots and kettles that were hard to come by was important. A clock was a treasure; a book, above price—even for a man who could sign only "his Mark."

Through these early wills we today can know the social background of the frontier—the dress, the business, the economic situation when whiskey was an honored medium of exchange; when soldiers' bonuses were bartered for land grants; when slaves were bought and sold and bequeathed to friends and relatives or set free to make their own new lives.

Some wills are scribbled; others are formally inscribed; some are pompous; others are humorous, even eccentric. But all of them, even though ink-soaked, broken, or faded, are majestic bits of paper. They are the very voices of people with whom we share across the years hopes, frustrations, successes, and prayers.

For her book Miss Chalfant read one hundred of the Allegheny County Will Books, and then selected wills from the first three; all of her selections are wills preserved in the vaults of the Register of Wills. Through them she was led to read colonial newspapers, journals, histories, genealogies, tombstones—anything which could add to her understanding of the will-makers and the Pittsburgh in which they lived. To her the wills bequeath a rich legacy—richer than money—for us who have followed them into the "Western Country." It is, she shows, a legacy of faith and vision and high adventure, which like them we can cherish and enrich and pass on to those who follow us into the frontiers of hope and opportunity.

AGNES L. STARRETT

Editor, University of Pittsburgh Press

TABLE OF CONTENTS

LIST OF ILLUSTRATIONS

Foreword

The land around the "Forks of the Ohio" is probably our country's richest historical field. This land, because of its natural resources, its terrain, and the kind of people who settled it, became a gateway through which the American way of life pushed farther and farther west.

It was, in its earliest history, a prize coveted by both French and English. And during a series of bitter conflicts each of these nations possessed it in turn.

The major conflict over the land started when the French built a chain of forts extending from the St. Lawrence to the Mississippi, intending to fence in the English against the sea— and eventually to push them into it. For a while victory went to the French, but when England, with the help of colonial troops, took three of the French forts in 1758, France's chain was broken. And when Quebec was captured in 1759, France turned over to England her claim on Canada and all her claims east of the Mississippi. From that time on our own country's language has been English.

From the first, the site which is now Pittsburgh was the center of Indian trade. One of the many Indian trails from the east to the west was known as "Nemackolin's Path." Both George Washington and General Braddock used and improved that trail which, later, became "Braddock's Road." The opening up of Braddock's and later Forbes's Road made easy the emigration from beyond the Allegheny Mountains.

People settled in Western Pennsylvania, either because the beauty of the country appealed to them or because industry attracted them. Sometimes they found opportunity to build a ferry where roads crossed rivers; sometimes the need for more boats suggested their settling down at Brownsville or Elizabeth and going into the boat building business. Pittsburgh grew and prospered, as villages and towns sprung up all around it, or as people followed the highways through it to locate on new lands beyond the rivers.

The "Point"—land jutting out into the rivers—was the pioneer scene of events and inventions and enterprises which have helped make America great. Fort Pitt was a stronghold throughout the French and Indian War and throughout the border skirmishes. It was an arsenal of supplies during the American Revolution and this it has been in all wars since. All we have left of old Fort Pitt is Bouquet's little blockhouse in the Point Park. Thousands of travelers, from the beginning of the nineteenth century, have come and still come in and out of Pittsburgh. Today's rebuilding of the Point—the recreation area which marks the old fort and the other historical sites there—will bring more visitors to Pittsburgh. Pittsburgh will be honored as it should be by those who follow the old trails of history.

The men and women who lived in the shadow of the early fort cleared the wilderness. They pioneered in making America strong and good. Some of them are not recorded in the usual histories and have long since been forgotten. Perhaps through the wills in this book we shall be able better to appreciate what even these forgotten individuals did for us, and perhaps through their last wishes we can realize how very fortunate we are to be living here at the "Forks of the Ohio" in the shadow of their "Endless Mountains," in our own city of Pittsburgh, which their courage and vision helped build.

Allegheny County's Oldest Wills

JOHN BREDY—*If I Should be Killed by the Indians . . .*
Dated April 14, 1788—Recorded March 31, 1789

When the population of Pittsburgh was little more than 500, when families on outlying farms had to be on guard against marauding Indians and prowling animals, the first will was recorded in the newly created Allegheny County.

The Frontispiece illustration is from a photostat, made in earlier years, of the first will; now the 7½ by 6-inch document is crumbled and worn. Mending tape about three-quarters of an inch wide covers its broken folds and reinforces its ragged edges. The handwriting of the will seems to be that of John McLaughlin, one of the witnesses, and not the handwriting of John Bredy himself.

In the name of God, Amen, this fourteenth day of Aprile one thousand Seven Hundred and Eighty Eight I John Bredy of franklin County and State of Pennsylvania Lay man being Now on my Journey from the Mouth of Yough River to post Vinston on the Wabash River and Calling to Mind the Mortality of my body & Knowing that it is Apointed for All men once to Dye, I Maick this my Last Will and testament, that is to Say first of All I Recommend my Soul to God, & as tuching my Wourldly Estate Wherewith it hath pleased God to Bless me With, I do by thease presants Appoint John McKee my

3

Whole and Soal Executor and I give him All my Wourldly Estate Real & Personal to be his own and to be at his own Disposal for Ever, if I Should Die or be Killed by the Indians before I Come Back only he is to pay All my Just Debts given under my hand this Day and year Above Written.

Presant

Georg Armstrong

John McLaughlin

Whether John Bredy was killed by Indians, as he feared, we do not know. The mouth of the Yough River to which he was journeying when he made the will, even then, was a danger spot. It had been dangerous, off and on, for more than thirty years.

It was not until Mad Anthony Wayne won the battle at Fallen Timbers, 1794, that the settlers in Allegheny County were entirely free from the fear of Indian attacks. In the *Pittsburgh Gazette* of the 1780's there are frequent accounts of people murdered by Indians. This seems very strange today when what remains of the Indians in Allegheny County are the pleasant and musical names they gave to our rivers and mountains: Allegheny, Monongahela, Ohio.

The executor and the sole beneficiary of Mr. Bredy's will, John McKee, was the founder of New Town at the mouth of the Yough, a town later called "McKee's Port."

JAMES WHITAKER—*I give to Elinor . . . her liberty.*

Dated June 16, 1788—Recorded June 15, 1789

The second will recorded in Allegheny County is that of James Whitaker, dated June 16, 1788, at Washington County. Although this will is numbered *1*, in the records, it was not probated until June 15, 1789. The will of John Bredy was probated on March 31, 1789, and so it is actually the first Allegheny County will to be recorded. Calling the Whitaker will Number *1* is not a serious error; for the Whitaker will actually follows the Bredy will in sequence in the hand-copied books filed in the Register's Office; but there is something very good about having Number *1*, a will to free a slave.

Mr. Whitaker made his "mark," but he did not put down the usual X; instead, he wrote something like a capital M or like an Indian Sign; Indian autographs were well known at that time in Western Pennsylvania. Whatever it is, James Whitaker's mark is distinctive and it probably had meaning to him, even if we cannot see its significance. Mrs. Whitaker, when she was required to "sign" as executrix of her husband's will, made the same kind of mark, but hers was a bit smaller.

From the text of this will we infer that Mr. Whitaker had come from Maryland and had probably earned in war service the money he mentions in the following bequests:

. . . I give to my daughter Charlotte one hundred pounds lawfull money of that money that is at Maryland when it is gained by law.

. . . I give to my daughter Elizabeth one hundred pounds of the same money that is at Maryland when it is gained by law.

. . . I give to my son James eighty pounds of the same money which is at Maryland when it is gained by law.

Also I give to my son Samuel eighty pounds of the same money which is at Maryland when it is gained by law.

His will begins directly with bequests. There is no preamble to the following paragraphs:

To my dearly beloved wife Catherine whom I constitute make and ordain sole Executrix of this my last will and Testament, her feather bed and furniture, a cow and calf, mare, saddle and bridle, a Negro boy and a Mulatto girl, the half of the Saw Mill Except she marries again, and the Third of all my lands, messuages and Tenements her life time.

Also I give to my son Aaron one Third Part of my land, viz., the East "end" and beginning at Whitesells Run and running square across the Monongahela after the death of my dearly beloved wife.

Also I give to my son Abraham one-third part of the land square through beginning where my son Aaron's part leaves off, a horse, saddle, bridle, a cow and calf, a feather bed and furniture.

Also I give to my son Isaak the third part of the land square through the beginning where my son Abraham's leaves off likewise the half of the Saw Mill and at his mother's death the whole of the Saw

Mill and a mare, saddle and bridle a cow and calf, a feather bed and furniture.

That James Whitaker had other land possessions appears in this advertisement from the *Gazette*, February 16, 1788:

TO BE SOLD FOR CASH

Five hundred and 95 acres of valuable improved land, situate on the Monongahela river, 8 miles from Pittsburgh. The improvements are, a good square log dwelling house, stables, an excellent peach and apple orchard, good meadow, 100 acres of clear land under good fence, and saw mill in good order. An indisputable title will be given the purchaser. The terms are one half to be paid in hand, for the remainder a credit will be given for seven years, the purchaser giving bond, bearing interest with approved security.

In addition to the "lawfull" money given to his two daughters, his favorite, Elizabeth, was also given "a horse, saddle and bridle, a cow and a calf and a feather bed and furniture." Besides, after her mother's death she was to come into possession of "Cass, the mulatto girl."

Mr. Whitaker's will concludes with his bequest to his slave. "Also, at my death, I give to Elinor, a negro wench, her liberty."

ALLEGIANCE TO PENNSYLVANIA

Although this item is not a will, it seems appropriate to include it among the earliest bequests in Allegheny County.

Oath of Allegiance to Pennsylvania
Pennsylvania Archives: second series, v. 3, p. 7

We, the subscribers, do swear (or affirm) that we renounce and refuse all allegiance to George the Third, King of Great Britain, his heirs and successors, and that we will be faithful and bear true allegiance to the Commonwealth of Pennsylvania as a free and independent State, and that we will not at any time do, or cause to be done, any matter or thing that will be prejudicial or injurious to the freedom and independence thereof, as declared by Congress, and also that we will discover or make known to some one justice of the peace of the said State all treasons and traitorous conspiracies which we now know or

6

hereafter shall know to be formed against this or any of the United States of America.

Among the Western Pennsylvanians who took this oath of allegiance were John Negley (the record shows the name spelled Neglee), a Virginian, and Stephen Lowrey, from Maryland. General Negley's pledge is recorded as of July 3, 1777, and Colonel Lowrey's is recorded as of July 22, 1777. Their oaths stand as symbols of loyalty for all who lived in Pittsburgh, to Pennsylvania and to the nation.

THE MOUNTAINS AND THE RIVERS

Even yet we are reminded that tribes of Indians roamed our hills and valleys and paddled silent canoes on our rivers, because the names they gave them are still there. These names, too, are a heritage, real and lasting.

They called the Point, where the two rivers meet, "Da-un-daga"—meaning the *forks*.

Some authorities tell us that the name "Allegheny" was given to the mountains by the first English settlers, who got it from the Indians (the Alligewis), and that the word means *endless*.

At first, the Ohio and the Allegheny Rivers were regarded as one river, the Allegheny being but a part of the Ohio. The French spoke of this long stream as "LaBelle Riviere," which is a literal translation of the name the Seneca Indians had for the *Ohio*, or "Ho-he-yu": *Beautiful River*. Allegheny County, of course, was named after the mountains, not the river, and the river got its name from the mountains, too.

It was the Delaware Indians who gave us the name for the Monongahela River. In their language, it has been said, the word meant: "falling-in banks; or high banks or bluffs, breaking down and falling off in places." How descriptive it is! And who would care to exchange for any other name the musical syllables *Monongahela*.

It is indeed appropriate that the hills and rivers, our oldest and most enduring heritage, should bear the names given them by the Indians.

7

Four Early Intestates

The earliest settlers of Penn's Woods in their first body of colonial laws provided for the just distribution of the estates of the deceased. When the first Provincial Council enacted the Great Law, at Chester, on December 7, 1682, among the rights it guaranteed to the individual was the right to hand down private property. A man's *will*—the selection of his heirs—has been respected in Pennsylvania ever since.

The Great Law also insured equitable distribution of the estates of intestates. Where no will was made real estate was to be distributed among all the direct heirs of the deceased. One half the land purchased after debts were contracted was reserved for the payment of those debts. Land purchased before the debts were contracted could not be attached for the payment of debts.

The legislators created at Philadelphia an Office of the Register of Wills to carry out the civil functions which in England were performed by ecclesiastical tribunes. Until the Revolution the power of appointing deputy registers in the other counties remained with the Register-General.

After the *Declaration of Independence* had annulled the authority of the King of England, the Pennsylvania General Assembly created new offices "for the probate of wills and granting letters of administration." An act of March 14, 1777, appointed registers of wills for the eleven counties then existing, and subsequent appointments were made as needed until the office eventually became elective. Among the first registers named was James Kinkead of Westmoreland County, which then embraced all of the Pennsylvania land west of the Laurel Mountains.

It was not until ten years after the appointment of registers, however, on September 29, 1787, that the *Pennsylvania Intestate Law* was passed. This law set up legal procedures for the distribution of the estates of persons who died without making a will, and these procedures then became part of the records of the early will books. Intestate proceedings continued to be recorded in Allegheny County Will Books until 1885, when they were transferred to the *Record of Inventory and Appraisement*.

John Boyd—*Intestate*
Recorded February 17, 1789

Page 1 of Allegheny County Will Book I is an itemized inventory and valuation of the property of an intestate, the first act of Allegheny County's first register of wills. Prior to September 24, 1788, when Allegheny County was erected, records of wills made in this area were kept in the offices of Westmoreland and Washington County registers. Samuel Jones began his official duties on February 17, 1789, when he recorded the case of John Boyd.

John Boyd was manager of Pittsburgh's only newspaper, the *Gazette*, and partner of its editor, John Scull. Early in August of 1788 Boyd stirred the community by committing suicide. And so, Samuel Jones's first grant of letters of administration made Ann Boyd administratrix of her husband's property. His transcription reads:

Allegheny County, vs. Samuel Jones, Register for the probate of wills, and granting Letters of Administration, in and for the Co. aforesaid in the Commonwealth of Pennsylvania.

To Ann Boyd, Greetings. Whereas John Boyd late of the Town of Pittsburg in the Co. of Allegheny and State of Pennsylvania, Lately died Intestate (as is affirmed) he having whilst he lived and at the time of his death divers Goods, Chattels and Credits within the said State and County, by means whereof the full desposition and Power of Granting the Administration of all and singular the Goods, Chattels

9

and Credits of the said decedent and also auditing the accompts calculations and Reckoning of the said Administration, and a Final dismission from the same to me is manifestly known to Belong; I desire That the Goods, Chattels and Credits of the said decedent may be well and truly administered converted and disposed of to Pious Uses, do hereby Grant unto the said Ann Boyd (in whose fidelity in this Behalf I very much confide) full Power by the Tenor of these Presents to administer the Goods, Chattels and Credits of the said decedent within the said Counties; and also to ask, collect, sue for, Levy, recover and Receive the Credits whatsoever of the said Decedent, which at the Time of his death were owing to him did in any wise Belong, and to pay the debts in which the said Decedent stood Obliged, so far forth, and the said Goods, Chattels and Credits will extend, according to the rate and order of Law, Especially of Well and truly Administering the Goods, Chattels and Credits of the said Decedent, and making True and Perfect Inventory of all and singular the Goods, Chattels and Credits of the said Decedent, and Exhibiting the same into the Register's Office at Pittsburgh, at or Before the Ninth day of March now ensuing, and Rendering a True and Just Account, Calculation and Reckoning of the said Administration on or before the Seventeenth day of February which will be in the year of our Lord one Thousand and Seven Hundred and Ninety. And I do by these Presents ordain, Constitute and Depute you the said Ann Boyd administratrix of all and singular the Goods, Chattels and Credits of the said Decedent within the limits aforesaid, Saving Harmless and forever Indemnifying me and all other Officers against all Other Persons by Reason of your Administration Aforesaid, and saving to Everyone their Rights.

In Testimony whereof I have hereunto set my Hand and Affixed my seal of Office at Pittsburg the Seventeenth day of February in the year of our Lord, One Thousand Seven Hundred and Eighty nine.

(Signed) Samuel Jones, Register (SEAL)

John Boyd's death was not reported in the *Gazette,* a weekly which concerned itself with news that was not common knowledge to the community. News of happenings east of the Alleghenies, articles concerning foreign courts, and advertisements for runaway slaves and lost cattle filled the pages and crowded out gossip. But in the issue of the paper dated August 9, 1788, the name of John Boyd was missing beside that of "John Scull, Printer." That places Boyd's death sometime during the preceding week—probably August 8, the day the appraisal of his estate was made.

The executors appointed by the county, George Wallace and Adamson Tannehill, figured John Boyd's assets as follows:

1	large cherry tree dining table	3£10s0d
1	Breakfast table	2£ 0s0d
1	writing ditto	7s6d
6	split bottom chairs	12s6d
1	bedstead	15s0d
1	small Oval glass	12s6d
3	pickters	7s6d
6	cups and saucers (Queensware)	3s6d
1	crame jug and sugar dish (Queensware)	1s9d
3	brass candlesticks, 1 pr. snuffers, old	15s0d
1	tin coffee pot	2s0d
1	frying pan	7s6d
1	bake iron	5s0d
1	Hatt brush	1s3d
6	Knives, 6 forks	5s0d
9	Queensware plates	6s0d
2	wooden buckets, old	3s0d
1	small milking pale and tub, old	2s6d
1	sweeping brush, 1 furniture brush, 3 blacking do.	4s9d
1	garden how, 1 small ax, old	11s3d
4	butter boals, Sunday Queensware (old)	5s0d
1	flint glass and stan for do. (old)	1s0d
1	man's saddle (old)	15s0d
1	pr. plated spurs	7s6d
1	pr. saddle bags	11s3d
1	curry comb	1s6d
1	small bracket	6d
13	French books, stitched	13s0d
7	small French books	2s4d
	Swedenburgh's works	6s0d
7	books, English	15s0d

1	cow and 2 calves	5£12s6d
48	Christian Relegen	15s0d
912	quills	4£10s0d
8	doz. papers of ink powder	3£ 6s8d
	Sealing wax	4s0d
9	Mathas Catch	4s6d
2	Queensware pint bowls	1s6d
4	tin cups	1s4d
1	small iron pot	7s6d
1	small iron coffee mill	5s6d
1	vinegar cruet	1s0d
1	bay mare	5£ 0s0d
	Total,	28£11s7d

. . . appraised by Adamston Tunnehill and George Wallace, the 8th day of August, 1788: 'We do hereby certify that the above and within Appraisement is just and True to the Best of our Knowledge as Witness our hands . . .'

Geo. Wallace
A. Tunnehill

Sworn Before me, Sam'l Jones, Regr.
February 17, 1789

The *Gazette's* February 21 issue printed two legal notices:

All persons who have any demands against the estate of John Boyd, deceased, are requested to bring them in, properly attested, to Ann Boyd, Administratrix.

The necessity of settling the accounts of the late partnership of Scull & Boyd makes it indispensibly necessary for those who are indebted to make speedy payment, either to Ann Boyd, or the subscriber.

Produce will be received in payment, if settled by the 1st of April next. John Scull.

Nothing further was published concerning John Boyd, except repetition of the above notices, until the November 28 *Gazette*. In that issue, because the deadline was nearing for final administration of the estate, his widow inserted the following notice:

The necessity of settling and closing the accounts of the late partnership of Scull & Boyd makes it indispensibly necessary that those indebted should make payment either to John Scull, or the subscriber, on or before the 14th day of January next. The administrator flatters herself a strict compliance will be paid to this notification as she will be under the necessity of putting all the debts unpaid at time into proper hands for recovery.

Ann Wilson, Administratrix.

N.B.—Country produce will be received in payment, if delivered before the above specified time.

That Ann Wilson was Ann Boyd, the *Gazette* of April 18 attests:

Married, on Thursday evening last, Mr. William Wilson, merchant, to Mrs. Ann Boyd, both of this town.

     ✿   ✿   ✿   ✿   ✿

What caused young Boyd to walk out of the Water Street printing shop, climb the bluff which is now the site of Duquesne University, and there hang himself? That has been a topic of speculation through the years.

John Boyd left century-old Philadelphia to come to Pittsburgh on the persuasion of Hugh Henry Brackenridge, one of the frontier town's leading citizens. He bought the share of the *Gazette* which had belonged to Joseph Hall, first partner of John Scull who died soon after the paper was established, in 1786. On January 1, 1787, Boyd's appointment as manager was announced by *The Printer*, a title by which John Scull liked to be known. A year and a half later Boyd took his life.

Was he disillusioned to find that Brackenridge's glowing descriptions of the town did not conform to the facts? Certainly, Brackenridge did exaggerate a bit to induce immigration to Pittsburgh. And to influence John Boyd to come here, to bring him to the *Gazette*—the newspaper Brackenridge had helped to establish and to which he had contributed valuable literary assistance—was to further that purpose. This is the description Brackenridge wrote of Pittsburgh which Boyd read:

In the fall of the year and during the winter season there is usually a great concourse of strangers at this place, from the different States, about to descend to the westward, or to excursions into the uninhabited and adjoining country. These, with the inhabitants of the town, spend the evening in parties at the different houses, or at public balls, where they are surprised to find an elegant assembly of ladies, not to be surpassed in beauty and accomplishments perhaps by any on the continent. It must appear like enchantment to a stranger . . . halls lighted up with splendor, ladies and gentlemen assembled, various music and the mazes of the dance.

As a "stranger" John Boyd had come, and for himself had found little of the gaiety mentioned. The first year was uneventful as far as recreation was concerned. The work was tiresome; the old wooden hand press made only one sheet of newsprint at a time and it was difficult to operate. Boyd had believed the statesman's exaggerated words and had relied upon them. But instead of "about fifteen hundred, this number doubling almost every year," he found in Pittsburgh only four or five hundred inhabitants.

And when it was midsummer again, his second summer in Pittsburgh, was John Boyd remembering another Brackenridge description?

There is not a more delightful spot under heaven to spend any of the summer months than at this place.

This place, indeed! How Boyd must have yearned for his Philadelphia home and friends.

Yet he had honestly tried to make a success for himself on the newspaper. The following letter from a reader (*Gazette*, June 9, 1787) indicates the respect in which he was held:

Messrs. Scull & Boyd,

It is particularly pleasing to find your paper meritoriously growing on the public esteem. Mr. B.'s address to the public is not only entertaining, but in the highest degree useful; by such means only can we, who are by our own local situation, removed a considerable distance from the seat of government, receive information of what is doing in the great world, know who are our friends, what political measures are framed

14

either for or against us, and other useful information, very necessary for us to be instructed in.

In your paper of the 19th ult., Mr. B. gives us a relation of the business transacted in the house of assembly relative to the public roads in this state, to which the yeas and nays are annexed; were it not that Mr. B.'s authority is respectable, particularly so as he is a member, no person would give credit to that account, but as it is, we are much puzzled to conceive on what principles our western members voted against the measure. . . .

Besides trying to get citizens to support the building of roads, John Boyd had tried to interest his fellow townsmen in a lending library. He published the terms and privileges of membership in several issues of the *Gazette*. It must have been discouraging to him that the project was dropped for lack of subscribers.

We know, then, that Boyd was a good newspaperman, and many of the items listed in the inventory of his estate show him to be a man of culture and refinement. The treasures brought from his old home to grace the new one must have provided a handsome dowry for Ann to take to William Wilson, merchant, when she married him within nine months after John Boyd's death.

JOHN DOUSMAN—*Intestate*

Recorded May 6, 1789

A simple listing of a man's possessions may reveal a lot about his way of life. The inventories spread out on the pages of the early will books, while they lack the personal touch that characterizes a will, still tell us much about the early settlers of Allegheny County. A man's wealth usually was made up of livestock, farm implements, produce, household goods, and clothing. Typical is the "true inventory of all and singular the goods and chattels of John Dousman, deceased, late of the Town of Pittsburgh":

14 old sheep and 3 lambs	6£ 7s6d
One old cow	2£10s
Two small feather beds	6s
Tow boxes	6s3d
4 small Potts and one bake oven	13s6d
2 small brass kittles (one of them patched)	8s6d

15

	A tea kittle	6s
	A small frying pan (fractured)	1s6d
	An old spinning wheel	5s
10	pewter plates and 2 small basons	13s4d
	A pewter dish	13s6d
1	coffee pot and a tea pot	5s
1	bucket, 1 churn, and milk pail	3s6d
6	geese	7s8d
1	skimmer, 1 ladle, and a flesh fork	2s
1	pair dog irons	7s6d
	A table	2s6d
	A pair of smoothing irons	10s
2	chairs	3s
	A bag	2s6d
	A heckle	15s
	A pair sheep shears	2s6d
	One falling axe	5s
2	bolsters and 2 pillows	5s
1	pair stilliards out of repairs, not better than old iron	2s

Sundry crockery vases—1 cracked pint, 1 quart mug, a vinegar cruet, 1 mustard pot, 2 teacups and 3 saucers, a half pint decanter, 2 cream mugs—all of them long in wear— 5s

Tinnwear—viz: half gallon measure, 2 qt. mugs, 2 tinn cups and gill measure and 2 Tea canisters long in wear 2s

4	pewter spoons and 2 porringers	1s
	A looking glass	1s3d
3	knives, different kinds	9d
	Pair snuffers on iron candlestick	6d
9	old books, viz., "Paradise Lost" 2 spelling books, Dutch testaments, psalm books, etc.	7s6d
2	bedsteads of trunks	5s
3	old barrels and washing tub out of half barrel	4s
	A branding iron and pair old hinges	2s

Total, 26£6s4d

Letters of administration gave Catherine Dousman, widow of the deceased, full power to settle this estate "and collect whatever is owing to John Dousman" within one year. And the estate, simple though it was, left her articles, even down to the "fractured frying pan," valuable and hard to come by on the frontier.

Robert Montgomery—*Intestate*
Recorded March 27, 1789

Robert Montgomery had a much larger estate than Dousman's when he died without making a will. The inventory added up to 115 pounds, 13 shillings, 10 pence (about $323.93 in our present day currency).

1	bay horse	6£10s
1	sorrel do.	3£
1	sorrel colt	3£
1	black heifer	2£
1	red, white face	2£
1	brown calf	15s
1	brindled cow	4£
1	black & white cow with a bell	15s
12	hogs (two sows and ten pigs)	3£10s
1	double Tree with a large clevis	7s6d
3	falling axes	1£2s6d
4	sickles and one sythe	10s
	two pairs of Hems with tew Traces	6s
1	Plow and Plow Irons with 2 clevices and Links	2£
1	stove	3£
2	Plow bridles with one pair of Hems	5s
1	riding bridle	5s
	One Tuill wheel and swifts	5s
1	churn and 2 corn hoes	11s6d
1	horse hide and one calf ditto	7s6d
2	Pots, 1 bake oven & 1 small skillet	2£12s6d
1	frying pan	15s
1	spinning wheel	15s
1	gun a round bore	7s
1	tub 3 pails & 2 coal hoes	10s

2 bags		7s6d
2 meat barrels and a keg		12s6d
2 pewter		1£
Tins and spoons		6d
1 cutting knife		2s6d
Cloathes of Robt. Montgomery, deceased		1£
Weavers reeds		4£9s
Bed & Cloathes, bedstead & curtains		2£
1 man's saddle & 1 woman's do.		1£
1 chair		1s10d
1 chair and Pot Rack		1s10d
1 coffee pot		3s
1 gray mare		12£
1 hammer		2s
2 yds. of tow linen		4s
16 bushels of wheat at 4s		3£4s
15 ditto		3£
14 gallons of whiskey @ 3s		2£
3 notes on Alexr. Long, each 19£19s1d, paid in whiskey at 3s per gal.		30£12s1½d
One due bill of Wm. Barr		12s4½d
flax and wollen yarn and tow yarn		2£4s
	Total,	115£13s10d

Mr. Montgomery's "3 notes on Alexr. Long," *paid in whiskey*, is the largest single item of value in the inventory. Surely, the administrators would be happy to find that item; for whiskey was at that time more reliable than money as a medium of exchange.

JOHN ORMSBY, SR.—*Intestate*
Recorded October 13, 1855: *Proceedings Index,*
Allegheny County, v.30, p.142

In early Allegheny County, as today, some people were careless about making a will and neglected to assign to their heirs the property that should have been theirs. Without a will a man's property can seldom be distributed as he might have intended it should be, and certainly not as promptly. John Ormsby, Sr., neglected to make a will, and as a result one of his heirs had to wait fifty years before she received her share of the estate.

Mr. Ormsby died in December, 1805. He left a son, Oliver; a daughter, Sidney; and a granddaughter, Mary Swazey. Oliver and Sidney shared in the property until they, too, died intestate; when it passed on to other hands. Mary Swazey didn't get a settlement until October, 1855, as the following records of the Allegheny County Orphans Court show:

To the Honorable, the Judges of the Orphans Court of Allegheny County.

The Petition of Christian Ihmson, Assignee of Mary Swazey, granddaughter and one of the heirs of John Ormsby, Sr., late of said county, deceased.

Humbly showeth:

That the said John Ormsby, Sr. died intestate, seized inter alia, of a certain contract or parcel of land situate on Beck's Run in Upper St. Clair Township in said County of Allegheny, known as the "BERGEN OP ZOON" tract, and bounded and described as follows, to wit, Beginning at a post on the line of a tract called "Mount Oliver" thence by land patented to Charles B. Bradford, Esq. south seventy-six degrees east one hundred and forty-eight perches and one fourth, thence by the Sugar Tree Hill tract south two hundred and fifteen perches to a Black Oak, south thirty-four degrees, east sixty-four and one-half perches to a sugar tree on Beck's Run, thence up said Run south fifty-seven degrees west one hundred and fourteen perches, south eighty-seven degrees, west sixty-six perches, south forty-five degrees, west thirty-eight perches to a sugar tree, thence by land now or formerly of Robert Wilson, south fifty-nine degrees, west fifty-four perches to a Hickory tree, thence by "Mount Oliver", north eight and three-fourths degrees, east three hundred and sixty-six perches to the place of beginning:

Containing three hundred and seventy acres and one hundred and fifty-four perches and allowance:

That the said John Ormsby, Sr. left issue, two children, *Oliver,* and *Sidney,* who was intermarried with a certain Isaac Gregg, and a granddaughter, the said Mary Swazey, who was the daughter of John Ormsby, Jr., the son of the said John Ormsby, Sr., who died in the lifetime of his said father.

19

The said Oliver Ormsby, Sidney Gregg, and Mary Swazey being
the heirs at law of the said John Ormsby, Sr., deceased.

Oliver Ormsby died intestate, leaving issue:

1st. *Jane,* who was intermarried with Robert Ormsby, of Louisville,
Kentucky, and who together with her husband are since deceased,
intestate, leaving issue three children, to wit:

Sarah, intermarried with William McKnight, Jr.

Jane, intermarried with Dr. Morgan, and

Oliver Ormsby.

2nd. *Sarah N.,* who was intermarried with Asher Phillips.

3rd. *Mary,* who was intermarried with Elias Phillips.

4th. *Josephine,* intermarried with Edward M. Yurd and since deceased,
leaving issue Josephine O., a minor.

5th. *Oliveretta,* who was intermarried with Clifton Wharton, the said
Clifton being since deceased.

6th. *Caroline.*

7th. *Oliver H. Ormsby.*

8th. *Sidney,* who was intermarried with John H. Page.

That the said Isaac Gregg and Sidney, his wife, died intestate,
leaving issue:

1st. *Sarah,* who was intermarried with Moses F. Eaton.

2nd. *Isaac Gregg.*

3rd. *Oliver O. Gregg.*

4th. *Sidney, Jr.,* who was intermarried with John Mowry.

That the said Petioner by divers good and lawful conveyances became seized in fee of all the interest of the said Mary Swazey being the
one undivided third part thereof, in the premises aforesaid:

That the interest of the said Isaac Gregg, one of the said heirs, has
become vested in William Phillips.

Your Petitioner therefore prays your Honors to award an inquest in
Partition of the premises aforesaid to and among the children and rep-
resentatives of the said intestate, in such manner and in such proportions as by the laws of this Commonwealth is directed, if such partition
can be made without prejudice to or spoiling the whole; but if such partition cannot be made thereof as aforesaid, then to value and appraise
the same and make report of their proceedings herein according to law.

And he will pray &c, &c.

(Signed)   C. Ihmson

No. 6. October 1855. Petition for Partition in Orphans Court, In the matter of the Partition of the real estate of John Ormsby, deceased. Allegheny County S.S.

Christian Ihmson, the Petitioner above named, being duly sworn, saith that the facts set forth in the foregoing petition are true to the best of his knowledge and belief.

Sworn and subscribed before me this
13th day of Octr., A.D., 1855.

(Signed)   Thos. Steele

And now, October 13, 1855, The within Petition presented in open court and in consideration thereof an inquest is awarded for the Partition as prayed for. . . .

P. C. Shannon and William Sprouse,
Attys. for Partitioner.

The foregoing legal document is interesting not only for showing how complicated is the procedure to settle properly an intestate's lands, but also because John Ormsby, Sr., was a prominent figure in Allegheny County before and after the Revolutionary War. For his services to the new government here he is said to have accumulated the acreage for which, a century later, a granddaughter's share was being claimed by process of law.

A small part of Ormsby's real estate holdings was bought directly from the Indians. All of it fronted the south side of the Monongahela River for miles, becoming known as Birmingham, East Birmingham, and part of lower St. Clair Township, including the Borough of Ormsby. The original patents were named "Barry Hall," "Bergen Op Zoom," "Ormsby Villa," and "Mount Oliver."

In Jordan's *Colonial and Revolutionary Families of Pennsylvania*, v.4, p.442, we find the following biographical data:

"John Ormsby, Sr., was educated at the University of Dublin. He was an officer in the British Army and came to Western Pennsylvania with General Forbes in the march against Fort Duquesne." After that he was offered several commissions here; he declined

21

all of them because of ill health, although, for a time, he was active at Fort Pitt. John Ormsby was prominent in early Allegheny County affairs: as its leading merchant; as a patriot in the Virginia-Pennsylvania boundary dispute, when he locked horns with Dr. Connally and came off the worse; and as a trustee in Trinity Episcopal Church. He was a large landowner. The last piece of ground to which he laid permanent claim, however, is marked in Trinity burying place by a 72 by 36-inch slab—No. 37 in the verger's record. The inscription on the stone reads:

On the 19th day of December, A.D., 1805, the remains of the venerable John Ormsby, aged 85, were interred agreeably to his desire with the ashes of his late wife. Mr. Ormsby may truly be styled the Patriarch of the Western Ormsbys. He migrated to Fort Duquesne about the time the British took possession of it; at which time he was Commissary of Provisions and Paymaster of Disbursements (sic) for the erection of Fort Pitt. Subsequently he entered largely into the Indian trade; and in the year 1763 was plundered of all his property, his people murdered, and himself shut up in Fort Pitt during the siege. Mr. Ormsby was a large stockholder in the Indian Grant which would have remunerated him for all his losses by the Indians, had not the Revolution taken place; notwithstanding, he was a staunch Whig, and gloried in our Independence.

Of his five children, only one of them—Joseph B. Ormsby—recorded a will; the others, like their father, died intestate. Dr. Nathaniel Bedford, one of Pittsburgh's earliest physicians, whose first wife was Jane Ormsby, laid out his American "Birmingham" on tracts of land received from her part of her father's estate. But there is no evidence that this inheritance came to him from her by direct will—at least, no will of hers is recorded.

John Ormsby, Sr., as he moved through the Pittsburgh settlement in his various activities and pursuits, was surely a colorful personage, "noted for his immaculate breast and sleeve ruffles, the brightness of his shoe and knee buckles, and especially for his dress sword at his side." (See *Western Pennsylvania Historical*

22

Magazine, v.9, p.138) It seems strange that a man who was meticulous in other details should neglect so important a matter as making a will, especially when the will made by his young son Joseph (who died only two years before his father's decease) would have been a reminder of such a duty to the Ormsby heirs. But, like many other people throughout the years, Mr. Ormsby passed on leaving disposition of his property to law and litigation.

Dictated Wills

Many of the early wills in Allegheny County were not written in the hand of the maker, but were written by someone who took down the words of the person making the will. When the scribe was an attorney the will was likely to be filled with legal phraseology. But more often than not the man who was unable to write his own will, either through illness or illiteracy, had one of his neighbors write it for him. Such wills, bearing the signature or "mark" of the maker and witnessed by other friends and neighbors, were copied into the will books in the same manner as holograph wills. In many cases only close scrutiny of the original document serves to distinguish the dictated will from one actually written in the hand of the testator.

It is a rare privilege to hold the original documents, gently open broken folds, and look for the makers' signatures or marks. Sometimes the text is written so much like the testator's signature that only a careful comparison of individual letter formations shows that the will is not a holograph. Other times the formal phrasing and stiff, carefully-formed letters are followed by an X or a quavering signature. In such wills the analyst must rely upon the text itself, rather than upon the phrasing or appearance of the document, to determine the personality of the author. But no matter how much the paper has deteriorated or the ink faded these early wills are to be venerated for the destinies they have directed and the witness they bear of men active in the settlement of Allegheny County.

The first two wills mentioned here are dictated and nuncupative (no statement actually signed by the testator exists). Nuncupative wills usually were made on the deathbed and relayed to the register of wills by those present to hear the last wishes of the deceased.

The wills following the first two are arranged chronologically as they were recorded in the will books, and they bear either the signature or the mark of the testator.

RICHARD TETTRINGTON—*His will as he declared to them.*
    Dated, Presqui' Isle, January 26, 1797—Recorded June 3, 1797

Although Richard Tettrington died without making a will, he entrusted the care of his children to those who were with him when he died. These were his fellow artificers at Presque Isle; they relayed the information to the commanding officer of the post whose sworn statement appears in the will book:

I certify that James Irwin, an Artificer, and James (?), also an Artificer, at this Post, came before me the 26th day of January, 1797, the date on which the said Richard Tettrington died, and confirmed upon oath the above to be the substance of his will as he declared to them.

    Presquisle, 26 Jan., 1797
        Russel Bissell, Capt. 2 Reg.
        Commanding at Presquisle.
        No magistrate.

Presque Isle, or Presqui' Isle, was the name given by the French to the first fort they built at the entrance to the Ohio Valley, on land claimed by Great Britain, Virginia, and Pennsylvania, now occupied by the city of Erie.

GEORGE STROCHAN—*Who told this affirment to remember . . .*
    Dated November 17, 1804—Recorded November 19, 1804

The last instructions of George Strochan were made known to the Register by a friend who was present at the deathbed.

Be it remembered . . . and says he was in the house of George Strockan on Saturday, the seventeenth day of this instant, about one hour before the decease of the said George Strockan, who told this affirment to remember that he (the Deceased) left all his property (as this affirment believes) to his Old Woman, pointing to his wife. This affirment then asked the said George Strockan if he would leave anything to any of his friends, and he answered No; but that Hugh Caldwell should make a deed to his Old Woman for the land. This affirment then asked the said George Strockan who should settle his affairs after his death. He answered, you and my Old Woman.

GEORGE FORBES—*Being in a frail state of body but of a calm tranquil mind . . .*
Dated April 6, 1789—Recorded July 24, 1789

George Forbes made a brief will and signed it with his mark. The original document, one of the earliest in the county records, is stained and torn; one piece is broken off entirely where a fold is worn through. The single sheet of paper on which the will is written measures 12¾ by 7½ inches.

The will was witnessed by William Gray, John Shaw, and W. H. Beaumont.

I, George Forbes, of the Town of Pittsburgh and State of Pennsylvania, being in a frail state of body but of a calm tranquil mind, duly considering the uncertainty of human events, do make and constitute the following writing to be my last will and testament.

In the first place, I recommend my soul to the care of Almighty God and when he so pleases to separate it from my mortal part I request that my body may be decently interred at the discretion of executors herein mentioned.

Secondly, I give and bequeath to my brother-in-law, James Todd and my sister Catherine, his wife, my lot in the town of Pittsburgh to hold the same to them and their heirs and assigns forever.

Thirdly, all my money and securities for money or other debts that may be due me, after payment of my just debts and funeral charges, I give unto my mother, my two brothers and my sister that are now living in that part of Great Britain called Scotland, share and shares alike, or to the survivor or survivors.

Fourthly, I give unto the aforesaid James Todd all my Tools, cloathes and wearing apparel.

And lastly, I do nominate and appoint him, the said James Todd, to be the Executor of this my will.

BENJAMIN KUYKENDALL—. . . *provided she makes no waste.*
Dated September 26, 1789—Recorded November 6, 1789

The cleanest and best preserved of the original wills we have examined is that of Benjamin Kuykendall, written on parchment. After handling many fragile papers, it was a delightful experience to touch and admire this beautiful legal document. Although the signature has several blots on it—at the central joining of the *k's* and at the base of the double *l's* in the last syllable of *Kuykendall*—it is legible and boldly drawn. The parchment, probably lamb's skin, measures about 15 by 12 inches. The fact that it has lasted in excellent condition for more than a century and a half is a tribute to Mr. Kuykendall's choice of writing materials.

The will makes three bequests of real estate. First, to the youngest sons:

I leave and bequeath my youngest sons Benjamin and Nathaniel Kuykendall all that messuage or Tenement with all its appurtenances situate on Monongahela River whereon I now live.

Then to his daughters Mary, Elizabeth, Susanah, Sarah, Margaret, Christina, and Rebecca:

all my lands and tenement in Kentucky situate on Kentucky River forty miles from the mouth of said River to share and share alike.

And to his youngest daughter Annotchey:

all that messuage or Tenement I hold situate on Racoon Creek, Washington County, Pennsylvania.

Next, Mr. Kuykendall charges Sarah, his wife, with the responsibility of the estate, and

support of the children under age until they are of age, with the product of the Farm (and Mills) whereon I now live, with all my Farming Uten-

27

sils, viz., waggon, horses, Ploughes, etc., etc., etc. . . . provided she
makes no waste or destruction thereof while she remains a widow.

Did he need to make that last statement? Most wives, knowing
how hard property and products were to earn and hold, were
frugal and appreciative, without being reminded.

Benjamin Kuykendall left his eldest son, Moses, who was
living in Kentucky, "seventy-five pounds in Pennsylvania currency"
and made him one of the executors of the estate. The other executors were Mr. Kuykendall's wife, Sarah, and his brother, Nathaniel.

Although Kuykendall was a Pennsylvanian by birth, he
pledged allegiance to Virginia in 1776 and made his home in
Augusta Town, where he had built an inn. Later he was selected
by Richard Yeats as one of the Virginia justices of the Court; and
in April, 1780, he was sworn in as sheriff of Yohogania County.
As sheriff, he was severely beaten when he tried to make an arrest
at Razertown during a fight that followed the last session of the
Virginia Court. The reason given for his bad treatment was that
he had agreed to support the establishment of the Mason and
Dixon line. Later, he was glad to return to Pennsylvania.

WILLIAM TROOP— . . . *and likewise all debts owing to me.*
     Dated August 1, 1776—Recorded September 15, 1790

This will of a "farmer" of the "County of Yachagenia" is not
easy to read, because the fragile 13 by 8-inch porous paper is ink-
soaked, and where the text is not obliterated by the ink, it has faded
until it is almost illegible. It is short and leaves everything to Mr.
Troop's wife:

. . . after my just debts are paid and discharged, I bequeath unto
my loving wife, Mary Smittens, all my estate, lands, goods, cattle and
horses, and likewise all debts owing to me.

The Troops had probably shared everything together on their
farm—the heavy work, too, because many women labored with
their men in the fields in those days—so it is not such a surprise
to read that William Troop bequeathed to his wife Mary "all debts
owing to me." But it was not so easy for a woman to round up
creditors and settle a husband's debts. The brevity of the will, how-

ever, implies full confidence in Mary's business abilities. In leaving everything to his wife, without strings attached, Mr. Troop was more generous than most husbands of his day when a widow's legacy, usually, was just for the period of her widowhood.

One of the witnesses to the will wrote its text. He was John Thomson. The other witness, Neal McCaughey, thought a bit of explaining was justified. So, when the two friends presented Mr. Troop's will for probate, included in the oath he took that the testator "was in his right senses" at the time of signing, Mr. Mc-Caughey's statement before the register of wills is to this effect:

Further this deponent saith that the within mentioned Mary Smittens was wife to said William Troop at the time the within will was wrote and seigned, but, according to a Scotch custom, she was called by her first name as before marriage.

Just an old Scotch custom, yet it might have caused difficulty in administering Mr. Troop's estate had not his true Scottish friends taken it upon themselves to set matters straight fourteen years after that will had been signed by William Troop's X.

William Troop was one of the applicants who got land in what is now the Squirrel Hill district, when the proprietary government of Pennsylvania opened its land office for the sale of lands in Western Pennsylvania.

COURT JOHNSON— . . . *except her feather bed.*
Dated May 19, 1790—Recorded January 20, 1792

The will of Court Johnson is on heavy paper of the laid pattern so common in old Allegheny County wills. The document, which bears his signature, is not torn or broken, but the paper is badly stained and faded. It measures 12 inches across and a little more than 12½ inches in length. The executors named by Mr. Johnson are his wife, Hannah, and his friend, Isaac McMichael. To Mrs. Johnson is bequeathed:

The plantation whereon I now live, the whole of every kind that I am possessed of at this time, the farming utensils of all kinds and sorts whatsoever, and the household furniture, every part and parcel thereof, during the time of her life, if she remains a widow. And if it should so happen that the said Hannah should marry herself to another man, my will is that she leave the plantation whereon I now live and the whole moveable estate, except her feather bed and furniture thereunto belonging . . . .

Poor Hannah! Her reward for a lifetime of work—if she did remarry—was to be the feather bed (she had probably made it herself, accumulating the feathers from tedious pluckings of ducks and geese through many years) "and the furniture thereunto belonging" which, without much doubt, would be quilts she had pieced together in her rare moments of relaxation. And, what was worse, Mr. Johnson had not once referred to her as "my beloved wife," which was customary in drawing up a will.

While he may not have been given to terms of endearment, Court Johnson's next bequest shows decided favoritism toward his eldest son and his first daughter:

My will is that if my lawful wife Hannah remains a widow that after her death the tract of land and the moveable estate is to be sold and out of such sale the first payment Jonathan Johnson is to have 20 pounds more and above any one of his brothers . . . Catharine Johnson . . . to have her choice of one milk cow and one bed and furniture over and above any one of her sisters and to be kept on the plantation whiles she lives with her mother.

The old Pennsylvania laws allowed the oldest son a double share if the children's share of the property were divided equally.

Mr. Johnson's large family were "to have the property equally divided between them," that is, after seeing that Jonathan and Catharine got the extras their father directed they were to have. Other parts of this will list his sons as Jonathan, David, Andrew, John, and Joshua; and his daughters as Catharine, Mary, Sarah, Ann, and Rachel.

JOHN MCDONALD—*One-third of ye rents and mean profits.*
Dated February 13, 1787—Recorded December 3, 1792

John McDonald's will was written on a single sheet of laid paper, 13 by 8⅛ inches. He signed with an X. After bequeathing

30

his plantation to his son Thomas, he left to Johanna, his "loving wife":

One-third of ye rents and mean profits of the above plantation during her life together with all my movable estate to be disposed of by her at her death as she thinks proper.

The eldest daughter, Rachel Hoy, received an annual income: "five pounds, to be paid in produce at market price each year after my decease."

Another daughter, Hannah Custard, received one payment: "five pounds to be paid in three years after my death."

Previous to September, 1786, John McDonald had conducted a general store at "Bell-Mont" in Peters Township. A notice in the *Pittsburgh Gazette,* September 2, 1786, shows his ambition to enlarge that business as well as the packet trade he carried on for a number of years:

It is evident that there is no speedier way of transporting any country produce or merchandise from Washington to Pittsburgh. Said boat is also the most speedy and sure way of transporting the Pittsburgh *Gazette* to the subscribers on Youghiogany, Peter's Creek, Mingo Creek, and Pigeon Creek.

Realizing the trade he might get from the mills up the river, McDonald suggested carrying the weekly newspaper (which evidently he could not read) on his trips between Pittsburgh and his own landing. And, in that same issue of the *Gazette,* he continues his advertisement by saying:

The subscriber also proposes by the assistance of his neighbors to erect at his landing a large storehouse for the reception of country produce &c. for public good, at Peters Creek, Washington Co.

—John McDonald
Bell-Mont, Aug. 30

In his will, John McDonald chose as his executors his son, Thomas and Henry Hulce. Witnesses were Joseph Hulce and John Douglas.

SAMUEL ALEXANDER—*And a looking glass to Elizabeth.*
Dated April 3, 1794—Recorded August 29, 1794

Four months after Samuel Alexander's will was probated, the following notice appeared in several issues of the *Gazette*:

All persons indebted to the estate of Samuel Alexander, merchant, deceased, or to the partnership of Alexander & Creigh, at this place, are requested to make payment in four weeks from this date to the subscribers administrators, or to James Nailor, at the store—and all those who have any demands against said estate or partnership are requested to lay in their claims that they may be adjusted.

John Creigh, Wm. Alexander, John Wilkins, Junior—Administrators

N.B.—At the store belonging to said partnership is a neat and general assortment of Dry Goods and Groceries which will be sold either wholesale or retail on the terms for cash.

Evidently the partner could not resist the opportunity to advertise in a postscript to the administrator's notice.

But it was not so simple to settle Mr. Alexander's affairs, for several months later in the *Gazette* of March 4, 1795, a more drastic notice appeared:

All persons indebted to the partnership of Alexander & Creigh are desired to make immediate payment to the subscriber, or to Mrs. Isabella Alexander, at Pittsburgh.—All those that neglect this notice may expect that bonds, notes and book accounts will be put into the hands of proper officers to bring suits according to law.

John Creigh, Surviving partner. Pittsburgh, Feb. 14, 1795.

Like most of the other merchants in early Pittsburgh, Mr. Alexander had doubtless given credit and even cash to his fellow citizens without security. And that probably accounts for at least part of the debts the executors found hard to collect in settling the Alexander estate.

Among Mr. Alexander's legacies to his family were:

To my beloved wife, Elizabeth, her bed, drawers, and pewter. The sorrel horse, her choice of any of the cows. The House I live in during her life, also during her life yearly one hundred weight of good sufficient merchantable Pork to be paid her from my son Thomas and 100 of good merchantable Pork from my son Joseph out of my real estate.

His sons were to pay Mrs. Alexander yearly:

15 bushels of merchantable wheat—that is each 7 bushels and a half—also each 10 bushels of rye and 5 of corn yearly. And every year during her life to be paid by them out of my real estate. I allow my son Joseph to sow my wife a bushel of flaxseed yearly on good ground.

All his clothes were willed to Joseph, also "half of the wagon," the other half being given to his other son, Thomas. Wagons were costly. To bequeath dual ownership of the wagon indicates not only the value placed upon it by Mr. Alexander, but also confidence that harmonious relations would be maintained in his immediate family.

I allow the remainder of my cows and sheep to be equally divided between my two daughters, Elizabeth Stewart and Rebecca McCurdy, and a looking glass to Elizabeth.

That extra legacy, "a looking glass," indicates some favoritism toward Elizabeth, for mirrors were luxuries at that time.

Mr. Alexander signed his will with an *X*. Twenty-three years later another Alexander will, signed with an *X*, was recorded in the will books. It was that of Elizabeth Alexander, Mr. Alexander's widow. We set aside chronological sequence momentarily to treat her will here.

ELIZABETH ALEXANDER—*My set of Silver teaspoons.*
Dated July 20, 1813—Recorded December 16, 1817

Mrs. Alexander bequeathed "One Dollar" to each of her sons, Joseph and Thomas, and to a daughter, Rebecca McCurdy, "my body cloathes." The other daughter, Elizabeth Stewart—she who had inherited the looking glass—was not living then, evidently, for no mention is made of her. But to the Stewart grandchildren Mrs. Alexander leaves:

33

To Mary Stewart, my set of Silver teaspoons and my pewter plates and dishes, my feather bed with the White tick, together with the best cloths belonging to it.

To Nancy Stewart, my feather bed with the striped tick and all the bed cloths belonging to it.

To Andrew Stewart, my mare, or thirty dollars, as he pleases.

Elizabeth Alexander did not have much to give, but the bequest of silver teaspoons was probably as much appreciated by Mary Stewart as the looking glass had been by her mother.

John Rardon—*For their ingratitude I do leave and bequeath . . .*
Dated March 16, 1796—Recorded April 5, 1796

What an unpleasant situation—to be unloved, unwanted, and sick! Possibly a combination of just such circumstances prompted John Rardon's eccentric will:

I do make and appoint John Urtheson my whole and sole heir, and to him I leave all my worldly substance as he has proved my friend in distress and supports me in sickness and in health. Each of the heirs of my body has got . . . and turned me out from amonst them and would not harbour me any longer, and for their ingratitude I do leave and bequeath to them as follows:

to son Thomas I do leave one penny to by snuff, and to each of others one penny. To Ann, my housekeeper, as she was the mother of all mischief and got her full pay when we parted, I will leave her 2 pence to give to the doctors for setting her crupper bone which I am informed she got broke.

It is a fair example of a "spite" will—one which marks its maker queer, and provides the reader amusement. Perhaps we should not laugh or condemn Mr. Rardon. After all, if his will amuses us, possibly it is because of its human quality and because we identify ourselves with his emotions. It might be well to recall here the Roman saying, *De mortuis nil nisi bonum.* ("Concerning the dead, say nothing but good.")

Just twenty days after John Rardon signed with his mark— his will was recorded in the Register's Office.

Adam Deemer—*He is to support his Mother and the . . . children.*
Dated September 3, 1797—Recorded February 2, 1798

Adam Deemer's will deserves extended treatment here because it is typical of the way a farmer of Allegheny County made
provisions for the care of his family after his death. He reserves
to his wife:

The privilege to live in house we now live in until another one is
built and a room prepared for herself if she chuses, the bed and beding
she now lays on, saddel bridle with the horse called Tom; likewise
ten milch cows, three sheep; the grain in the barn to go to the use of
the Family as usel and the thirds of the grain raised on Adam's part of
the land with the third of the hay for the use of the four youngest children, that is to say Jacob, Dorety, Andrew and Sarah, with their mother
while a Widow or during her life if she remains such. I give and devise
to my son John Deemer, one hundred acres of land with the allowance
on the lower end of the place where his improvement now is him paying
thirty pounds in the manner following—that is to say fifteen pounds the
first of January next, the remainder in one year after—to my two daughters Christina and Mary I give and bequeath to Christina her choice of
one milch cow and the Heffer and Steer she now cleams—ITEM I give
and bequeath to my son Adam one hundred acres of land where I Now
live with the allowance and improvements thereon, with four head of
Horse creatures the Horse Geares one plow and Irons, one harrow with
the other farming Utensils belonging to the place; as he is to suport his
Mother and the above named children during her widowhood and
their minority; also fifteen pounds to Jacob when of age. I also give and
bequeath the Waggon to Adam. ITEM I give and demise to my son
Jacob one hundred and three acres with the allowance on the upper end
of the place him paying my son Andrew teen pounds when Andrew
bes of age. ITEM I give and bequeath to my daughter Dorety fifteen
pounds when she is of age. ITEM I give and bequeath to my daughter
Sarah fifteen pounds when she is of age. ITEM I give and bequeath to
my son Andrew twenty pounds at my death to be put out to interest
for his use. I also allow the above named four children to be learned
to read and write— and the dresser furniture for my wife's use during
her life. It is my will and I do allow that if my estate are more than will
pay what is above mentioned to be divided in the form and manner

35

following, that is to say to my five daughters Christina, Mary, Margaret, Dorety and Sarah, with my son Andrew to have an eaquel divide with my five daughters. And I nominate appoint, ordain and constitute my dearly beloved wife Dorety and my beloved son John Deemer to be my only and sole executors of this my last will and testament in Trust for the interest and purposes in this my Will contained. And I do hereby disallow, revoke and disannul all and former Testament, will, legaties and executors by me and in my name in any wise before made willed and bequeathed; ratifying allowing and confirming this and no other to be my last Will and Testament. In Witness whereof I have herewith set my hand and seal this third day of September in the year of our Lord One thousand seven hundred and ninety seven.

his

Adam   X   Deemer

mark

Jos. Scott
John Manor

The bequests are of the usual kind: the wife's maintenance and comfort are provided for "while a Widow or during her life if she remains such"; the care of younger children is entrusted to the older children; the eldest son gets a larger portion of the estate because he "is to suport his Mother and the above named children during her widowhood and their minority"; the boys are to receive twenty pounds and the girls fifteen for the reason that the girls are assured of a home but the boys will have to look out for themselves once they leave the parental roof. The father "allowed" money from the estate to be used for "the above named four children to be learned to read and write"—just an elementary schooling, but more than he had known. His sons and daughters, he hoped, would be able to make *their* mark in the world better than he had been able to do.

Farmer Deemer thought of every contingency that might confront the members of his family when he was no longer alive to look out for them. The grain and hay must "go to the use of the Family as Usel," with specific instructions that it was to be used for the four youngest children and their mother. Two sons were given generous legacies of ground, but they were to pay for it a stipulated sum to their sisters and younger brother each year. And, if the estate totaled more than had already been bequeathed, Mr. Deemer's five daughters and his youngest son were "to have an eaquel divide." That concern is typical of our early will-makers, who always tried to provide the most for those less able to stand alone. Typical, also, is the naming of a wife and eldest son as executors of the will.

"His mark," not his signature, attested the will made by Adam Deemer. But his evident inability to write has not detracted from the good content of his will. Since he did not write the document himself, the spelling and language errors cannot justly be attributed to him, although he probably would say "Dorety" instead of *Dorothy,* and "bes" for *become,* as the scribe writes, if he had picked up the lingo of an unfamiliar tongue.

SAMUEL CULBERTSON—*To my beloved wife Elizabeth . . .*
Dated March 2, 1799—Recorded April 25, 1800

ELIZABETH CULBERTSON—*Widow and relict of Samuel Culbertson.*
Dated May 20, 1799—Recorded April 25, 1800

Samuel Culbertson and Elizabeth Culbertson, man and wife, died on the same day—October 19, 1799. Samuel's will had been drawn up first, and when Mrs. Culbertson made her own will, before her husband's death, she disposed of his property as though it were already hers. In the end, the estate of both the Culbertsons was distributed by a court-appointed administrator, because the executor named in both wills renounced his executorship in the face of the double death.

Filed with Samuel Culbertson's will in the county's records is the following memorandum—"given on March 2, 1799, by Samuel Culbertson to his executors to help them settle his estate, on his deathbed":

In my trunk at Casawago is some papers viz. Receipt for taxes paid on my father's estate which has a right to be deducted being incurred before the sale of the land and lies as a charge against the legatees. I think I have paid my sisters Hancock and Glow their part of what

37

monies came into my hands, there is three statements or gales of Nineteen or Twenty pounds cash yet due to them what I have Rec'd of my sister Lindsays deceased I allow to be paid out of what is yet due to myself. What I call my real estate is first the tract I intended to live on in Allegheny Co. on French Creek adjoining lands of James Herington and Captain Buckhanon. Also two tracts settled in partnership with John Hancock. On the waters of Sandy, there is one other tract on which Joseph Mattacks settled that was given up to Fields for 100 Dollars. I think I should have the half of that sum for my part.— this is what I have bequeathed to my wife which is my last will Testament.

It was not to be his deathbed immediately, however, a lingering illness kept him there seven more long months.

After directing the disposal of his wearing apparel, including a "Surtoot Coat," and bequeathing "my Cow and Gun that is at Cuswago," Mr. Culbertson gave "to my beloved wife Elizabeth the residue of my real and personal estate."

Elizabeth Culbertson, in making her own will two months after her husband had made his, listed his property in her bequests. Her main consideration was an extraordinary bequest to her father. He was to be:

reimbursed and paid all moneys by him expended about my union with the said Samuel Culbertson, deceased. . . . my negro woman and child and all other lands claimed by my late husband in said county to be sold at the discretion of my executors.

And finally, she left to her father a bay mare which, she states, is to be considered "as part of said reimbursement."

Because women owned nothing unless it had been given to them directly, her husband's will provided Elizabeth Culbertson with her first chance to repay a debt to her father. The Culbertsons were in comfortable circumstances, but Elizabeth's pride would scarcely permit an acknowledgment and explanation of a wedding debt!

Mrs. Culbertson's other bequests were to her brother Edward —"my riding horse, called Ball, given by my father"—and to her husband's half-brother, James Share, "the tract of land situate in

Alegheni County whereon he last lived or settled on the waters of French Creek."

Secure in the belief that her estate would be settled as she wished after her death, Mrs. Culbertson continued to care for her invalid husband, expecting his death almost any time. Spring (with its promise of freedom from the things that had worried her) faded into summer, and summer disappeared into the chilly autumn time—the dreary, endless months taking their toll of her strength—until, at last, she expired with her husband in mid-October. What an ironic end to all her plans, which had been so carefully laid!

When Edward Work, who had been appointed administrator of his sister's will—as well as that of her husband—renounced that responsibility, the county appointed others to administer these two estates. In Allegheny County's Bond Book No. 1, Page 197, we read:

Know all men by these presents that we, James B. Clow, Robert J. Clow, of Allegheny County, and Edward Cook of Fayette County, all in the Commonwealth of Pennsylvania, are held and firmly bound unto the said Commonwealth in the sum of three hundred dollars, lawful money of the United States, to be paid to the Commonwealth, to which payment well and truly to be made, we bind ourselves and each of us jointly and severally, for and in the whole, our and each of our Heirs Executors and Administrators firmly by these presents. Sealed with our seals, Dated the nineteenth day of Octr. in the year of our Lord one thousand seven hundred and ninety nine.

The condition of this obligation is such that if the above bounden James B. Clow, Administrator of all and singular the goods, chattels, rights and credits of Elizabeth Culbertson, late of Allegheny County, Deceased, do make or cause to be made a true and perfect Inventory of all and singular the Goods, Chattels, rights and Credits of the deceased have or shall come to the hands, possession or knowledge of him the said James B. Clow or into the possession of any other person or persons for him, and the same so made, do Exhibit or cause to be exhibited into the Register's Office in the County of Allegheny at or before the nineteenth day of November next ensuing, and the same goods, chattels, rights and credits of the said Deceased at the time of his death, which at any time after shall come to the hands or possession of the said James B. Clow or into the hands or possession of any other person or persons for him, do well and truly Administer according to law, and further do make or cause to be made a true and just account of his Administration at or before the nineteenth day of October next ensuing, and all the rest and residue of said goods chattels and Credits which shall be found remaining upon the said Administrator's account, the same being first examined and allowed of by the Orphans Court of the County of Allegheny, shall deliver and pay unto such person or persons respectively as the said Court of the aforesaid county by their decree or sentence pursuant to a true intent and meaning of the last will and Testament of the said Elizabeth Culbertson, Deceased. Then the obligation to be void and of none effect or else to be and remain in full force and virtue.

Sealed and Delivered in the presence of
L. Stewart
Saml. Jones

James B. Clow (SEAL)
Robt. J. Clow (SEAL)
Edw. Cook (SEAL)

This is one of the earliest examples of Letters of Administration issued by the Orphans Court of Allegheny County. It is handwritten on legal size laid paper, and an identical document was also written for Samuel Culbertson—both witnessed by the same men, both estates having the same administrators. These papers are folded and affixed to the decaying pages of our first bond book. A little later, printed forms with spaces for necessary writing replaced such papers.

PETER ROWLETER—*I order and direct all my just debts to be paid.*
Dated June 2, 1797—Recorded September 11, 1800

Peter Rowleter was an honest man. The first item in his will shows what he considered of primary importance: "First, I order and direct all my just debts to be paid of every kind whatsoever."

He took care of his own obligations promptly and he expected his debtors to do the same. Notice the vigor of this statement in the *Pittsburgh Gazette,* February 4, 1797, just a few months before he died:

All persons indebted to the subscriber, by bond, note, or book account, are requested to make payment by the 15th of February next; those who neglect this notice may expect to be dealt with in the most summary way.

—Peter Rohletter
Perry's Town
Jan. 26, 1797

Mr. Rowleter's prompt and full payment of accounts in the ledgers of Smith & Douglass contrasts with many a larger debt of well-known men of that day—some of whose obligations never were taken care of. The Rowleter store bill often was discharged in terms of service, for instance, a credit entry of Peter Rowletter's (Ledger *A,* 1773):

By making 6 Blanket Coats....................................18s
By making a Coat for E. Douglass..........................7s6d
By our Assumption for Henry Geiger......................12s6d
By Sundry work, mending, & C, for E. Douglass...............9s6d

In this way Rowleter paid his debts to the last sixpence; "making a Coat for E. Douglass" balances "a pair Leggons for Son" on the ledgers of Smith & Douglass. Since much of the tedious mending and the careful tailoring work must have fallen to the lot of Mr. Rowleter's wife and two daughters, they deserve their reward for helping pay the family's bills.

I do give and bequeath unto my beloved wife four Dollars per month out of the monies due me by Geo. Wallace during her life. Also the House and two Lotts with appurtenances thereto belonging in Perrystown with all Beading and other furniture that I may be possessed of at my Death during her life time and she is not to dispose of any part of said furniture, the same is to be Inventured and she accountable for it ware excepted.

I do give and bequeath unto my daughter Cathrain Lovjoy, wife of Benjamin Lovjoy, the sum of two Spanish milled dollars.

41

I give and bequeath unto my daughter Polly Powers, wife of James Powers, the sum of two Spanish milled dollars.

Hard money was scarce in those days, and was a legacy of real value.

Peter Rowleter was not a man to neglect anyone, and his last provision—to go into effect "after the death of my wife, should she survive me"—takes into account the Rowleter grandchildren:

Real and Personal estate of every kind whatsover shall be disposed either by public or private sale as may best answer the Purpose by my Executors hereinafter mentioned, and the monies arrising therefrom to be equally divided between the children of my daughters Cathrain and Polly.

And the aforesaid Legatees shall be Intitled to Receive their Parts of said Estate as they arrive at age and my said Executors are hereby Directed to put the monies arrising from the sales of my said estate out at Intrust on sufficient Security for the use of my Legatees.

And I do hereby appoint James Power my son-on-law and Geo. Wallace Executors of this my last will and testament, hereby revoking all former wills by me made.

Peter Rowleter's will has deteriorated very little; in fact, it is not even much soiled. But his signature zigzags along the paper's tiny laid marks as though his feeble hand had no control of the pen. Folded, the old document measures about 12¾ by 7½ inches.

Peter Rowleter, one of Pittsburgh's staunchest if lesser-known citizens, was among the signers for the creation of Allegheny County in 1788. And it is not unusual that we should find his name on the first tax roll of Pitt Township, in 1772. From what we know of Peter Rowleter, he would not have wanted to be left off that roll.

JANE WATSON—. . . *before it is too late.*
Dated February 15, 1805—Recorded February 8, 1806

The quality of Jane Watson that comes through in her will is her assertion of character. When she was asked to sign with her mark the will which had been drawn up for her, it was not the usual *X* she made on the indicated line. Instead, she made her own peculiar word sign—which looks something like a large capital *W* with embellishments.

Then there is the admonition coupled with her bequest to her daughter Elizabeth:

> a quarter of a dollar, in the hope that she will think of Heaven, and amend her ways before it is too late.

To her brothers she left her treasures: her "spectakles" and the "spectakle case" to David, her "staff" to Alexander. Can't you just see the stern, straight-laced old lady, leaning on her "staff" and looking askance over the top of her "spectakles" at the frivolous goings-on of her daughter?

Mrs. Watson's gifts to her brothers are given, she states, "as a token of my love." A little suggestion of love for the daughter might have helped more than the "holier-than-thou" warning.

The original of this will, measuring 13¼ by 8½ inches, is faded with age. But the paper is not torn or broken, and has come down to us as an intact expression of its maker.

EPHRAIM JONES—*To each of my eldest sons a Ferry.*
Dated, Jones's Ferry, December 13, 1806—Died June 29, 1808

Before there were bridges in Pittsburgh, ferry owners did a good business. The first ferry was established in 1773 with the Pittsburgh landing at Wood Street and the south side landing at the foot of Coal Hill. ("Coal Hill" was Mt. Washington—which was so steep that coal for the town had to be tumbled down the hillside in bags.) Another ferry, the one that later came into the hands of Ephraim Jones, was established before 1788 on the banks of the Monongahela River opposite Fort Pitt. The Pittsburgh landing was right at the Point. These ferrys came very close to landing at the places where the Duquesne and Mt. Washington inclines are today.

Ephraim Jones passed the ferry opposite the Fort to his son James:

> To my son, James Jones, I give the lower ferry in the borough of Pittsburg called Jones's ferry, situate between Liberty and Penn Streets.

43

Son Thomas also inherited a ferry, and the Jones boys carried on the business until after the Civil War. The family name was retained by the company which took over the business at that time, chartered as the Jones Ferry Company.

A codicil to Ephraim Jones's will, dated February 8, 1807, reads:

Having given to each of my eldest sons a Ferry & as stipulated in the different paragraphs in the above will I now declare it is my wish and desire that each is to have free liberty of landing on the others ground and their right to extend to them severally their heirs and assigns forever. And further having given my son Thomas the ferry where I now live subject to his paying at a certain period two thousand dollars to my executors it is fully understood that said two thousand dollars is to be paid independent of all other accounts and that all our accounts are to be considered as balanced at my death, and the said Thomas to have no credits toward said two thousand dollars being a transaction or dealing between us.

To my son, John . . . tract of land on Chartiers Creek purchased of Jones Richardson, joining lands of General Nevill with the appurtenances thereunto belonging . . . and by deeding to my executors within four years after my death the sum of four hundred dollars with interest on the same for the purchase hereinafter mentioned.

To my son, Ephraim Jones, I give a lot of ground on the side of the coal hill joining to William Herd.

To my son, Presly Jones, a lot in the Borough of Pittsburg marked No. 1 in Turnbull's plan, situate on Liberty Street.

As to my beloved wife Rachel Jones, she shall choose whether to live with my son Thomas at the Ferry or with John at Chartiers Creek, that however she may elect she is to be made comfortable in a room and that my Executors pay to her annually during her life the sum of eighty dollars out of the funds hereafter to be mentioned.

. . . one bed and bedding, one chest of drawers, two tables, half a dozen chairs, and any things they think may be necessary for her comfort.

This paragraph in Mr. Jones's will indicates the source of the "funds hereafter to be mentioned":

The money arising from the debts due me, from the sale of my personal property, and the two thousand eight hundred dollars stipulated before to be paid by my three youngest sons—after securing the payment of eighty dollars per annum to my wife Rachel—be equally divided between my five youngest children, that is Polly Plummer, Marshal Jones, Ephraim Jones, Eleanor Jones and Presly Jones, except that Polly Plummer shall receive less than the others by one hundred pounds because of her having already received a considerable amount.

Ephraim Jones's signature was witnessed by John Park, Peter Mowry, and Robert Johnson; the codicil, by James McDonald, Robert Johnson, and Presley Nevill. Only a blank space is left in the will book for its date of recording; but according to Zadok Cramer's *Pittsburgh Magazine Almanac* for 1808, Ephraim Jones died on June 29 of that year.

WILLIAM BOGGS—*Sell 4,000 acres of land I hold in the state of Virginia.*
Dated August 7, 1808—Recorded September 1, 1808

William Boggs was one of five brothers who emigrated to Pennsylvania in 1799 and settled on the east bank of the Allegheny River. They were pioneers in that part of the country, and William Boggs acquired extensive land holdings. The last few years of his life he spent as a partner in the merchandising firm of Wrenshall & Boggs.

When it came time to make his will, William showed great generosity to the children of his brother David. He parcels out the land wholesale, beginning with his nephew William Boggs, "son of David and Mary Boggs":

two tracts of land in St. Clair Township and in the Manor of Pittsburgh, marked No. 6 and No. 7—No. 6 containing as per deed 151 acres and 152 perches and the allowance of 6pCt. for roads & and the other containing 260 acres 130 perches and the same allowances. I also give to my said nephew William Boggs a part or parcel of another tract of land marked No. 3 in the said Manor of Pittsburgh and adjoining to the aforesaid Tracts No. 6 and 7 which part or parcel I suppose to contain about 70 acres and which I leave to be laid off at the discretion of my Executors to the best advantage of my legatees these tracts or parcels of land.

45

I also give and devise to my nephew David Boggs, son of David and Mary Boggs, a tract of land lately purchased at Sheriff's sale, sold as the property of a certain John Sheriff, deceased, supposed to contain about 73 acres. Also another tract of land, laying within the Manor of Pittsburgh and adjoining the aforesaid tract purchased at Sheriff's sale, which tract now bequeathed is also a part of No. 3 situated in the Manor and containing as before expressed 271 acres 88 perches which now described, I calculate to contain about 70 acres, and is to be laid off at the discretion of my Executors. I also give to my said nephew David Boggs one Moiety or half part of a tract of land . . . in partnership with my brother David Boggs for the use of my said nephew, heirs and assigns forever.

I also give to my niece Agnes Boggs, daughter of David and Mary Boggs, the remaining part of Lot or tract No. 3, after deducting the parts which are before bequeathed to my two nephews David and William, which part now bequeathed I calculate will contain about 130 or 140 acres.

I also bequeath to my niece Peggy Boggs, daughter of said David and Mary Boggs, one tract or lot of land marked No. 2 in the Plan of the Manor, containing 100 acres, also another small piece of land adjoining the above containing about 37 acres. The said Agnes and Peggy to hold the same to them their lives &c.

It is my will that the aforesaid legatees, male and female, shall be put in possession of their different legacies when they arrive at legal age or when they marry, and should any or all of them die before arriving at maturity, it is my will that their portions descend to the next heirs.

Having purchased in conjunction with my brother David Boggs from the executors of General John Neville, dec'd, a body of lands on Peters Creek and made a payment in part, I bequeath to said brother David Boggs all my interest in the said purchase, that is to say he is to enjoy the whole himself on paying up the balances still due.

. . . to sell 4000 acres of land I hold in the state of Virginia when it can be done with advantage: I desire them to collect all my debts as soon as convenient and pay all the debts I justly owe: All my personal property and all property whatever not before disposed of I give to my brother David Boggs to enable him to carry on the business of his family and raise the same.

I further do nominate and appoint my trusty friend Col. Presly Nevill and my brother David Boggs to be the Executors of this my last will and Testament, with legal and effectual powers to carry the same into full effect.

This will was written in a good hand on a sheet of paper measuring 16 by 10 inches. William Boggs's first attempt to sign his name was not to his liking; he scratched out the first part of it, then rewrote the entire name just below the crossed-out letters. One month after he signed the will, it was recorded.

JAMES CARNAGHAM—*One streaked Cow, four sheep of her own choice.*
Dated December 12, 1808—Recorded December 28, 1808

The will that James Carnagham dictated, not much more than two weeks before his death, was forthright and to the point. It combines the clear thinking of a man of purpose with the simple expression of an uncluttered mind. The will states that James Carnagham, "of Deer Township":

. . . by the laws of Nature nearing my latter days, do for the purpose of doing justice to my children and preventing trouble Ordain and make this my last will and Testament. That is I do give and bequeath to my dear and Lawfull wife Mary one feather bed and bedding, one Bureau, one Sorrel Mare, one Sadle and Bridle, one streaked Cow, four sheep of her own choice. Also she is to have the household clock during her natural life and at her death it is to be the property of my son James. I also bequeath to her during her natural life if she remains my widow the one-half of the tract of land on which I now live which half is to be taken off the west side of said tract and in case of marriage or decease it is to become the property of my son James. I also bequeath to her one bound female servant, the one-half of dresser furniture belonging to the house of her choice, the bed, bedding and dresser furniture to be at her disposal, also all other property beside the land and clock to be at her disposal. I also bequeath to my daughter Sarah Cowan one Sorrel horse at my decease and two years after twenty-five Dollars. I also bequeath to my son James the one-half of land on which I now live which half is to be taken off the east side of said tract. I also bequeath to my said son James all other property of which I am possessed besides the aforementioned bequests, as also all Book debts, credits, dues and demands in any wise belonging or appertaining to my estate and he my son James is to defray all the expense in settling my estate aforesaid also the discharge of all just debts due by me. I also bequeath to my daughter Jean—out of the before mentioned bequeath made to my son James—one feather bed and bedding, one Cow at twelve dollars one horse or mare at the value of forty dollars, the bed, cow and horse to be delivered to her at her marriage and one year after her marriage she is to receive as above fifty dollars in property and fifty more in money. She is also to get as soon as convenient one Bureau.

Mr. Carnagham appointed his wife and son James executors. He signed the will with his name and affixed his seal of red wax, some of which still remains. The document measures 12¾ by 15½ inches.

JACOB WEITZELL— . . . *according to the Laws and customs of Pennsylvania.*
Dated July 10, 1809—Recorded July 13, 1809

A high respect for the Laws and customs of Pennsylvania is evident in Jacob Weitzell's will, for he makes frequent references to them. He even begins with the legal-sounding term, "Imprimis," but the rest of the will is in the language he would use in dictating his will to its writer.

IMPRIMIS.—I order so much of my goods and chattels to be sold as will pay all my just debts after my decease. Item. I will and bequeath to my beloved wife Catherine one hundred and fifty acres of land which is the upper place called John Perries Cabbin during her widowhood, as also two horses, two cows, a heifer, four sheep and six geese . . . and her Tea Ware, together with the farming utensils and I allow her to build a good convenient house on the said land to enable her to raise my younger children, as also fifty dollars a year out of the yearly income of my estate, and also her bed and bedding and saddle.

And further I allow my sons Phillip and Geo. to have and to hold my Lower place for the term of five years, they to keep the same in good and sufficient repairs over and above an equal share with the rest of my children. And I give and bequeath to my daughter Elizabeth her bed and bedding, one young Mare, Saddle and Bridle, and one Cow over and above an equal share. And I order the house and land I now live on to be rented, together with four acres of meadow off the Lower place—which I have allowed to my two sons Philip and Geo.—and after the expiration of the said five years I wish my house and land I now live on and the Lower place to be valued and appraised according to the laws of Pennsylvania, as in cases of intestate estates, and the money therefrom arising to be equally divided among all my children. And on the death or marriage of my said wife I order that the one hundred and fifty acres be valued and appraised as aforesaid, and the money therefrom arising to be equally divided between all my children or the survivors of them and after ye valuation of the lands made, any of my children may take the whole of my lands at valuation or any part thereof according to the Laws and customs of Pennsylvania as above mentioned. I order my two sons Jacob and Joseph to be educated and appointed to Trades such as they may chuse.

Another instance where Jacob Weitzell revealed his respect for the law is found in a notice appearing in the *Pittsburgh Gazette,* June 13, 1795, fourteen years earlier:

Whereas I gave a bond to a certain Jacob Yoder in December in the year one thousand seven hundred and ninety one for upwards of Fifty Pounds in consideration for a Tract of Land, and whereas the said Yoder was to make me a good and sufficient title to said land which he has not done, I hereby forewarn all persons from taking an assignment on said bond as I am determined not to pay it unless compelled by law.
—Jacob Witzell.

Mr. Weitzell's wife and his son George were made executors of his will. The document, bearing his signature, is of linen paper measuring 16 by 10 inches. It was witnessed by Richard Morrow and Samuel Drake.

WILLIAM RIGDON—*I bequeath . . . my plantation.*
Dated May 22, 1810—Recorded May 31, 1810

Most of the early settlers of Western Pennsylvania called their lands *plantations.* At that time the word meant *settlement* or *colony.* All through these early wills we find references to plantations, as in the will of William Rigdon. He divides his land among his wife and three sons, beginning with this bequest to his wife Nancy:

one third of all my present estate in such things as she shall make choice of, and they shall be entirely her own in life and at her death; moreover, I bequeath to her the dwelling house together with the buildings contiguous to it and also the third part of my land to be chosen compactly together by her on any part of my plantation and to be converted by her at her discretion to her own use during her natural life or as long as she remains my widow. She shall be entitled to Timber for all necessary repairs upon her part of the place from whoever it may be convenient.

His son Carvel was to receive:

one hundred acres of land on the Southeast end of my plantation to be laid off upon John Larimer and John Murry's line and to be cut off from the residue of lands by a straight line from Northeast to Southwest but not to interfere with his mother's part during her natural life or widowhood.

My son Sidney is to have one hundred acres of land on the North side of my plantation upon James Walker, Edward Riggs and Thomas Rigdon's lines, and to be struck off from the remainder of my land in the most convenient manner by a line—nevertheless his division is not to interfere with his mother's part.

To Loammi, the remainder of my land, be it more or less, but not to infringe on his mother's part.

William Rigdon's three hundred and fifty-eight acres were granted to him in 1785 in what was then Washington County, later becoming part of Allegheny County. His brother Thomas settled one hundred and fifty acres.

After dividing up the land in his will, William Rigdon gives all the farm profits to his wife, for the following reasons:

My son Carvel is now an apprentice. My son Loammi is in learning and have not got through his studies, and my son Sidney under age. Therefore, I give and bequeath all the profits of my Plantation to my beloved wife until my three sons are clear of the above imbarriements to enjoy it themselves.

My daughter Lacy is to have two thirds part of my personal estate to be husbanded for her interest in the best manner prudence may dictate by my executors; and furthermore, I give and bequeath unto her three hundred dollars to be paid to her by my three sons, Carvel, Loammi and Sidney Rigdon, after the death of my wife Nancy Rigdon . . . thirty-three and a third dollars each at the close of one year after their mother's decease. . . .

Lacy never received a single payment of the three hundred dollars she was supposed to receive after her mother's decease; that is, if the terms of the will were followed. For her mother outlived her by a number of years, dying at the age of eighty in 1838.

Another wish of William Rigdon's for his offspring apparently never materialized. That was his ambition for Loammi:

I have designed my son Loammi to be a Phisician. I wish him to be conducted through the learning and studies at the expense of the monies that I have appropriated for that purpose and under the care and discretion of my executors.

All we know about Loammi is that he married, had a son, and died. There is nothing to indicate that he ever became a physician.

The rest of the Rigdon family became Mormons after Sidney, the youngest son, discovered a copy of Spaulding's *Manuscript Found* while he was an apprentice in a printing shop. Inspired by its passages, he became an ardent Mormon missionary and a close associate of the Prophet Joseph Smith. He assisted the Prophet in a translation of the Scriptures and, with him, was tarred and feathered by an angry mob in Hiram, Ohio. Sidney Rigdon served as First Counselor to the Prophet in the first presidency of that church from March 18, 1813, to June 27, 1844 (*Utah Genealogical and Historical Magazine*, 1936, v.27, p.145).

The original of the William Rigdon will is on laid paper, 15 by 12½ inches, and has broken through the lengthwise fold into two parts. Witnesses to the signing were Thomas Rigdon and Ebenezer Gallaher.

JAMES RYAN—*And should he not live so long* . . .
    Dated October 26, 1810—Recorded December 23, 1812

James Ryan, "formerly a subject of the King of Great Britain, but now of the United States of America, of the Township of Pitt, Allegheny County, and State of Pennsylvania," signed his will with his mark. After leaving instructions that his body was to be buried on his own plantation "in a plain decent but becoming manner," he went on to his bequests:

After my decease Ambrose Ryan my second son to enjoy an absolute fee in and to my real estate . . . provided allways that he the said Ambrose . . . discharge the following legacies to the near value of the said estate within three whole years from the day of my decease, to wit, that after my decease in the space of three whole years—my oldest son William Ryan I give and bequeath one hundred dollars and I do hereby enjoin my executors to see that my son Ambrose pay the same to him the said William Ryan or his heirs.

I give and bequeath to Jane Guffey, my oldest daughter, at the time limited above, one hundred dollars and that out of my real fund my son Ambrose pay the same to her . . .

Item—I give and bequeath after the term of three whole years be expired after my death unto Rebecca Carroll, my second daughter living, the sum of one Dollar to be paid unto her. To Isabella Large, my third daughter now living under the restriction above one Dollar. To Sarah McDonald, the sum of fifty dollars, to each of my daughters for divers goods considerations I give and bequeath one Dollar at three years after my decease, to wit Matty Booker and Nancy Booker.

Item—I give and bequeath unto my grandson James Ryan son of Ambrose Ryan one horse Colt which at this time is one half year old and I do enjoin his father to keep the same in trust for him or the avails thereto till he comes to years of eighteen, and should he not live so long then to the said Ambrose.

52

James Ryan's homestead, comprising two hundred and fifty-six acres when it was deeded to him in 1785, went by the name of *Peleponesus*. The log structure that stood there for many years was replaced by a colonial brick house in 1820. Bricks from that house have been used to build the present Ryan homestead, which stands on the old site in Penn Township.

Mr. Ryan's will was witnessed by James McCutcheon, John Thompson, and James Rogers. The executors were Samuel Nerr and Thomas May.

BRETON BRUNOT—*I am a subscriber for the Encyclopedia and British Classics.*
Dated January 23, 1815—Recorded April 11, 1815

The will of Breton Brunot, signed in big, bold letters as "B. Brunot," is the testament of a man of proud lineage and high standing in the community. Himself a physician, his father was Dr. Felix Brunot, foster brother of Marquis de la Fayette, who had come to America as a member of the medical staff of Lafayette's military expedition. The younger Brunot's will reads:

In the name of God, Amen, I Britton Brunot being of sound mind and memory, but being weak in body, do make this my last will and testament in manner following, to wit, after all my lawful debts are paid, I give and bequeath all my real estate to my dearly beloved father Felix Brunot to be by him disposed of at his decease in such manner as he may think proper; to him I likewise give and bequeath all my personal property whatever, excepting my library, mahogany Bookcase, and desk, which I give and bequeath to my brother Felix Brunot; and as I am a subscriber for the Encyclopedia and British Classics, it is my wish that my said brother Felix should continue to take the remaining numbers until the said books are complete, and it is my will and desire that all the remaining numbers be paid for out of the estate bequeathed to my father. I do relinquish any claim I may have against my said brother Felix for any debt or demand which I now have against him. As witness my hand the twenty-third day of January, A.D., eighteen hundred and fifteen.

—B. Brunot

(Witnessed by: S. Douglas, John Gorman, and Dennis S. Scully.)

I do hereby declare the above disposal of my property to be my last will and testament and do hereby appoint my father and brother Felix executors thereof. Signed and acknowledged in the presence of us who at the request of said Testator did subscribe our names thereto.

—B. Brunot

(S. Douglas, John Gorman, Dennis S. Scully.)

Dr. Brunot died on April 2 of that year, according to a 72 by 34-inch stone slab in the churchyard of Trinity Cathedral. The text on that old marker is of more than casual interest:

Dr. Breton Brunot, April 2, 1815, 25 years. He was an ornament to his profession, a friend of the poor, a fit companion of the virtuous and a useful member of society.

Farther down on the stone slab is this tribute from an un-known admirer, dated 69 years later:

A.D. 1884.

One, who in childhood, was often told of the virtues of the de-ceased, has renewed his crumbling grave stone a few years longer to mark the spot where his moldering remains await the coming of our Lord.

At the time this second inscription was made, a nephew of Breton Brunot's, Dr. Felix R. Brunot, was serving out his last years as trustee of the Western University of Pennsylvania after a life of service to the entire community. He may have added the later cutting. The Brunot name, inscribed and venerated in stone, re-mains alive in the deeds of those who bore it.

Little else seems to be known about young Dr. Brunot, except that he was one of the witnesses to the will of the well-known Dr. Andrew Richardson. That presupposes a friendship between the two men and, certainly, Breton's father—Dr. Felix Brunot—and Dr. Richardson would have had a lot in common. Politics, perhaps, in addition to the medical profession? For, as everybody knows, Richardson was a "Democratic Republican"—and Breton Brunot selected three prominent members of that party to witness the signing of his will.

The first Dr. Felix Brunot, foster brother of Lafayette, who had settled in Philadelphia after the Revolution, came to live on an island in the Ohio River in 1797. That island had formerly belonged to John McKee and had borne his name, but ever since Dr. Felix Brunot settled there it has been known as *Brunot's Island*. This founder of the Brunot name in America lived to the ripe age of eighty-six, venerated for his skill as a surgeon and remembered by the medical profession for his successes in new treatments.

The person who actually wrote Breton Brunot's will insisted on spelling his first name as "Britton," probably because it sounded like that. The document measures 12¼ by 7½ inches, and is well preserved.

JOHN JOLLIFFE YARNALL—*At present belonging to the United States Navy . . .*
Dated November 6, 1813—Recorded May 23, 1816

There is a very significant relationship between the date on which John Jolliffe Yarnall signed his will and the phrase which appears in its preface—"at present belonging to the United States Navy." The War of 1812 was at its height. It was a dangerous year for sailors. The date on which the will is recorded leads to a conclusion borne out by a search of the Naval records of the U.S. Congress—John Jolliffe Yarnall died in the service of his country.

Lieutenant Yarnall was one of the heroes of the War of 1812; he brought honor to his country and to his family. The circumstance of his death was one of the ironies of the war. But we shall begin with his will. The main provision follows:

I desire that my Executors shall, after the payment of my just debts, invest the whole of my surplus Estate in Bank Stock or other Publick Securities for the express purpose of becoming a fund for the more comfortable maintenance of my aged Mother, the Interest or lawful increase whereof I hereby give & bequeath unto my said Mother, same to be applied exclusively to her use and benefit during her natural life.

The will was written on a heavy sheet of foolscap paper,

signed by Lt. Yarnall, and witnessed by Townsend Speakman, Samuel Pettigrew, and Everard Bolton, Jr. Named as executors were John's brother, Amos, and his brother-in-law, Aquila M. Bolton.

Two months before he signed his will, Lt. Yarnall had distinguished himself in the Battle of Lake Erie, September 10, 1813. Capt. Oliver H. Perry, commanding the flagship *Lawrence,* takes personal note of Lt. Yarnall's valor in his official report to the Secretary of the Navy a few days after the battle *(U.S. Congress, American State Papers, Naval Affairs, v.1, p.295):*

The *Lawrence* . . . sustained the action upwards of two hours, within canister distance, until every gun was rendered useless, and the greater part of her crew either killed or wounded. Finding she could no longer annoy the enemy, I left her in charge of Lieutenant Yarnall, who, I was convinced, from the bravery already displayed by him, would do what would comport with the honor of the flag.

Lieutenant Yarnall, first of the *Lawrence,* although several times wounded, refused to quit the deck.

Capt. Perry made a perilous passage by rowboat to the *Niagara,* from whose decks he maneuvered the defeat of the enemy.

Lt. Yarnall was awarded a Gold Medal for his part in the action, but it was not until the summer of 1819, four years after his death, that his family received the medal. This fact comes to light in the examination of two letters recorded in the *Pennsylvania Archives: sixth series, v.9.* The first of these was from the Navy Department to "Thomas Sergeant, Esqr., Secretary of State of Pennsylvania, Harrisburg":

Navy Department
March 2nd, 1819

Sir:

I have had the honour to receive your letter of the 23rd. ultimo, written at the request of the Governor of the Commonwealth of Pennsylvania, for the purpose of ascertaining the address of certain officers of the Navy of the United States, to whom the Legislature of Pennsyl-

vania had awarded gold medals in honour of the brilliant action of the
10th September 1813 on Lake Erie.

Capt. Oliver H. Perry is the commanding Navy Officer at Newport,
R.I.—Capt. Jesse D. Elliott is at present in this city; and Lieutenant
John J. Yarnall was lost in the U.S. Brig Epervier; his Mother and relatives reside, it is believed, in Pittsburgh, Pa., particular information respecting them may be obtained from the Honble Abner Lacock, one of
the Senators in Congress from Pennsylvania.

With the highest respect,

I have the honour to be,

Sir,

Your most ob: servant,

Smith Thompson.

The second letter is addressed to "His Excellency William
Findlay, Esq., Governor of Penn'a, Harrisburg," and is signed
"Phebe Yarnall," John Yarnall's mother:

Pittsburgh, 5th of 11th mo., 1819

Honoured Friend,

I have the pleasure to acknowledge the receipt of thy letter of the
7th ulto. accompanying, by the hands of Ephraim Pentland, Esq. a copy
of Resolutions of the General Assembly of Pennsylvania, expressive of
their sense of the brave and gallant conduct of my son, the late Lieutenant John J. Yarnall in the brilliant victory of the 10th of September
1813 over the British Squadron on Lake Erie. Amidst the sorrow of
heart to which I have been inevitably exposed by a dispensation depriv-
ing me of my son, the sympathy expressed in thy communication and
my confidence in believing that his memory will be preserved and
cherished in the annals of our nation and in the affectionate recollection
of its patriotick citizens afford a consolation which, be assured, I
though not altogether a Spartan, know how to appreciate.

The Style of execution both the penmanship and the frame in
which it is set is as striking to every other eye as the memorial itself is
affecting to a mother's. For the manner in which this framed copy of the
Resolutions, as well as the Medal, has been presented, accept the thanks
of

Thy friend

Phebe Yarnall

57

Lt. Yarnall had perished aboard the U.S. brig *Epervier* in the Navy's last mission of the war. The Treaty of Ghent had already been signed when the *Epervier,* with several other vessels, was sent to the Mediterranean to deal with the pirates of the Barbary Coast states. After a successful encounter with the enemy, the *Epervier* was returning to the United States in July, 1815, with a copy of the treaty signed by the Dey of Algiers. It was last sighted off Gibraltar July 12, but apparently foundered in an Atlantic storm, for it never reached the states.

John Jolliffe Yarnall, in his will, had provided for "the more comfortable maintenance of my aged Mother." In his service to his country, he provided her with something she probably cherished more—a lasting memory of a gallant and honored son.

NATHANIEL BEDFORD—*All that tract and parcel of land . . . adjoining the town of Birmingham.*
Dated March 17, 1818—Recorded March 24, 1818

Dr. Nathaniel Bedford, pioneer physician of Pennsylvania and Pittsburgh's first doctor, made his will exactly a week before it was probated. His signature, irregular and shaky, betrays his physical condition. The writing takes up both sides of the first double sheet of 10 by 15⅛-inch paper. The second sheet contains only a few lines of writing at the top, and the register's statement below. A large, round-headed pin, apparently hand made, held the pages together the first time we examined it; but upon returning for a second examination sometime later, we found the pin missing. Outside of that, the will has come down to us in fairly good shape, although discolored and frayed at the edges.

Dr. Bedford had inherited large tracts of land from his first wife, Jane Ormsby. This ground was on the south side of the Monongahela River, where he laid out his American "Birmingham." The will disposes of his real estate as follows:

I give and devise to my wife, Mary Bedford, and her heirs, all that tract and parcel of land whereon I now live situated adjoining the town of Birmingham aforesaid, containing sixty acres more or less, including a piece of land lately purchased by James Brown, together with the buildings, coal banks, improvements and appurtenances thereto belonging, to have and to hold the tract of land aforesaid with the appurtenances, to the said Mary Bedford and her heirs . . . The remainder of my real estate, after satisfying the debts and legacies above-mentioned, I order and direct my executors and their survivors to part and divide equally between Bedford Mowry, son of Doctor Mowry, and Nathaniel Bedford Bingham, son of my sister Martha Bingham, wife of John Bingham of Birmingham in England.

The "Doctor Mowry" mentioned in this will was Peter Mowry, Nathaniel Bedford's first apprentice. Bedford Mowry became a physician, too, but died early in life.

Mary, according to some of Dr. Bedford's biographers, had been "lady's maid" to his first wife, Jane. His bequest to her contained, in addition to the sixty acres:

all moveable property including all my horses, cattle and stock of every kind, garden utensils, watches, time pieces, plate and household and kitchen furniture of every kind whatever.

He exempted from that bequest "all my books, maps and manuscripts," which he gave to Peter Mowry, with the further interesting exception:

excepting Wilson's Ornithology, Deleplaines, and Bible, which I bequeath to my wife, Sarah Bedford.

Who was "Sarah?" Was this the "Mary" referred to earlier as his wife, called now by another name, or just a slip of the penman? The question remains unanswered.

Dr. Bedford was a scholarly man, thoroughly educated in the medical profession. His diploma hangs now in Carnegie Library's Pennsylvania Room. This is its text:

London, April 3d, 1770

These are to certify that Mr. Nathaniel Bedford hath diligently attended our Lectures on the Theory & Practice of Midwifery and on the diseases of Women and Children.

Wm. Moore.   Thos. Debman.

On the back of the framed diploma is the following notation:

This diploma is the property of Dr. Wm. B. Mowry. His great-uncle Peter studied medicine under Dr. Bedford—and the diploma was handed down from him to Dr. Robert B. Mowry and from him to Dr. Wm. B. Mowry, his son.

Originally a surgeon in the British Army, Dr. Bedford was attached to one of the English garrisons at Fort Pitt. Prior to 1784 he resigned his commission and entered into private practice in Pittsburgh. He is said to have lived in style in his beautiful home at the corner of Seventh and Liberty Streets, the grounds of which extended back to Penn Avenue. Like an English nobleman, he had his servants, his horses, and a pack of hunting dogs. But an advertisement in the *Pittsburgh Gazette,* dated February 18, 1797, suggests that he was, at times, pressed for money which was due him:

Doctor Bedford requests those who are indebted to him on the score of his profession, or otherwise, to make speedy payments. He makes this call on his friends with reluctance. But in consequence of certain new engagements that will require the command of considerable sums, he will be under the disagreeable necessity of putting in suit all monies, without distinction, that are now due to him and shall remain unpaid by the 15th of March next. Further indulgence cannot be given.

Pittsburgh, January 14, 1797.

After his second marriage Nathaniel Bedford moved to the south side of the Monongahela River and lived on the land he came by through his first wife, Jane Ormsby.

Besides his contributions to the community as a physician, Dr. Bedford was one of the original trustees of the Pittsburgh Academy, now the University of Pittsburgh, when it was chartered on February 28, 1787. He also served as one of the assistant burgesses of Pittsburgh after the first borough elections on May 19, 1794. He was a vestryman of Trinity Episcopal Church; a plaque in the graveyard of that church witnesses his accomplishments and gives his date of death as March 21, 1818.

A strange coincidence is found in the fact that near Dr. Bedford's grave, along the west wall of the burying ground, is the headstone of one of Dr. Bedford's most noted patients. The inscription reads:

MIO-QUA-COO-NA-CAW
or
RED POLE
Principal Village Chief
of the Shawnee Nation
Died at Pittsburgh
Jan. 28, 1797
Lamented by the United States

As surgeon at Fort Pitt, Nathaniel Bedford attended the Shawnee chief when he fell victim to an epidemic of influenza. Red Pole was buried with full military honors—a conciliatory gesture to the Shawnee nation. At that time it was customary for the attending doctor to head a deceased patient's procession to the grave, followed by the pallbearers with the corpse. It is not known whether Dr. Bedford actually participated in this ceremony; but there is no doubt of the fact that doctor and patient, white man and red man, eventually came to share the same plot of ground.

GEORGE McGUNNEGLE—*A certain deed of Perpetual Lease.*
Dated March 7, 1820—Recorded August 6, 1821

George McGunnegle lived to be eighty-five. That was a long span of life in a period when men—on the average—died some twenty to thirty years younger. Mr. McGunnegle seems to have been a robust fellow, judged by his varied activities. He was an artisan and a realtor. And his many newspaper notices show that he moved often, locating his shop in at least three different places in less than two years. In the *Pittsburgh Gazette* of November 2, 1787, appeared the following notice:

George M'Gunnigle, White and Black Smith has opened his shop at the house lately occupied by Capt. Alexander Fowler, in Second Street, Pittsburgh, where all kinds of Smith work is made in the neatest and best manner, and at the lowest price. He hopes by attention to his business to merit the countenance and favor of the public.

—George M'Gunnigle

N.B.—All kinds of locks repaired, also trusses for ruptures, warranted good.

August 1, 1789:

The subscriber respectfully informs the public that he has moved his shop to the house formerly occupied by Mr. Marmaduke Curtis, in Market Street, where he carries on the Black & White Smith business. He has furnished himself with a very good horseshoer and country smiths and likewise makes locks, keys, hinges of all sorts, pipe tomahawks, scalping knives, boxes and pins for vizes, grates, polished and unpolished andirons, shovels, tongs, pokers, chaffing dishes, bread toasters, ladles, skimmers, flesh forks and skewers, with all kind of iron work for a kitchen, currying combs, plates, saddle trees, makes crapeing, curbing and pincing tongs, rupture belts, grinds swords, razors, scissors, and pen knives, cleans and polishes guns and pistols. As he is determined to do any of the above work on the most reasonable terms, he flatters himself he will engage the attention and favors of the public.

—George M'Gunnigle

September 15 . . . makes bed screws and branding irons of all sizes and does several other pieces of business in the White Smith line, too tedious to mention. He also carries on the Blacksmith, in the shop late occupied by William Braden, in partnership with James Beard, who is perfectly well qualified for horse shoeing or any kind of work in that way, also make horse, cow and sheep bells.

—George M'Gunnigle

N.B.—Two Apprentices wanted to the aforesaid business; also a quantity of old brass, for which a generous price will be given.

The property that Mr. McGunnegle acquired as a realtor, he willed to his children.

To David the large brick house situate in the Diamond or Public Square of the city aforesaid now in the occupancy of Ephraim Pentland, Esq. (subject nevertheless to the payment a judgment now remaining against me unsatisfied in the court of Common Pleas of the County of Allegheny in favour of said David amounting to 5951-33/100 dollars in Fee Simple.)

To James the smaller brick house situate in the Diamond or Public Square aforesaid, together with the back dwellings and lot of ground occupied by and the same is now rented by Phillip Gilland, Esq., as also the lot of ground fronting on Liberty Street in the city aforesaid, together with all the incumbrances thereon (as now in the possession of Richard Getty, in fee simple forever,) subject, nevertheless, to the payment of all my debts not otherwise provided for, as also to the payment of the annuity to my daughter Eliza M'Gunnigle hereinafter mentioned.

I give and devise to my daughter Eliza M'Gunnigle all my furniture and household utensils of every kind or description whatsoever, as also an annuity of one hundred dollars to be paid to her yearly out of the property devised to my son James, from the time of my decease during her natural life, provided she should continue single and unmarried, but in case she should become married, then my will is that the said annuity cease and determine. I also give to my said daughter Eliza one gold ring of the value of ten dollars.

The other daughters who each received a gold ring—a precious luxury in those days—were "Anna Moore, Elinor Gibson, Mary Davis, Rosamond Gilland, Margaret Gilland, and Catharine Johnston." Mrs. McGunnegle apparently did not live long enough to share in her husband's bequests.

Two other sons, John and George, each received $50 for "a suit of mourning." And then, before signing his will, George McGunnegle made this addition in his bequest to James:

It is my express intention and I do hereby devise to my son James all my right title and interest of, in and to the ground rent reserved to

63

me in a certain deed of Perpetual Lease made by me to Abraham Long of a lot of ground fronting on Penn Street in the city aforesaid to have and to hold the said yearly ground rent with all the rights and privileges thereunto appertaining.

George McGunnegle, a frequent advertiser in the local newspaper, sometimes used that medium for selling or renting some of his real property. For example:

The subscriber proposes selling about 20 feet of the LOT he now lives on, fronting the Public Square and corner of Diamond Alley. If not sold before the 18th day of August next, he will, on that day, dispose of it by public auction to the highest bidder. Any person wishing to purchase may know the terms by applying to the subscriber.

George M'Gunnegle

Pittsburgh, July 17, 1796

N.B.—He will give good encouragement of a journeyman Blacksmith & also wants an Apprentice to said Business.

March 2, 1805

To be rented and possession given the 1st of April next. Two new log houses in Penn Street, between St. Clair Street and Cecil's Alley. There are in each house two rooms on the first floor and two on the second, with a well lighted garret, and a good cellar. The situation is pleasant, being so convenient to the Allegheny River. Also, to be let forever, twenty-seven feet of ground adjoining the above-mentioned houses on the same street. For terms, apply to either of the proprietors.

George M'Gunnegle
Philip Gilland

The ponderous IMPRIMIS, SECUNDO, TERTIO, QUARTO, QUINTO, SEXTO, and SEPTIMO, which set off the paragraphs in his will, are as solidly fixed in this document as if they had been hammered out on the anvil by the powerful arm of Blacksmith McGunnegle. But also illuminating as to Mr. McGunnegle's character were his first instructions to his executors, James

64

Brown and William Hays, that his body was "to be interred in the Protestant Episcopal Church of said city."

ROBERT MAGEE—*All my Estate . . . excepting the sum of three Dollars.*

Dated November 25, 1822—Recorded February 1, 1823

Robert Magee was Scotch-Irish; his will, adequate to the last degree, was yet a masterpiece of economy. It follows complete:

In The Name of God Amen.

I Robert Magee of the City of Pittsburgh County of Allegheny and State of Pennsylvania, being of sound mind, memory and understanding, but growing weak in Bodily Strength, and considering the uncertainty of this life, and knowing that all men must die, do make and publish this my last will and testament in the following manner, to wit. I give and bequeath to my beloved Son Christopher Linem all my Estate both real and personal to be enjoyed and possessed by him and his heirs for Ever, excepting the sum of three Dollars, which I give and bequeath to my three sons Thomas, Samuel and Matthew, to be Equally divided among them, And I do, hereby, nominate my said Son Christopher Linem and appoint him to be Sole Executor of this my last will and testament—In witness whereof I have hereunto set my hand and Seal, the twenty fifth day of November, A.D. one thousand Eight hundred and twenty two.—

Signed sealed and published
and pronounced and declared by
the said Testator as and
for his last will and testament
     In the presence of
     John Taylor
     Andrew Watson, Jr.
     Wm. Pentland
Robert Magee

One look at the handwriting of this will leaves little doubt that it was written by John Taylor, who has a very clear and firm script. Written on good stock, it measures 12¼ by 15⅛ inches.

The paper is folded down the center, and the writing is contained on the right hand side of the fold.

Robert Magee, progenitor of the Pittsburgh family, came from Derry County in Northern Ireland. He settled here in 1788, and thereafter became active in the Jeffersonian party. In 1802 he was assistant to the chief burgess, Isaac Craig, and in 1803 he was Clerk of the Market. His descendants, notably Christopher L. Magee (1848-1901), have kept alive the Magee name and leadership in city and county politics.

Robert Magee was a vestryman of Trinity Episcopal, and his body lies in that churchyard. On a metal slab, 35 by 72 inches, is a long record of the Magee descendants beginning with the death of Robert Magee, January 30, 1823.

Angus McBain—*The bed tick . . . from Scotland.*
　　　　Dated January 29, 1822—Recorded November 26, 1823

Angus McBain signed his will with a word-symbol faintly reassembling the letters of his first name. His bequest to his niece emphasizes his Scottish ancestry:

I leave and bequeath to said Cady McDonald the two best plaids which are in my chest and the bed tick she brought with her for me from Scotland, and one half of the citching furnature . . .

The other half of the kitchen furniture went to Mr. McBain's brother Daniel; and a second brother, John, who lived in Scotland, came into the largest bequest:

I wish and request that the obligations which I hold on Sundry Individuals may be collected as soon as may be practicable which amount to some more than Fourteen hundred dollars all of which I leave and bequeath unto my brother John in Scotland and his heirs and my brother Daniel and his heirs and my said nice Cady McDonald in three equal shares. . .

A codicil, signed shortly before his death, November 11, 1823, gives final evidence of the soft spot Angus McBain had in his heart for his niece, for it is concerned solely with her:

I will and bequeath unto my nice Caty McDonald who now lives with me, in consequence of her faithful and affectionate attention to me in my distress, the sum of Sixty dollars in cash . . . besides her share of my estate as bequeathed to her in my said last will. . .

Appointed executors were William Watson and Thomas Hind. Witnesses to the will were Matthew B. Lowrie and Nancy Cameron, and Mr. Lowrie and David Pride witnessed the codicil.

Holograph Wills

A holograph will is one which is written by the testator himself and signed by him. The only way to tell whether a will is a holograph or not is to examine the original document, for the recorders who copied the old wills into the will books made no distinction between holographs and other manuscript wills. They are given equal status within the framework of the law, as long as they are properly signed and witnessed. But to the historian—or to anyone who is privileged to read the old manuscripts in the original—a holograph will takes on added interest. For when a man phrases his own will and sets it down in his own hand, more of his personality is bound to find expression in the pages he writes.

After all, though, the phrasing and handwriting of a will are only the *added* interest. The provisions a testator makes for the welfare of his family, the education of his children, and the equitable distribution of his estate—in such matters are bound up a man's character and way of life, and in them is revealed the depth of his judgment and foresight. These things we look for in a will, besides the homely turn of phrase or quirk of nature. And in the holograph wills that follow, presented in the order they were recorded, we find much that was vital to men who lived on a growing frontier.

WILLIAM BUTLER—*I will . . . the education of my sons.*
Dated May 12, 1789—Recorded August 1, 1791

William Butler expressed himself with clarity and purpose, in a distinct hand and in numbered paragraphs. The firm manner in which he handled the provisions of his will is best illustrated in the following paragraph:

> I will, order, and direct that all my children have a genteel education at the discretion of my executors hereinafter named, but that the education of my sons Richard and William Butler do not exceed the Lattin language.

Mr. Butler was making it clear that while he wanted his children educated, and was willing to provide the means for it, he did not want his two sons to neglect practical pursuits for learning that could not be put to use. In this he reflected the general attitude of the times, and must be given credit for providing for education as well as he did.

Mr. Butler was fair, as well as firm. His wife, his two sons, his three daughters, all receive "each an equal share and portion of all my personal estate of whatsoever kind, share and share alike . . . each an equal share and portion of all my lands, Tenements and Hereditaments I shall die possessed of."

The firm hand evident in William Butler's will is best understood when we learn that he was most proud of his rank as an officer in the Revolutionary War. When he identifies himself in the opening lines of his will, it is not as the Indian trader he had been most of his life. Rather, it is as the "late Colonel commanding the Fourth Pennsylvania Regiment in the service of the United States of America." And he had a right to be proud of his career as an officer, for the men who had served under him boasted of his bravery. The qualities that raised him to the rank of lieutenant colonel must also have included firm but fair leadership.

For leadership in family matters after his death, William Butler relied upon his wife:

> My beloved wife, Jinny Butler, shall have the conduct and management of all my real and personal estate to manage the same as she shall

think the most suitable for the mutual advantage of herself and children during her widowhood. And it is further my will and I order and direct that in case my beloved wife Jinny Butler should intermarry after my decease that then and in such case she shall cease to act as an executrix or have anything to do with the management of the children's estates.

Again, the fair and generous provision, followed by the restraining hand.

Among Mr. Butler's other bequests was one of forty pounds Pennsylvania currency "to my honoured Father and Mother, Thomas and Elinor Butler." And to his "beloved and much esteemed brother, General Richard Butler," a full suit of mourning. William and Richard lived in adjoining houses said to be the first substantial buildings around Fort Pitt. Within a year after the Colonel's death the General was killed in a skirmish with the Indians near Fort Recovery, Ohio. But the Butler name lives on in the name of a city, a county, and a Pittsburgh street.

William Butler's will, measuring 15 by 12½ inches, was witnessed by George Wallace, Matt Ernest, William Tilton, and George Adams. A slab of stone in the churchyard of the Trinity Cathedral is believed to mark Colonel Butler's last resting place, although the name has long been worn off.

EBENEZER MITCHEL—*Money for land in Caintucke.*
Dated October 9, 1788—Recorded March 5, 1792

Mr. Mitchel's will shows little education, but no lack of foresight. The quaint spelling and absence of punctuation fail to obscure the purpose of his will. There are definite reasons, for instance, behind the way he divides his property:

my three sons is to have equeal shears and doghters to have each of them haf as much as any of my sons and my wife being now pregnant if she has a son it is to sheare as the rest of my sons and if a doghter as the rest of my doghters.

Upon the boys would be placed the burden of the family's welfare when the father died. They would have to provide for the mother, and for the unmarried girls. In addition, they would have wives and children of their own to care for. Mr. Mitchel knew the sons would need the extra share of land, and he provided that the unborn child should have the extra legacy also if it were a son. The recording date of the will indicates that the father lived to see the new child take its place among the other Mitchel children —David, John, Mathew, Jean, and Isabil.

In another clause of his will Ebenezer Mitchel reveals the true spirit of the pioneer and the vision that brought him to the frontier. For he is looking far into the future when he makes this bequest, "that my executors or other fit persons chosen for that end as soon as it can be done lay out my childrens money for land in Caintucke or some other new country."

That "some other new country" covered a lot of territory Mr. Mitchel would never know, but he looked forward to his children's going there, and he knew enough about frontier land to know that it would rapidly increase in value.

That Ebenezer Mitchel was fair in the treatment of his daughters is very evident in the section of the will providing for the education of his children:

Also I do order that my executors do put my sons to treads and provide that they be sufficiently schooled in the time of their apprenticeship by their masters and also that they see to the schooling of my doghters.

The apprenticeship and schooling of the boys would better enable them to earn a living. But the education of the girls, at a time when it was seldom provided for, would only bring them personal benefit. Yet Mr. Mitchel wanted them to have it.

Mr. Mitchel wrote his will on a piece of paper 12⅝ by 7¼ inches in size. He identifies himself as a resident of the "Steat of Pennsylvania and County of Westmoreland," although on the date he signed it he was actually a resident of Allegheny County. Allegheny had been erected from part of Westmoreland County by act of General Assembly two weeks before.

ROBERT CALLENDER—*All the property . . . which was hers previous to our marriage.*
Dated November 15, 1802—Recorded November 23, 1802

The customs of the time guided the form of Robert Callender's bequests. His legacy was to go mainly to three women—his wife, his mother, and his sister. Therefore, his bequests reflect the law of that time that women could own property only when it was willed directly to them. This is the reason that Mr. Callender found it necessary to leave to his wife, the former Harriet Butler, "all the property of whatsoever kind which was hers previous to our marriage and to which I have now by that marriage any interest or claim."

The same type of bequest to his mother gave her "all my Plate which is Family plate," which Robert had probably inherited upon the death of his father with directions to keep it in the family.

It is known from the land records of the Pennsylvania Department of Internal Affairs that Robert Callender had been an extensive land owner. During the Revolutionary War Mr. Callender, then a captain, had been through this part of the country as commander of the Seventh Company of the First Battalion of Pennsylvania Provincials. Later he returned and secured a patent for six hundred acres along the base of Wills Mountain, including the William Todd mansion on the present Lincoln Highway north. But when it came time to make his will, Mr. Callender probably thought it would be better to leave his three women cash holdings rather than large estates they might have trouble managing. So he instructed his executors—John Wilkins, Jr., George Wallace, and Alexander Addison—to convert his property to cash and set up trust funds for the three women. His wife was to receive: "a legacy of five thousand dollars provided that the same exceed not one-third of my estate after the disposition aforesaid."

The "disposition aforesaid" included a "trust for the payment of my just debts and funeral expenses."

The rest of the property was to be divided equally between his mother and his sister, Mary Thompson. Being a "Counsellor at Law," Mr. Callender knew what he was doing when he attached a provision to his bequest to his sister stating that the trust fund was "for her children after her decease, not being subject to the management of her present or any future husband, or subject to any debts of such husband."

By making the gift to his sister so definite, he gave her absolute control over her legacy and the power to hand it down to her children when it came time to make her own will.

Yet another provision in Robert Callender's will throws light upon his judicious nature. "To avoid disputes," the passage reads, "my mulatto servant William is to be free immediately after my decease."

Mr. Callender wrote his will in neat, clear letters, on four sides of a folded sheet measuring 16½ by 15 inches. It was witnessed by Jeremiah Barker, Isaac Meason, Jr., and Alexander Addison.

JAMES IMBRIE—*Be careful in raising sufficient quantity of flax yearly for the Girls.*
Dated December 20, 1802—Recorded March 4, 1803

James Imbrie was a widower with five boys and six girls to think about when he wrote his will. His instructions to them were set down with touching care, and it is interesting to see how he tried to make provisions for each one. Two of the older boys, James and Robert, were intrusted with the management of the farm:

James and Robert or either of them shall be careful in raising sufficient quantity of flax yearly for the Girls, out of which they, viz., the Girls, are to supply the Boys with what is sufficient for common use; and the Overpluss to be considered as their own property.

The movable property was to be appraised:

for the use of John, George, Effy, Jean, Margaret, Catherine, Elizabeth and Mary . . . and all profits or increase arising from that property as also profits issuing from the cultivation of the Farm shall be equally divided among the whole, including James and Robert.

The eldest son, David, was treated according to his special inclinations, which was a remarkable consideration for a father harassed as Mr. Imbrie must have been:

73

My eldest son David who haveing near finished his education shall continue in the family as formerly until Providentially provided for, otherwise to enjoy boarding and clothing, but when leaving the family is to have the third of the English Library, and I bequeath to him the horse Bucephalis, saddle and bridle.

Bucephalus was named for the favorite war horse of Alexander the Great. A boy inheriting such a horse would undoubtedly prize him very much.

The eldest girl, Effy, was to have "her choice of a Bed and Bedding above the rest." The three youngest daughters, who probably would need more care and instruction than Effy would have time to give them, were taken care of by this direction to the executors, "dispose of my three youngest daughters into such familys as they judge for be for their advantage."

Mr. Imbrie further directs that the schooling of his children "must be duly attended to, the expense of which is to be out of the product of the place." The two youngest boys were to be "put to trades agreeable to their inclinations."

This was the organization by which the family could be kept going. Further provisions were made for when the children grew older:

Further, it is my will that my Plantation in Mill Creek be sold at the time that George is to be put to a trade or at any time between that and the year 1817, at which time he will be of age; and the amount equally divided between the two youngest boys and the six girls.

James and Robert, the older boys, were to receive a special reward for managing the farm: "my tract of land in the Connecticut Reserve equally divided between them as their share of my real estate."

Two codicils followed the will, afterthoughts to Mr. Imbrie's careful planning.

I do hereby constitute, ordain and appoint Hugh Miller and John Neilson, Elder guardians of my children.

It is further my will and pleasure that all wearing apparel, consisting of body cloathes, shall not come under the appraisement with other effects of the house, these being distributed already.

74

James Imbrie's signature—witnessed by William Fraiser, James Craig, and James Neilson—is partially obscured by a large ink blot over the letter *J*. But the text is clearly written, and all contained on a document measuring 15¼ by 12½ inches. How important was this single sheet of paper, both for what it told of the past and planned for the future!

JOSEPH B. ORMSBY—*All the advantage I might derive from the sales of this cargo.*
Dated, New Orleans, La., May 30, 1803—Recorded June 10, 1803

One of the holograph wills examined was in the form of a letter. It was dated "New Orleans, La., May 30, 1803," and addressed to John Ormsby, Sr., a prominent Pittsburgh merchant. The letter was signed by his son, Joseph B. Ormsby, and read:

My dear honored, much beloved Parent, your son has left you, by the mandate of Him who governs all. It is perhaps for the best, I hope so, and trust fully that I shall be saved. My dear father, do not lament the loss of me, but let my dear worthy excellent sister and brother, with their sweet offspring, console you. May I request that my dear father will grant, will pay attention to the best wishes of his son's in giving John Ormsby Gregg all that property which was destined by you for Joseph Blakeney Ormsby, viz., the piece of land on the Monongahela and the lott in the Town of Pittsburgh. I wish also all the advantage I might derive from the sales of this cargo may be extended to you, my dear father, and that you may live to enjoy it. Any advantages of any kind whatsoever I might have derived in living that can be transferred, I wish extended to my dear John Ormsby Gregg, but wish that he not dispose of the property so given at any time, but to derive every advantage from it, and could wish him an elegant education, especially in French and Spanish. I wish all my wearing apparel, books, flute, bureau, and in fact everything I am possessed of may be delivered to John Ormsby Gregg, with the following emcumbrances, viz., Ten dollars to Mr. Henry Woods and Twenty dollars to Hugh H. Brackenridge, which is all the money I owe unsettled and which I wish paid.

Nephew John Ormsby Gregg, ten-year old son of Sidney Ormsby and Isaac Gregg, did not live to benefit by his fond uncle's

75

bequests. A 72 x 36-inch stone slab in the Trinity burying ground is witness to this:

JOHN ORMSBY GREGG, August 13, 1807
14 years old.

Amiable and accomplished, an affectionate son . . . suddenly cut off in the bloom of youth and health. Thus, too, were blasted the fond and ardent hope of affectionate and devoted parents.

The signature of an unknown witness, a James Huston, attested the will of the dying Joseph B. Ormsby. The script is written in neat, flowing letters with heavy shading to embellish capital letters. A pressed flower—a rosebud, judging from the imprint—stains a corner of this unique will. The paper, 9¾ by 7¼ inches, bears chain lines across the tiny laid marks and a curious watermark of an upright animal, with a torch or staff, and the letters . . . *OIR*.

This letter was duly recognized as young Ormsby's will after Register Samuel Jones called in some friends of the testator— William Wilkins, Jeremiah Barker, and Henry Brackenridge:

who being duly sworn according to law, Deposeth and saith that they were well acquainted with the handwriting of the above named Joseph B. Ormsby, and that to the best of their knowledge the foregoing Letter or instrument of writing and the signature of "Jos. B. Ormsby" thereunto subscribed is the proper handwriting of the said Joseph B. Ormsby. . .

Joseph apparently planned to take a profit in New Orleans, for he bequeaths the expected proceeds from the sale of his cargo to his father. Pittsburgh storekeepers found the New Orleans market very important as an outlet for their excess produce, which they took in trade from the farmers. The use of the eastern markets was prohibited by the high cost of transportation over the mountains and the low value of the products to be sold. But it was comparatively easy to float the produce down river, where it found a ready market under French prices. At the time of young Ormsby's last trip the Louisiana Purchase had just been signed, largely because of the demands of the up-river merchants for a permanent market in New Orleans. These same merchants had forced the French governor of New Orleans to reopen the market after a short closing in 1802 by threatening to take forcible possession of the city.

Joseph's father died two years later, intestate, which set off the proceedings for the settlement of his estate described on page 20.

JOHN NEVILL—*The last requests of my dear and incomparable wife.*
Dated April 20, 1802—Recorded August 10, 1803

General John Nevill served in the French and Indian War, in Dunmore's War, and in the Revolutionary War. He was socially prominent, and one of the wealthiest men in town. His political feud with Hugh Henry Brackenridge is known well in Pittsburgh history. But what we are concerned with here is the way his will reveals his personality, for herein is the most intimate view of him possible. The impress of his character is unmistakable from the outset:

Whether a form or preamble is really necessary in a will, I do not pretend to judge, but I have such a confidence in my two children that I hope and believe that nothing more would be necessary for their mutual agreement in the division of my estate than merely to see my last will and bequests in the most plain and simple manner it could be expressed, more especially when I declair that this is not only my will and desire but that it was among some of the last requests of my dear and incomparable wife, their Mother, in all of which I have not varied one shilling to the best of my knowledge, nor would I have done it, had I had an inclination, but I had none. For in this as in all other matters we were perfectly agreed, and were ever happy.

Therefore suffering no bodily Pain or affliction at the present but that of the loss of my dear and beloved wife, being of sound mind and memory, do make and constitute this my last will and Testament in the manner following:

First, I bequeath my Soul to God, hoping for his mercy through the only merits of our Lord and Savior Jesus Christ.

77

My body I desire, if I should die in any Place convenient to the tomb of my late adorable and incomparable loving wife to be buried by her side, but not be at any Great or unnecessary expense in removing each other, that in all humility praying that as we have ever lived in perfect unity and happiness, to have part together in the resurrection of the just.

John Nevill then divides his estate between his eminent son, Presly, his daughter, Emelia Craig, and his eldest grandson and granddaughter, Morgan Neville and Hariot Craig.

Although John Nevill's will was dated April 20, 1802, it actually had been written five years earlier, just after the death of his wife:

Signed and sealed as my last will and testament this twentieth day of April Eighteen Hundred and Two, being all written on June the seventh, Seventeen Hundred and Ninety-Seven, just after the death of my wife but not signed till this day.

The tender phrases which reveal Mr. Nevill's devotion and respect for his "dear and incomparable wife," and the sentiments he pauses to give expression to, make the yellowed, tattered sheets of this will a love story of singular appeal.

Mr. Nevill wanted no fuss made about his funeral. He wanted it to be:

without any punctilious ceremony, no signs, I hope, of outward mourning by my relatives or friends, not even black or white gloves, nor any bits of black rags tied around the hats, arms, or legs—an apeish custom I have long disliked.

Near the end of his will, he states his desire for the quiet settling of his affairs with even more feeling:

. . . and the next and last is merely a request from me to my heirs and executors, Presly Nevill and Isaac Craig, that they will within thirty days after my decease exchange reciprocal instruments of writing, which I think may be done in a very few words, to settle the outlines of these my bequests in any manner it may seem meet to them. This, I hope, will

keep this, my last and only will, from ever being sullied by the merce-
nary, ingenious or quibbling fingers of lawyers; and then, I hope and
wish, it may rest as quiet as the coffin that contains my poor forgotten
body.

Did Mr. Nevill's plainly-stated aversion to lawyers have anything to do with the fact that Hugh Henry Brackenridge, his political foe, was the town's leading attorney? Well, at any rate, his
wish was not to be granted, for during the last century and a half
his will has been so worn by handling that it has had to be supple-
mented by an early photostatic copy of it.

It seemed almost sacrilegious to touch this fragile document
long enough to get the feel of the maker's reality and to describe
the paper he left us. John Nevill, himself, seemed to be hovering
nearby, protesting at the "quibbling fingers" which followed his
handwriting across the unruled 15½ by 10¼-inch paper, searching
out his last thoughts and wishes.

TARLETON BATES—*Pay . . . my debts and burn my body.*
    Dated January 7, 1806—Recorded January 14, 1806

Tarleton Bates wrote his will the day before he was killed in a
duel. It was not witnessed, and was very brief:

This is my last will—I Constitute Henry Baldwin, very dear friend,
whole executor. He is to sell all my estate, real and personal, except
Clothes and my watch. This last I give him with any money he may be
indebted to me and the proceeds of my Estate he is to pay, first my debts
and burn my body, or at least bury it without any direction. Next, to
Support James at school & finish his education by the Study of the Law
at Litchfield if there be a Sufficiency, Otherwise my Brother Frederick
will make up the deficit. And any Residue to go to my adored Mother.
    Signed at Pittsburgh, being written wholly by myself this seventh
day of January in the year of Our Lord, One Thousand and eight hundred & six.

                                                    Tarleton Bates

"James" was Tarleton's younger brother. With the brief business of his will taken care of, Tarleton must have spent his remain-

79

ing time pondering the circumstances which had drawn him, un-willingly, into the forthcoming duel.

Young Bates was associate editor of the *Tree of Liberty*, standard-bearer of the Democratic-Republican party in Allegheny County. Henry Baldwin was editor. The rival newspaper, *The Commonwealth*, took issue with the editorials of the *Tree*, and also with its staff, and particularly with Tarleton Bates. Ephraim Pent-land, editor of *The Commonwealth*, intensified his invective after the re-election of Governor Thomas McKean, who had received strong backing from Bates, until Bates sought out his tormentor and assaulted him. As Tarleton Bates put it, in a notice in the *Tree*, he had "corrected the licentiousness of the press with the liberty of the cudgel."

Pentland then sent Tarleton a challenge to a duel by a young Irish merchant named Thomas Stewart. When Bates refused to fight, Pentland made him out a coward on the pages of *The Commonwealth*. Bates published his defense in the *Tree of Liberty*, and the Irishman Stewart took offense at a reflection upon himself contained in Bates's argument. He personally renewed his chal-lenge. This time Tarleton Bates accepted.

The duel was fought on the bank of the Monongahela near the foot of present Bates Street in Oakland on January 8, 1806. Stewart's second shot mortally wounded Tarleton Bates, and he died within the hour. The *Tree's* editor, the man named executor in the victim's will, had this to say in the paper a few days later:

> Thus perished one of the best of men, who by a long series of sys-tematic persecution was drawn to this dreadful fate. The public has lost an invaluable servant, society one of its brightest ornaments, the poor their best friend.

Tarleton Bates was buried in Trinity churchyard, in an un-marked grave—as he had directed. The funeral was attended by the largest crowds ever seen until that occasion, for the Virginian aristocrat had been very popular in Pittsburgh. He had lived in the finest homes—as clerk to Major Isaac Craig and later to Gen-eral James O'Hara—and was prothonotary of Allegheny County at the time of his death. He was about twenty-eight years old when his career was cut short by a ball from a duelling pistol. This was the last duel fought in Western Pennsylvania.

Tarleton Bates's will occupied the first half of a sheet of paper measuring 12¾ by 7¼ inches. The rest of the sheet contains the following sworn affidavit:

Allegheny County, SS

Be it remembered that on the Eleventh day of January Anno Domino 1806, Before me, Samuel Jones, Esqr., Register for the Probate of Wills in and for Allegheny County, came John Woods & Thomas Collins of Pittsburgh and being duly sworn deposed that the foregoing paper, purporting to be the last will and testament of Tarleton Bates thereto subscribed is also in the proper handwriting of the said Tarleton Bates and further saith not.

In Testimony whereof I, the said Samuel Jones, have hereunto set my hand and affixed the Seal of my office the day and year afore written.

Samuel Jones, Regr.

Henry Baldwin, Executor,
Sworn before me, January the 14, 1806.

Samuel Jones.

JAMES BURKE—*As life...is especially precarious in a Sea Voyage...*
Dated January 9, 1807—Recorded January 25, 1807

The will of James Burke presents another view of the precariousness of life in his time. It is necessary to read the whole will in order to get the story.

This is the Last Will and Testament of me James Burke formerly of the Kingdom of Ireland and now of the Borough of Pittsburgh in the State of Pennsylvania.

Whereas my brother Michael Burke late of the City of Dublin in the Kingdom of Ireland, Merchant before his decease, made his last will and Testament whereby he devised and bequeathed most of his property to me.

And whereas my dear and affectionate wife Rachel Burke, formerly Rachel Perrins, after her marriage left her friends in England and accompanied me to America, taking all chances of fortune with me—and whereas our property at the time of our marriage and in contemplation of going to America have failed—and whereas in consequence of my

81

brother Michael's death it becomes necessary for us to leave America and go to Ireland to receive and possess whatever property I may be intitled to by devise bequest or succesion from him—

But as life at all times uncertain is especially precarious in a Sea Voyage it becomes my duty now when in life and health to make the best provision I can in case of my death for her who left all and followed me seeing next to my creditors it is my duty to do justice to her in my life and after my death as far as providence has put means in my hands—

Now therefore under all these considerations I, the said James Burke, Do by this my Last Will and Testament devise and bequeath to my said beloved wife Rachel her heirs executors administrators and assigns all my estate and property, real and personal and mixed, to which I am in any respect intitled to either in my own right or the will of my said brother Michael or in Succession to him of whatever nature such Estate and property may be whether Lands houses Stockgoods Bonds Notes debts book accounts or any Other Estate property or claim Whatsoever, that she in Case of my death may have enjoy demand Claim and Recover the same as fully as I myself could do were I alive.

Such is my will. Provided however that any Real Estate which may be devised to me by my brother Michael shall be held by my said wife Rachel if she have no child by me living at the time of decease. Only during her life and after her decease the same shall all go to my Heirs and I do hereby appoint my said wife Rachel and my friend Archibald Taylor of the Borough of Pittsburgh aforesaid Executors of this my last will and Testament.

In Witness whereof I have hereto set my hand and seal at Pittsburgh this ninth day of January in the year of our Lord One Thousand Eight hundred and seven.

James Burke, (SEAL)

This writing contained in this and in the preceding page was Signed and Sealed by the above named James Burke and by him published and declared as and for his last Will and Testament in the presence of us who have hereunto subscribed our names as Witnesses thereto in his presence and in the presence of each other.

Alexr. Addison
Robt. Steele
John Taylor
Archd. Taylor

James Burke's will was recorded just sixteen days after he wrote it. Did he, then, perish on the sea voyage which had prompted him to write his will? Certainly he would not have had sufficient time to reach Ireland and possess his brother's property. And if his "beloved wife Rachel" had accompanied him on the voyage, as the will clearly states she was to do, did she perish also? If not, then it remains a mystery why she, as executrix, did not appear in the register's office when the will was recorded. Only the above four witnesses were present, according to Samuel Jones's notations in the will book.

Although these questions remain unanswered, there is no doubt that ocean trips, in those days, were dangerous. With one crossing already behind them, from England to America, James and Rachel Burke still were uneasy about the coming voyage. The brief time between the writing and the recording of this will, and the unusual omission of any reference to Rachel Burke when the will was recorded, are ominous indications that their worst fears were realized.

ANDREW RICHARDSON—*To provide against sudden death* . . .
Dated April 10, 1808—Recorded August 5, 1809

Knowing that animal as well as vegetable matter must die and knowing also that it is prudent to provide against sudden death which nowadays is very common, I pronounce this to be my last will.

With these words Dr. Richardson begins his will. The caustic tone was very natural to him, for he was one of the chief contributors to the *Tree of Liberty,* and his articles were always designed to "get under the skin" of the Federalists. But after permitting himself this little social comment, as reference to the untimely end of Tarleton Bates, Dr. Richardson becomes very sincere in his bequest to his wife:

I give all the estate . . . to my amiable, beloved and dutiful wife, Sally Richardson. I will not say in what manner she is to dispose of it for well I am convinced prudence will mark the disposal when the time arrives that she can no longer enjoy it. And further as a mark of my high

83

opinion of her good sense, I do hereby constitute and appoint her my sole executrix.

A high compliment indeed, in an age when a husband's bequests to his wife were almost always for the period of her widowhood alone. She was Register Samuel Jones's daughter.

Dr. Richardson was one of Hugh Brackenridge's companions in the creation of Pittsburgh's second newspaper, the *Tree of Life,* which became the instrument of expression for the anti-Federalists on August 16, 1800. Brackenridge gave the new paper its name from a passage in *Revelation* XXII:2: "And the leaves of the tree were for the healing of the nations."

Dr. Richardson contributed to the "healing" process with zest, and along with Brackenridge, Tarleton Bates, Henry Baldwin, and others, began giving political opponents the "treatment." The Democratic-Republican victory in the borough elections of 1804 was largely a result of their efforts.

Dr. Richardson's establishment on Market Street, between Water and Ferry, was a combination dwelling house, doctor's office, and drug store. It also contained a fine library of medical books, which must have induced his young friend, Breton Brunot, to visit there often. Breton Brunot, who became one of Pittsburgh's distinguished early physicians, appears on the elder doctor's will as a witness. The other witnesses were Delia Waters and Will Woods.

Dr. Richardson wrote his will with style and flourish, shading certain letters and underscoring the name of his wife—Sally Richardson—and his own signature with double lines. His words march in straight lines across the 16 by 17-inch manuscript, instruments of a man who knew how to use them with precision and effect. Long after his death, so his biographers say, he was remembered for his wit and humor as well as for his high collar and stock, and his precious gold-headed cane.

GEORGE WALLACE—*The plantation called Braddock's Field.*
Dated December 15, 1803—Recorded August 25, 1812

George Wallace was Allegheny County's first judge. Benjamin Franklin, president of the Pennsylvania Executive Council, appointed him President Judge of the Common Pleas Court of the county when it was erected in 1788. Although not a lawyer, he presided very capably until the Constitution of 1790, and then was re-appointed associate judge to Alexander Addison, First Law Judge of the district.

Judge Wallace's will was written in a good large script on a 13 by 8-inch page. It is not a polished composition, but it does give evidence of the same capable handling that made George Wallace a good judge. He directs that "after all just debts are paid":

all the residue of my real and personal estate (except such parts as hereafter excepted) shall be equally divided between my wife Jane and my children, Viz., George Wallace, Thomas Wallace, William Wallace, Henry Wallace, Irwin Wallace, Charles Wallace, and my daughters Arabella Wallace, and Eliza Wallace, sheare alike and the profits of such real and personal estate shall be for the use and Suport of the above-mentioned Legatees until each arrives at the age of twenty-one years, at which time they shall receive their part. And in case any of my children before-mentioned die without lawfull issue or die before they arrive at the age of twenty-one years in that case their shears if it be Boys shall be equally divided between my two daughters and in case it be a daughter, in that case equally among the surviving children or their heirs.

Secondly, Its my will that my wife shall remain in full possession of the plantation called Braddock's Field, with the appurtenances therein belonging, also the stock of every kind, Viz., horses, cows, hogs, sheep, etc., that I may have at the time of my death, also all kind of farming utensils and every kind of house furniture, together with all issues and profits of said Plantation for her use during her life time in case she never marries, then its to be equally divided between my surviving children or their lawfull heirs after the death or marriage of my wife Jane.

Thirdly. Its my will that my wife Jane shall keep the two negro women and their offspring, also the negro man that I now have or any other negroes that I may have at my death during her lifetime or marriage and after either to be divided between my surviving legatees or their lawfull issue.

Fourthly. Be it understood that I purchased an Out Lott in the Allegheny Bottom from Thos. Hutchins, Esq., and the deed is in the name of my son George. And in case George should claime said Lott in

85

his own right, in that case my executors hereinafter mentioned shall have it valued, and if he choses to receive it at such valuation he may, but in case said valuation shall be more than his part he must pay to the other surviving legatees the overplus to make their sheare alike.

Fifthly. It is my will that my son Thomas shall have four lots on the Allegheny River, three of them purchased from James Blain and one of them got in exchange from General Butler, to be valued and disposed of in the same manner as the Out Lott to my son George.

Sixthly. I do hereby appoint my most valuable Friends John Wilkins, Jr., Alexander Addison, and George Wallace, Jr., executors of this my last will and testament.

Appendix. The interest of my three percent stock standing in the books of the United States amounting to about One Hundred Dollars yearly be and remain for the use of my wife Jane during her lifetime or widowhood and after her death or marriage be divided among my within-named heirs.

The signature *Geo. Wallace* is very impressive to look at, being artfully shaded and completely encircled with a magnificent flourish.

The plantation called "Braddock's Field" was the site of the historic British defeat on July 9, 1755, now the site of Braddock and North Braddock boroughs. Judge Wallace owned and cultivated that tract of land and made his home there until his death.

ADAMSON TANNEHILL—*False swearing and vile slander can't reach me here.*
Dated April 25, 1815—Recorded January 4, 1821

Adamson Tannehill's will is a studied expression of rancor over an incident which marred his reputation at the prime of his life. In 1798 he was removed from the office of justice of the peace after he was convicted of extortion. Although later reinstated by Governor McKean, he never forgave his accusers. His resentment was still strong seventeen years later when he wrote his will, as the text of it will indicate:

I, Adamson Tannehill, of Grovehill, Allegheny County, and State of Pennsylvania, Do make and declare this instrument of writing, which

86

is written by me, when in a full and correct state of mind, and each signed with my signature, to be my last will & Testament—From the course of nature, added to the belief that I must die, and willing to give those who may survive me the least possible trouble respecting my worldly affairs:— I only desire that my body should be buried in a decent manner in my allotted graveyard at Grovehill—that all my *just* debts be paid by my wife which are but few, & the expenses that may accrue at my burial.— After this is completed, it is my wife Agness M. Tannehill shall inherit all my estate, real, personal & Mixed.— In making my will, as I do not calculate in pleasing every expectant, my great and primary object is to please myself.— I have but little to give, therefore would be attended with the greater difficulty of mincing it out among all who might expect a little of that little.— In a former will I had directed two Busts to be executed, & placed in the courthouse in Pittsburg as legacies to two of the most unprincipled scoundrels who ever appeared before a Court of Justice.— One of them is dead in reality, & the other dead to all feelings of moral principle—I now decline a continuation of that appropriation and direct it to be applied to a Tombstone & epitaph for myself, as follows, Viv.—

ADAMSON TANNEHILL
was born the 23 of May, 1750.

Died

on   , 18   aged   years

He served his Country, as an officer, during the American Revolution, with the confidence of his superior.

and

Honour to himself

But

In the year 1798 his character was spoiled *unjustly* by the slander of unprincipled men & virulance of party.

He has left this world with the hope of a better.

Farewell, vain world, I've seen enough of thee,
And am now careless what thou says't of me.
Thy smiles I court not, nor thy frown I fear;
My cares are past, my head lies quiet here.

What faults you saw in *me,* take care to shun
And look at home, enough there's to be done.
False swearing and vile slander can't reach me here—
Of each, when living, I had my share.

It is my will further, that if my beloved wife should have any remainder of my estate at her disposal after taking a comfortable living out of it, I devise to my ward Sydney Tannehill Mountain, whose education and care of I leave with my said wife, who is hereby appointed my sole Executrix to this my will and Testament. I also leave to Sydney T. Mountain all my Books of all descriptions.— My family graveyard shall be always reserved from sale.

Signed, sealed and acknowledged by the Testator in the presence of each of us jointly as his last will and Testament, to which we have subscribed our names thereto in the presence of each other this twenty-fifth day of April, 1815.

(Signed) A. Tannehill.

James Young
John Hannen

Mr. Tannehill felt so compelled to denounce the offense against him that he resorted to poetry for added emphasis, and directed that it be chiseled in stone.

Despite the blight on his name which weighed so heavily on Adamson Tannehill, he was elected to represent his district in the United States Congress for the 1812-14 term. He also served on the original board of directors of the first bank west of the Allegheny Mountains—the Pittsburgh Branch of the Bank of Pennsylvania, established in 1804.

Mr. Tannehill's will is written in a small, neat hand on three pages. His signature appears at the bottom of each page.

STEPHEN LOWREY—*My real estate in Maryland.*
Dated November 29, 1821—Recorded January 4, 1822

Stephen Lowrey was a citizen "of Butler County, formerly of Queen Anne's County, Maryland." His property was divided between the two states. But there was no doubt as to which state he owed his allegiance. As we know from Chapter I, he was among the Western Pennsylvanians who took the *Oath of Allegiance to Pennsylvania,* pledging his loyalty on July 22, 1777. At that time he was Colonel Lowrey, commissary in the Revolutionary army.

His will is concerned mainly with bequests to his two daughters:

I have had it in view to divide my property as equally as possible between my two children, Margaret Wright, the wife of Thomas Wright of Reeds Creek, Queen Anne's County, Maryland, and Sarah Collins, widow, now of Pittsburgh in the State of Pennsylvania. Having heretofore made considerable advances to the said Thomas Wright, I now devise and bequeath to him and to his said wife Margaret all the remainder of my real estate in Maryland consisting of Four lots adjoining the town of Hibernia—Queen Anne's County—together with all my negro slaves—my Library and all such books and papers and documents as have relation to said property devized & bequeathed, together with all debts due to me and judgments in my favor remaining unsatisfied in the State of Maryland, and also all my shares of stock in the City Bank of Baltimore now in the care of James Armstrong of Baltimore, of the house of Armstrong & Son of that city. They, the said Thomas Wright & Margaret, to hold the property thus devized and conveyed to them, their heirs, executors, and administrators and assigns, subject to payment of twelve dollars per annum for seven years after my decease to Mary Jeffries for the education of her son James, and also of a fee . . . services to Kinsay Harrison, Esq., and a Bill of Costs in the suit of The Reverend Joseph Scull & wife against Stephen Lowrey in the Orphans Court of Queen Anne's County.

To my daughter Sarah Collins and to her heirs, executors, & administrators, I hereby devize and bequeath all my estate, real, personal and mixed, in the State of Pennsylvania, intending to convey to her in the fullest manner all my lands, tenements & heridaments in said State, together with all the title—papers & documents connected therewith and the benefit of all contracts and articles of agreement in relation thereto and generally every right, title and claim of every description arising out of my ownership of said property so as to enable her to sue for, recover and enjoy the same as effectually as I have done during my lifetime.

And whereas the property so devized to my said daughter Sarah Collins will require vigilance and expenses in its management to the best advantage and may not be very productive . . . to provide for her such a fund as will be competent to her support and enable her to meet the expenses incident to the real estate devized, I do therefore give and bequeath to the said Sarah Collins twenty-six full shares in the Union Bank of Maryland and also all my Govt. of New Jersey Stock, commonly called the War Loan Stock amounting to about seven thousand dollars funded in the Loan Office of the United States and for the State of Maryland held in the City of Baltimore and any dividend or interest remaining due thereon and unpaid at the time of my death.

As I anticipate that all the difficulties attending to final settlement of my affairs will arise from that portion of my estate devized to Sarah Collins, I do hereby nominate and appoint the said Sarah the sole Executrix.

(Signed)   Stephen Lowrey.

Stephen Lowrey was seventy-five years old when he died and was buried in Trinity graveyard. His will was witnessed by James R. Butler, Edward Selden, and Richard Biddle.

SAMUEL JONES—*Being now about Sixty-eight years of age . . .*
Dated December 21, 1812

It is fitting to present last among the holograph wills that of Samuel Jones—Allegheny County's first register of wills. He served from February, 1789—soon after the county was erected —until February, 1818, a period of 29 years. During that time he recorded, dated, and affixed his signature to all of the wills which appear in Will Book I and most of those in Will Book II. His own will appears on Page 216 of Will Book II.

I, Sam'l Jones, being now about Sixty-eight years of age, Knowing that I have to die, Therefore I declare this to be my Last will and Testament in manner and form Following, that is to say, that I order all my just debts to be paid out of Estate after my decease; Secondly, I will and bequeath to my beloved Wife Sarah, all my real and personal Estate whatsoever I am now possessed of, to be holden by her, her

90

heirs & assigns forever, and after the decease of my said wife Sarah, I will and bequeath to my Grandson Samuel B. Jones, son of my Eldest son William Jones, the sum of One hundred Dollars to be paid to him after my said Wife's deceased, if so much should remain, and if more the overplus to be equally divided between my son William; my son Michael and my Daughter Sarah Richardson, and do nominate and appoint my beloved wife Sarah my Whole and sole Executrix of this my last Will and Testament. In Witness whereof I have hereunto set my hand and seal this Twenty-first day of December, one Thousand Eight hundred and Twelve. Sealed & Delivered, Published and Pronounced as the last Will and Testament of

Sam'l Jones   (SEAL)

Witnesses:

> Henry Panvy
> Jeffrey Scaife

Ironically enough, there is no recording date, and therefore we can not place the year of his death. But we know from Samuel Jones's publication *Pittsburgh in 1826*, his reminiscenses of the city, that he lived at least fourteen years beyond the dating of his will. At the age of eighty-two he was still active enough to take his pen and write cogently of his surroundings.

After scanning so many of these original old manuscripts, and seeking out the recording dates and other notations in the writing of "Sam'l Jones," it was with particular poignancy that we opened Packet 177 to read his will. It was brief. It was business-like. But the familiar signature at the end recalled to mind all who had appeared on so many other wills, and it made one wonder if Samuel Jones, too, hadn't been thinking of these as he signed his own will.

Slavery—Indenture—Apprenticeship

In the early days of Western Pennsylvania, work on farms and in shops and industries was performed by three kinds of labor: by freemen who bargained for their wages in the open market and could withdraw their service at will; by indentured servants or apprentices who were voluntarily or by court assignment legally bound to service for the time set down in an *indenture,* which was a written agreement drawn up between the contracting parties; and by negro slaves who were imported, bought and sold, held in servitude, and given freedom according to the law of the day.

SLAVERY

Up until 1820, when the Missouri Compromise made slavery illegal in Pennsylvania and in certain other states, anyone who could afford to buy slaves could own them and could dispose of them as he chose. Many questioned the morality of this right even before their attitudes were reflected in the legislation of 1780 and 1820.

Records of the time show, however, that human beings or their services were bought and sold at public auction or in the Pittsburgh market and were handed down in wills in the same practical way as milch cows, pots and pans, and clothing.

Many of the earliest settlers of Western Pennsylvania came from Virginia into what they considered Virginia territory and brought their negro slaves with them. And apparently all kinds of Pittsburghers, even ministers, held slaves and bequeathed them to their heirs, although there is evidence even in the earliest wills that Pittsburghers were beginning to be concerned about the inconsistence of slavery with the ideals of freedom and democracy on which they were building a fairer country.

In March, 1780, an Act for the "gradual abolition of slavery" was passed, which expressed the general concern and hastened the disappearance of slavery in Pennsylvania. The preamble to this Act deserves a place with the other noble declarations of freedom which are our pride and heritage in Pennsylvania. It is printed in the appendix of this book.

We rejoice that it is in our power to extend a portion of that freedom to others which hath been extended to us . . . we conceive ourSelves . . . extraordinarily called upon . . . to give substantial proof of our gratitude.

The Act provided that all slaves had to be registered by November first following the Act; any not registered could not be continued in slavery. No child born of slave parents after the Act could be held as a slave; he might be continued with the same owner as an indentured servant, but he could be bound only until he was twenty-eight years of age. Only with their own consent could families be separated and sold apart. By the Act, then, time would end slavery forever in Pennsylvania. And forty years later, in 1820, the Missouri Compromise prohibited slavery entirely in Pennsylvania and other states north of 36 degrees 30 minutes north latitude.

About the time of the Missouri Compromise, a heated debate between the editors of the *Steubenville Gazette* and the *Pittsburg Mercury* kept the evils of slaveholding before this section of the country. James Wilson, the Steubenville editor, contended that no man had a moral right to enslave another; John M. Snowden, of the *Mercury*, combated that statement. Citizens of Allegheny County, however, favored Pennsylvania's course of steadily getting rid of slavery not just in Pennsylvania but throughout the country. But even after the Missouri Compromise of 1820, Allegheny County still had, in 1821, ten slaves, unlawfully held. Only one slave was listed by 1828. The more advanced of the churches, realizing their duty to humanity, had kept the sin of slavery before the people and, in 1826, a meeting to organize an Anti-slavery Society was held in the First Presbyterian Church in Pittsburgh.

The *Pittsburgh Gazette*, January 19, 1837, took a firm stand and refused to print notices about runaway slaves. When a Tennessee slave-holder requested the newspaper to publish such an advertisement for him, John Scull, the *Gazette's* editor, wrote:

> We have reflected carefully upon the subject and have arrived at the deliberate conclusion not to publish such advertisements.

Not until 1870, however, were colored males of legal age allowed to vote in Allegheny County.

INDENTURE

The work of the farmers and mechanics required more skill than the usual slave was able to supply. And so because of the increasing need for workers with more technical skills and because of the rising sentiment against slavery, there was a demand in Western Pennsylvania for other kinds of labor. Advertising in the Pittsburgh newspapers called for the services of indentured servants and apprentices.

This indentured labor varied in kind. Some, especially in the unskilled and domestic fields, were former slaves who had been freed by their masters or by law. Some were skilled artisans who by their own action or by the action of others were bound for a certain number of years, but who could look forward someday to independence, perhaps with property, a business, and their own indentured help. Some had entered into voluntary servitude for payment of debts, according to older English law or later modification of it. People wandering around without giving satisfactory account of themselves often were seized on suspicion as runaway servants and, if nobody appeared to pay their fines, their services were advertised for sale for payment of prison charges.

A superior kind of indentured laborer was the "redemptioner." When ships docked at Philadelphia, their captains, or city merchants who had guaranteed the passage money, placed advertisements in the newspapers describing the passengers for sale, giving their nationality, age, sex, and the kind of service for which they were fitted. In this way many an immigrant established himself in the new country and in this way many good citizens and worthy business enterprises were established in Western Pennsylvania.

The apprentice was one bound by indenture or legal agreement to serve for a limited time in consideration for the learning of an art or trade. The name has continued to describe one who is learning an art or trade even since the practice of "binding" to a master has been discontinued. Parents and guardians in the early nineteenth century "bound out" children to serve by indenture because they wanted them to learn a trade, and orphans were "bound out" under Court order.

The services of any indentured person could be sold to new masters until the time of indenture expired or they could be passed on to heirs and assigns.

Laws were passed from time to time which protected indentured servants from abuse, limited their time of bondage, measured its value, and compelled owners to contribute toward their future independence. Sometimes, through discontent or restlessness, they ran away. Newspaper advertisements describing runaways were frequent and there were laws compelling their return.

But the system provided that the bound servant in time could become a master. In fact, many leading Pennsylvania citizens started in the new world as indentured servants, and the founders of many highly respected families started their careers as bound apprentices. The more highly skilled the indentured man or woman, of course, the sooner he became independent.

NEWSPAPERS

That all kinds of people owned slaves in Pittsburgh before 1820 and that slaves were bought and sold appears in the advertisements in the early newspaper as well as in the wills. The *Pittsburgh Gazette*, May 23, 1787, records an ad placed by the commandant at Fort Pitt to exchange a slave for provender:

95

To be Sold to Any Person Residing in the Country—a Negro Wench.—She is an excellent cook and can do any kind of work in or out of doors. She has been registered in Westmoreland County. Produce will be taken, or cattle of any kind.

> Enquire of Col. John Gibson,
> Fort Pitt.

She had been "registered" and therefore was a "slave for life," as allowed by the Act of 1780.

A similar advertisement shows that the notorious Dr. John Connally, who before the Revolution defended Virginia's title to Pittsburgh with a war which enabled him to rename the fort "Fort Dunmore," owned ten slaves while he lived here.

One placed by the editor of the *Gazette* on July 13, 1795, advertises for an indentured servant, not a slave, since his ad appeared fifteen years after the 1780 Act which prohibited a child born later being held a slave:

A generous price will be given for a Negro or Mulatto girl, from 8 to 12 years of age. (Apply to the PRINTER)

Often, too, the newspaper advertised for runaway negroes. The rewards offered, however, usually were for a lesser amount than would have been paid for the return of strayed horses or cattle. A typical notice is the following:

Pittsburgh Gazette, August 21, 1789

Run away on the 19th inst., from the subscriber living on Plumb Creek, Allegheny County, a negro man named Jack; he is about forty years of age, and his hair is not so curly nor so much wool as the most of negroes. It is supposed he is lurking about Pittsburg. Whoever will take up said negro and deliver him to his master shall receive two dollars reward, paid by Thomas Girty.

> —August 21, 1789.

James Robinson, whose son William was the first white child born north of the Allegheny River and became the first mayor of Allegheny, advertised May 15, 1804, in the *Gazette,* a "slave for life" (one registered November 1, 1780):

I will Sell a Likely Negro Man.—He is about 27 years of age, and a slave for life, and has been brought up a farmer. For terms, apply to the subscriber, living on the bank of the Allegheny River, opposite Pittsburg.

—James Robinson.

Another Pittsburgh paper, *The Tree of Liberty*, on September 26, 1801, carried an advertisement illustrating the sale of the unexpired time of servitude of a girl 21 years old, who must have been born just after the passage of the 1780 Act:

FOR SALE.—The time of a smart and very active mulatto girl, one-and-twenty years old and who has about seven years to serve. Apply to James Berthoud, merchant, Water Street, near Henderson's Ferry. Pittsburgh, 24th September, 1801.

James Berthoud, French colonist, was a member of the prominent shipbuilding industry of *Tarascon Brothers, James Berthoud Company*, which in 1802 started business on the Monongahela near the end of Try Street. Besides building ships the firm gathered cargoes for their vessels which traded around the world, import and export.

The *Pittsburgh Mercury* of November 18, 1813, lists the sale of a boy's unexpired time:

A Mulatto.—Subscriber will sell the unexpired time of a mulatto boy.—George Evans, Pittsburg, November 13, 1813.

George Evans was the son of Oliver Evans; he managed a flour mill on the Monongahela run by an engine his father invented.

General James O'Hara, whose will is printed in full on pages 199ff. because of its importance to the development of Pittsburgh, doubtless owned many servants. He frequently advertised for runaways. His description of their appearance and attire give us interesting sidelights on the costumes of his day.

Pittsburgh Gazette, February 23, 1787

ONE HUNDRED DOLLARS REWARD

Ran away from the subscriber, on the 11th of October last, an indentured Irish servantman, named John Buchanan, about 28 years of age, 5 feet 5 or 6 inches high, black complexion, of a very effiminate appearance, short black hair, speaks with the brogue, is very pregnant with little artifice, and a notorious liar, had on a blue broadcloth coat, with yellow buttons, moleskin jacket, black breeches, and a large cocked Castor hat; took with him two horses, one black, 15 and an half hands high, with a small star, his left hind foot white, marked on the right buttock U.S., almost worn out; the other a bay; he carried a case of holster pistols and a fuse; endeavored to change the horses in the Allegheny Mountains, on his way down the old Virginia road; he had then in company with him a young woman, who he passed for his wife; he was bought of Jeremiah Warder, Parker & Co. in Philadelphia, on the 27 of May, 1784; says he was born in Cork, and is a glovemaker. As he had access to a large store in Pittsburgh, it appears that he has carried off a considerable sum of money and other valuable property; it is therefore expected that he may escape to Ireland, should this be the case, the above reward shall be paid to any person that will have him apprehended, so that he may be brought to justice, and a reward of Forty Dollars shall be paid to any person that will have him taken up and secured in any workhouse or prison in the United States, so that his master may get him again, or that will deliver him to General Febiger, in Philadelphia; Walter Roe, in Baltimore; Michael McKown, in Martinsburg, Virginia, or the subscriber in Pittsburgh, and all reasonable charges.

Jan. 10, 1787 —James O'Hara

Pittsburgh Gazette, May 20, 1797

SIXTY DOLLARS REWARD

Ran away from the subscriber on the 8th instant, three indented Dutch servant men, of the following descriptions, *William Heymirick,* by trade a painter, a middle aged man, pretty well made, somewhat attached to company, brown complexion; had on and took with him a short brown coat and overalls, also a tolerable good long blue coat, and yellow cassimere waistcoat and breeches; he sometime ago bored his ears, one of which has been materially injured by the weight of lead attached to it; he wears his hair tied. *William Hammis,* by trade a blacksmith but professes the locksmith branch particularly, a robust, well made man, not exceeding twenty-five years of age, much inclined to idleness and smoaking, marked with the small pox, of a brown complexion, short hair, a forbidding look, he usually wore when at work a short coat and overalls but in all probability he will change them, having a number of good cloaths. *Peter Smith,* by trade a common blacksmith, a short corpulent man, very full faced, in whose mouth will the pipe ever been seen when striking the anvil or blowing the bellows, he usually wore a large flat crowned hat, speaks very bad English, a dark complexion, short hair.

The aforesaid servants have been travelling towards Greensburgh.

The above reward will be paid to any person or persons who will apprehend and secure the said servants in any gaol in the state, or elsewhere, or in proportion for any of them, and if delivered in Pittsburgh, reasonable charges, paid by

Pittsburgh, May 12, 1797   James O'Hara

These ads illustrate graphically how the services of these indentured workers were valued before 1800.

An example of the practice of selling an indentured servant much as a slave was sold is seen in this advertisement:

TO BE SOLD
(For ready money, only)

A German woman servant, she has near three years to serve, and is well qualified for all household work; would recommend her to her own country people, particularly as her present master has found great inconvenience from not being acquainted with their manners, customs and language. For further particulars, enquire of Mr. Ormsby's, in Pittsburgh.

There were numerous advertisements, too, for runaway apprentices. If they were jailed and not called for, they were put up for sale to take care of their gaol expenses. One apprentice had run off from his master several times and each time the master had

99

inserted a notice in the *Gazette* offering a reward for his appre-
hension and return. The third notice stated that the reward would
be only "Three Cents and no charges paid." The master, it would
seem, valued his apprentice's services less with each wandering.
Rewards seldom amounted to much, anyhow.

The following advertisement for an apprentice runaway is
typical of such newspaper insertions:

Commonwealth, May 12, 1812
SIX CENTS REWARD.

Ran away from the subscriber on Sunday, the 10th instant, an
apprentice to the blacksmith trade named James Nary. He is about 17
years of age; about 5′4″; red hair. Had on and took with him a home-
made corded coat; a pair of snuff colored cloth pantaloons, two linen
shirts; two pairs of shoes, one coarse, and the other fine, both new; a
roram hat more than half worn, and a pair of woolen socks.

The above rewards, but no charges, will be given to any person
who will bring back the said apprentice.
Pittsburgh, May 12, 1812.   GEORGE McGUNNEGLE.

N.B.—He is supposed to have gone toward Greensburgh and all persons
are forbid harboring him at their peril.

Advertisements were usually for "lads about fourteen to fifteen years of age," probably because their youth would make them
ready for learning and would mean that they could be bound for
a period long enough to make them most useful eventually.

Pittsburgh Gazette, January 4, 1792

Wanted, by the Printer hereof, a LAD of about 14 or 15 years of
age, that can read and write English, as an apprentice to the printing
business.

Wanted, Apprentice to bow-string manufacturing. John Cowan's
business in the s.w. corner of the Diamond.

Apprentices were much in demand in the busy industrial
Pittsburgh, and apprenticeship was a respected method of voca-
tional training. In spite of the advertising which suggests a rather
cold blooded marketing of service, it was a good way to usefulness
and independence in the early nineteenth century. The diversity

100

of manufacturers and businesses advertising for apprentices shows advertisements inserted by Cabinet-makers, Carpenters, Nailors, Hatters, Printers, Potters, Shoemakers, Tanners, Wheelsmiths, Black and Whitesmiths, Teachers, Shipbuilders, Millers, and many others. Pittsburgh's industrial progress was indeed well under way at the beginning of the eighteenth century.

WILLS

But it is to the wills, the real interest of this book, we turn for the most personal records of slavery and indenture.

James Whitaker of Washington County, whose will is discussed in the first pages of this book as one of the earliest recorded in Allegheny County, granted "Elinor, a negro wench, her liberty" at his death and bequeathed to his wife "a Negro boy and a Mulatto girl." Since he died in 1789, we may assume that these were all "slaves for life," his property, free to sell, or to bequeath, as he pleased.

ELIZABETH CULBERTSON—. . . *my negro woman and child to be sold*
at the discretion of my executors.
Dated May 20, 1799—Recorded April 25, 1800

Her will indicates that she was interested primarily in converting her property into cash for her heirs. Probably the executors would be discreet enough to recognize that the child was not a slave, because it must have been born after 1780 and, according to the terms of the Act, could not be separated from the mother without the mother's consent. Probably the purchaser would have to enter into an indenture agreement with the law concerning the servitude of the child.

DAVID DUNCAN—. . . *a Negro woman called Catherine* . . .
Dated December 30, 1791—Recorded April 18, 1792

He kept a tavern in which the trustees of the Pittsburgh Academy held their meetings, a busy place, but his only bequest of a slave was this one to his wife.

101

BENJAMIN KUYKENDALL—*Ned to dispose of as he pleases . . .*
　　Dated September 26, 1789—Recorded November 6, 1789

To his son, Nathaniel, went "my Mulatto man Ned," to another son, "a negro man Sam," and to his wife, "a negro wench
Nancy," for each of them "to dispose of as they please."

But there are other wills showing the concern of masters for
the future of their slaves. The wills of John and Margaret Clark
illustrate this concern.

JOHN CLARK— *. . . my mulatto slave Dido be set free . . .*
　　Dated February 4, 1793—Recorded July 26, 1797

MARGARET CLARK—*Three volumes of Davis' Sermons to Dido.*
　　Dated May 5, 1806—Recorded June 9, 1807

John Clark, a graduate of Princeton who came to Western
Pennsylvania after he was sixty, was a Presbyterian minister, pastor of Lebanon and Bethel, and a member of Redstone Presbytery.
His will left to his adopted son, William Jones, most of his library
and money to be educated at Canonsburg Academy. This legacy
bore good fruit; William Jones lived to be 90, had twenty children,
and was a minister for sixty years. But perhaps the Rev. Clark's
most significant bequest is, "it is my will that my mulatto slave
Dido be set free at ye death of her present mistress, providing she
behaves well to her mistress while she lives." And Margaret, seventeen years later, in her will, carried out her husband's wishes by
setting Dido free and beyond that, left to Dido:

One feather bed
One coverlid, one quilt
Two blankets
One pair of sheets and pillowcases
One chest
One spinningwheel and a Pot
Three volumes of Davis' *Sermons*
Doddridge's *Rise and Progress of Religion in the Soul*
Six pewter plates
Three pewter basons and a small soapdish

Eight spoons

One milk cow and one Ewe

The character of the gifts suggests that Dido had been taught to read, and along with her freedom a good master and mistress had equipped her materially and spiritually for the new life of freedom.

JOHN METZGER— *. . . to each negro slave a freedom suit . . .*
Dated February 24, 1798—Recorded June 5, 1798

John Metzger directed, "neither of my four negro slaves to be sold during their time of slavery," and each one of them "a freedom suit at the expiration of their servitude." They must have been indentured servants, not "slaves for life."

ROBERT CALLENDER— *. . . a black woman named Nell . . .*
Dated November 15, 1802—Recorded November 23, 1802

Robert Callender makes clear that he wishes to avoid family disputes, and so, "my mulatto servant William is to be free immediately after my decease." He makes clear, too, that a "black woman named Nell, whom I formerly gave to my sister, Mrs. Mary Thompson, is not to be considered as one on whom I have any claim or as part of my property."

JOHN CAMPBELL—*. . . the money arising by the sale of the slaves . . .*
Dated July 21, 1786—Recorded April 16, 1802

John Campbell was a partner in the fur trading firm of Simon and Campbell, a Virginia partisan in border claims, and a surveyor. In 1764 he laid out one of the earliest plans for Pittsburgh, four blocks on the Monongahela now included within Ferry, Water, Market Streets, and the Boulevard of the Allies, the third village to rise on the site since English conquest. He certainly considered his slaves his property to dispose of as he would, for he directed "that the rest and residue of the money arising by the sale of the slaves" was to be forwarded to his father in Ireland.

103

JOHN VANCE—. . . *my negro woman Rhoda . . . shall have her Indenture given up and be free . . .*
Dated August 29, 1812—Recorded November 11, 1812

Wills are not frequent which terminate the servant's obligation to the agreement drawn up by indenture. John Vance's bequest to his wife is one example:

If my beloved wife, Nancy Vance, should die before the expiration of the Indenture of my negro woman Rhoda that she shall have her Indenture given up and be free, on condition that she shall live peacably with my beloved wife during her life or the time of said Indenture of which my beloved wife is to be the judge. And if she sees fit may sell or dispose of her any way during the time of the Indenture, she to have her freedom in either case.

WILLS AND INDENTURE

During the Revolutionary War importation of foreign servants dropped, and gradually "Redemptioners" disappeared from the market. However, there were for a few more years a number of children growing up who had been sold out to service for long terms—not because their passage had cost so much but because parents or guardians bound them out to learn a trade. Mention is made in the wills of children's servitude and apprenticeship.

ISAAC GREER—. . . *my right and title to the indented children . . .*
Dated February 20, 1809—Recorded July 30, 1809

To his wife, Isaac Greer leaves:

my right and title to the indented children, Mordecai and Phoebe Price —said children to be fed, cloathed, schooled, and freedomed, according to Indenture, by my son Jesse. I also will that Mordecai serve my son Jesse when my wife may not require his services.

RICHARD TETTRINGTON—. . . *Joseph, whom I have bread up as a carpenter* . . .
Dated, Presqui' Isle, January 26, 1797—Recorded June 3, 1797

This will shows a father's faith in apprenticeship as education:

I do hereby constitute and appoint Mr. James Gossman of the City of New York, Master Carpenter, the sole Guardian of my youngest children—the eldest of whom, namely, John, I wish bound out as an apprentice to a Shoemaker; the next, namely, Adam, to be bound apprentice to a Tallow Chandler, and Matthew to be also apprenticed to a Taylor. And I further desire the sum of $340 of which I die possessed and all the worldly property I am now worth except as hereafter excepted (which property is to be converted into cash in the manner hereafter mentioned) to be remitted with all convenient speed to said Mr. Gossman, to be disposed of as follows—namely to apply as much thereof as he shall deem necessary to cloath and apparel in a decent manner said John, Adam, and Matthew, previous to their being bound out as apprentices, and the residue or remainder of said money to be applied towards the education and maintenance of my youngest son Richard in order to prepare him for some trade or profession . . . To my oldest son, Joseph, whom I have bread up as a carpenter and who I now consider to be able to provide for himself without any further aid of mine, I leave all the carpenter tools I die possessed of in order to enable him to carry on his trade.

Mr. Tettrington's instructions for apprenticeships are for his *younger* sons; his eldest son, Joseph, was to carry on the father's trade. It is interesting that to him the father pays the highest compliment by leaving him his own carpentering tools. For the youngest son, the one least prepared to stand alone at his father's death, the father indicates training for a profession. Richard Tettrington's will shows, as do other wills, that the father is concerned with each child, individually. An apprenticeship legacy was an honorable way of providing for the children's future.

105

EBENEZER MITCHEL— *... put my sons to Treads ...*
Dated October 9, 1788—Recorded March 5, 1792

I do order that my executors do put my sons to Treads and provide that they be sufficiently schooled in the time of their apprenticeship by their masters.

Mr. Mitchel's will provided the money to assure his sons the proper training in a trade. *Treads* was the Scottish word for *trade*.

JAMES IMBRIE— *... between the age of fifteen and seventeen ...*
Dated December 20, 1802—Recorded March 4, 1803

Mr. Imbrie made sure that his two youngest children were provided with resources for independent living.

JEREMIAH VANGUILDER—*... the children shall be bound out ...*
Dated November 15, 1793—Recorded December 13, 1794

Mr. Vanguilder directed his executors that

If necessity requires or if the estate is not sufficient to keep the family that the children shall be bound out in places they shall think most suitable.

Other wills left rewards to apprentices for especially good service. Such was the will of Able Wayman.

ABLE WAYMAN—*Unto John Stewart ... as soon as he is free ...*
Dated August 26, 1786—Recorded September 17, 1791

Unto John Stewart, who is now in apprentice to Matthew McCoy, Sadler, of Nobrsburgh, $50 to be paid by my executors as soon as he is free from said McCoy.

WILLIAM BLAIR—*If my brother David Blair's son ... conducts himself honestly and safely ...*
Dated July 4, 1827—Recorded March 28, 1828

If my brother David Blair's son Saul serves a regular term of apprenticeship to an honest trade and conducts himself honestly and safely until he arrives at the full age of twenty-five, to receive $50.

Fifty dollars was a lot of money, then. Such a large reward would encourage an apprentice to apply himself faithfully. William Blair, himself, was a brush maker. Doubtless he, too, had been an apprentice. He did not suggest that Saul be taken on as an apprentice in his own business, probably for the reason that bristles were becoming hard to get: transportation facilities to the east were so good that most farmers sent their hogs to the eastern markets.

Perhaps the most interesting will relating to apprenticeship is the will of James Kennedy Moorhead, who himself had been trained by the apprentice system.

JAMES KENNEDY MOORHEAD—... *for the benefit of apprentices and poor boys.*
Dated August 29, 1868—Recorded March 17, 1884

General James Kennedy Moorhead, prominent in city, state, and national business affairs, after his father's death decided to learn a trade. He apprenticed himself to a Quaker tanner in the Pequa settlement of Lancaster. By his diligence and honesty to his employer, the boy became foreman of the business long before his apprenticeship terminated. In 1828, he built a tannery of his own at Montgomery's Ferry. He did not operate it very long, having interested himself with his brother-in-law, Mr. Montgomery, in the Susquehanna Division of the Pennsylvania Canal. As the direct result of Mr. Moorhead's planning for a line of light packet boats, exclusively for passenger use, the Pioneer Packet line between Philadelphia and Pittsburgh was established. Making the Monongahela River navigable was J. K. Moorhead's finest achievement, and his greatest pride, as we learn in part of his will:

The larger portion of my MONONGAHELA stock is placed in the hands of my daughters, and so I wish it. The best years of my life have

107

been given to the construction and care of this improvement. When it was dilapidated and bankrupt, I had faith in its success—I therefore leave this to my daughters, in full confidence that it will produce a regular, steady income. Whilst it is not my intention to tie up or entail any portion of my estate, yet it is my wish and desire that they retain this stock as long as circumstances will permit, it being the greatest work of their father's life.

His will as originally drawn had left 100 shares of this stock to be used for a library "for the benefit of apprentices and poor boys." A codicil revoked that bequest because of the passing of the system of apprenticeship.

This bequest, as originally stated said:

Having in early life felt the want of proper books, it has long been impressed on my mind that I should make some provision for the benefit of apprentices and poor boys. Therefore, I give to the "Young Men's Mercantile Library and Mechanics Institute of the City of Pittsburgh" all books, pamphlets, maps, charts, and printed documents contained in my office library. Also one hundred shares of stock in the Monongahela Navigation Company, provided they accept the same from my executors, and agree that any and all poor boys, whether apprentices or not, between the ages of 14 and 21 years, residing in the city of Pittsburgh or that part of the County of Allegheny and lying south of the Allegheny and Ohio Rivers, including Neville Island, forming the district which I have for many years represented in Congress, shall have access to the said library and the free use of any books contained therein, subject of course to the rules and regulations in regard to the same. Also, that the proceeds arising from this bequest shall, from time to time, be invested in the purchase of mechanical, agricultural, and scientific works best adapted to their use.

Western Pennsylvania Hospital benefitted, however, as he changed that part of his will and made a Codicil to transfer the hundred shares of stock in the Navigation company to the endowment fund of the hospital's medical and surgical department: "the income therefrom to be applied exclusively to the support of free beds for charity patients," because, as his will stated:

the apprenticeship system, I regret to say, has almost entirely disappeared and the conditions have been thereby rendered useless.

Mr. Moorhead's will was not administered until after his death, early in 1884. By that time, apprenticeship had died, too. But the will stands as a permanent record of the value of the system as education for good citizenship.

Religion and Education

Now, we take a will pretty much for granted, recognizing it as a commonplace legal instrument for disposing of property after death. We may not know, however, that people did not always have the right to make a will, that such a right had to be assured by law. Modern wills are traced to ancient Roman wills—not the *Calata Comitia,* the Patrician Assembly which excluded Plebians, but another Testament which competed with it—and superseded it, eventually.

The law governing wills, as we know it today, developed from the early postobit gift. In England, particularly during the twelfth century, the will was limited to the disposition of chattels. If there was no will, the chattels were administered by the Church for the good of the dead man's soul and for laying his body in the earth with proper ceremony, which was usually in proportion to his worldly estate. The familiar expression found in our own early Allegheny County's Letters of Administration, ". . . of the said decedent may be well and truly administered, converted, and disposed of to Pious Uses . . .," is very likely a carry-over in language from the Church's administrative duties; certainly, the pious preambles are. The preambles vary in length; some are very long, some are very short.

The will of William Warden, one of the oldest, has a brief introduction, typical of this medieval influence.

110

WILLIAM WARDEN— *... I give and commend my soul to the hands of God ...*

Dated September 14, 1789—Recorded October 3, 1789

Therefore, calling to mind that it is appointed once to dye, principally, and *first of all,* I give and commend my soul to the hands of God that gave it, and my body I commend to the earth from whence it came, to be buried in a Christian-like and decent manner at the discretion of my executors, nothing doubting but at the General Resurrection I shall receive the same again by the mighty power of God; and as touching and concerning such worldly estate wherewith it hath pleased God to bless me in this life, I dispose of the same in the manner and form following ...

EZEKIEL MILLER— *... that I may be the better prepared to leave this world ...*

Dated January 31, 1828—Recorded February 27, 1828

In the name of God, Amen, I, Ezikeal Miller, of Allegheny County and State of Pennsylvania, being weak and sick of body but of sound mind and memory and understanding, (praised be God for it!) and considering the certainty of death and the uncertainty of the time thereof, and to the end that I may be the better prepared to leave this world when it shall please God to call me hence, do make and declare this my last will and testament in manner following (that is to say)— first and principally, I commend my soul unto the hands of Almighty God, my creator, hoping for free pardon and remission of all my sins, and to enjoy everlasting happiness in his heavenly kingdom, through Jesus Christ, my saviour; my body, I commend to the earth ...

HENRY LANG— *... in full assurance of its Resurrection ...*

Dated April 26, 1797—Recorded July 18, 1797

In the name of God, Amen, I, Henry Lang, of Versailes Township, Alleghany County, being through the abundant mercy and good will of God, though weak in body yet of a sound and perfect understanding and memory, do constitute this my last will and Testament, and desire it may be received by all as such. First, I most humbly bequeath my soul to God my Maker, beseeching his most gracious acceptance of it, through the all sufficient merits and mediations of my most Compas-

111

sionate Redeemer, Jesus Christ, who gave himself to be an Atonement for my sins and is able to save to the uttermost all that come unto God by him, seeing he ever liveth to make intercession for them, and who I trust will not reject me, a returning penitent sinner, when I come to him for mercy. In this hope and confidence, I render up my soul with comfort, humbly beseeching the most Blessed and Glorious Trinity, one God, most holy, most merciful and gracious, to prepare me for the time of my dissolution, and then to take me to Himself into that peace and rest and incomparible felicity which he has prepared for all that love and fear His Holy Name. Amen, blessed be God.

I give my body to the Earth, from whence it was taken, in full assurance of its Resurrection from thence at the Last Day. As for my burial, I desire it may be decent without pomp or state, at the discretion of my dear wife. I leave my wife my whole executor of all that I now possess, after all my debts and funeral. And every one of my children I leave one shilling Sterling apiece.

In witness hereof, I hereunto set my hand and seal this twenty-sixth day of April in the year of our Lord, one thousand seven Hundred and Ninety-seven.

Mr. Lang's will seems almost top-heavy with religious reassurance. It was recorded a little less than three months after he made it, which suggests along with his own phrase, "weak in body," that he expected death, soon. Surely the things that mattered even more to him than the material possessions to be distributed "at the discretion of my dear wife" are emphasized.

✻   ✻   ✻   ✻   ✻

Occasionally, a will-maker tries to joke when he draws up his last will and testament, knowing all the while that Death will have the last jest. The will of James Ryan, with its pleasant reiterations and unique phrasing, is such an example:

JAMES RYAN— *. . . seeing the taper of which I at present am supported nearly burned to the socket . . .*
Dated October 26, 1810—Recorded December 23, 1812

In the name of God, Amen, I, James Ryan, formerly a subject of the King of Great Britain, but now a citizen of the United States of

112

America, of the Township of Pitt, Allegheny County, and State of Pennsylvania, seeing that mortality which was begotten in iniquity and as of course seeing myself among the number of those who must once die; and that my probation in this Vale of Tears is fast proceeding to a close, therefore seeing the taper of which I at present am supported nearly burned to the socket, but at the same time enjoying at this present time a sound mind and perfect memory do, in order to elude in view of the aforegoing solemn considerations and perhaps sudden act of Providence and an unsettled or undistributed order of my estate of which I am seized, do make ordain constitute and declare this as my last will and testament. Imprimis, I hereby recommend my soul to that presiding divinity of whom as the cause I am the effect. Relying on the goodness whose condescension has been to lay his life for the ransom of an undone world. And from whose sufferings I hope to obtain pardon for my sins. Item—as for the house of clay wherein my soul inhabiteth, I desire and enjoin my executors to have it buried on my own plantation in a plain decent but becoming manner, and in so doing to avoid unnecessary expense.

Religious faith was strong in our ancestors here on the frontier. The "Scotch-Irish," who represented the greater number, were devoted to Kirk and School. To them education was as important as religion because the ordinary man ought to be able to read the Bible and every community needed a preacher well-versed in orthodox Christianity. Religion and education share equally in gifts not lightly given when so hard to come by.

JOHN CLARK— ... *for ye education of ... poor and pious youths for the Gospel ministry ...*
Dated February 4, 1793—Recorded July 26, 1797

John Clark's will, which has been mentioned before, not effective until his wife's death in 1806, is written on a single, large sheet of paper in straight lines and without paragraph indentations. Quaint spelling, the use of the long s and some scratched-out words make this will a bit difficult to read in manuscript. Because of its importance to education in Western Pennsylvania, we give the following excerpt to show Dr. Clark's plan in detail for the training of Christian ministers:

113

Whereas the American United States are indebted to me in a considerable sum, the certificates for which are in ye hands of Mr. Isaac Snowden, Esq., of Philadelphia, the interest of which I will to laid out (after ye Death of my beloved wife Margaret) for ye education of such poor and pious youths for the Gospel ministry, as the Reverend Messieurs James Finley, John McMillan, James Dunlap, Thaduce Dodd, and Joseph Patterson may judge to be fit objects for ye above purpose and to give such proportions to such poor and pious youth as they ye above named Rev. Gentlemen may judge duty. Provided, nevertheless, that if William Jones, whom I have brought up from his infancy, should upon examination give such evidence of his piety my wish is that preference should be given to him before others equally hopeful. Moreover ye above named Rev. Gentlemen are hereby empowered to appoint others to succeed them in this trust so that there may be a succession to this trust in this Presbytery. The Majority to whom this trust may be commited, may at any time meet & determine to whom and how much shall be granted to any one poor & pious youth; the whole to be notified.

MARGARET CLARK— . . . *I will and bequeath to the trustees of Jefferson College . . .*
Dated May 5, 1806—Recorded June 9, 1807

Margaret Clark, in her will, not only carried out to the letter her husband's expressed wishes, but showed herself completely in accord with his plan by establishing a trust for a college which is now Washington and Jefferson College. She said:

. . . and the remainder of my estate, real and personal I will and bequeath to the trustees of Jefferson College to be by them disposed of as they shall judge most conducive to the Good of the Institution and to the advancement of the Redeemer's Kingdom in the world.

Witnesses to her will were William Woods and Abraham Tidball.
Of the "Rev. Gentlemen" referred to in John Clark's will, John McMillan and Thaddeus Dod had belonged to the so-called *Four Horsemen of Western Pennsylvania,* appointed by the Presbyterian Church to look after religious observance and education in the Pittsburgh country. In addition to these two, the Reverend

114

Clark named three others — James Finley, James Dunlap, and Joseph Patterson. All five of these ministers were interested in promoting higher education, and the Reverend McMillan, especially, Dr. Clark trusted to make the right selection of young men to profit by the bequests. A letter of Dr. McMillan's, addressed to the Reverend James Carnahan on March 26, 1832, explains why this trust was good.

> When I had determined to come to this country, Dr. Smith enjoined it upon me to look out for some pious young men and educate them for the ministry; 'for,' said he, 'though some men of piety and talents may go to a new country, at first, yet if they are not careful to raise up others, the country will not be well supplied.' Accordingly, I collected a few who gave evidence of piety, and taught them the Latin and Greek languages, some of whom became useful, and others, eminent, ministers of the Gospel. I had still a few with me, when the Academy was opened in Cannonsburg, and finding I could not teach and do justice to my congregation, I immediately gave it up and sent them there . . .
>
> I am now in my eightieth year, and have outlived all the first set of ministers who settled on this side of the mountains, all the second set who were raised in this country, and several of the third.

What a wonderful record for the patriarch of Presbyterianism in Western Pennsylvania! Dr. McMillan's own pastorate at Chartiers lasted from 1788 until 1833. Dr. Dwight Guthrie's recent life of John McMillan shows how fruitful this long life was.

Certainly, the one thing which people who made these early wills cared about was education for children and dependents. Scarcity of material possessions and lack of schooling is reflected in some of the wills, but appreciation of books and of education is there, too. The early will-makers wanted their children trained to make their own way in life but, even more, they wanted them to know how to live in a truer kind of nobility. Parents then, as now, wanted their sons and daughters equipped with skills and trades to take their places in a changing world. But above all they wanted their children to go on living the right kind of life, with a sense of more than material responsibility to themselves, to those who had gone before them, and to those who would come after them. Even now, these early wills hold an essence of what matters to those who are alive, for our own rich educational heritage had its beginnings in the foresight of the Allegheny County pioneers.

SAMUEL HOLLIDAY— . . . *until they can read and write and go through the five common rules of arithmetic . . .*
Dated October 17, 1792—Recorded June 31, 1793

Here is the will of a father who recognized his children needed at least fundamentals of education, although like many of his neighbors then and now, he seems eager to have them begin to earn a living as soon as possible.

I allow them to be kept in school until they can read and write and go through the five common rules of arithmetic with a tolerable degree of proficiency.

This clause included his three daughters—a liberal attitude toward the education of girls which was not uncommon in earliest Pittsburgh. One early traveler remarked on the unusual number of schools for girls in early nineteenth century Pittsburgh.

And when my two sons, Thomas Berlin and William, are both of age, I allow them to pay my three daughters above-mentioned the sum of 40 pounds to be paid in produce at four yearly payments, the fifth payment to be paid two years after the youngest of them is of age.

Along with bequests of real estate, described by quaint boundaries, his clothes, saddle, and bridle, "also a piece of cloth I had for a coat," he left the boys two volumes of McHenry's *Comment on the New Testament,* which is one reason he hoped they could read.

And a bequest to his oldest son reveals that he was a smith— an important figure in the late eighteenth century and one of the most honored, even by savages. On the trails and outside the settlement he would do a profitable business in shoeing horses, mending firearms, and making all manner of necessary tools.

116

Ephraim Hughey— *... to be made perfect ...*
    Dated July 31, 1812—Recorded December 18, 1813

Mr. Hughey went a little further in outlining his son's education in trade or apprenticeship beyond the rudiments of book learning.

I leave my son Wilson Hughy that he must be learned to read and write well, to be made perfect in the five Common Rules of Arithmetic, to be clothed and kept free from expenses until fit to go to a trade or other business.

Jacob Miller— *... so that he will be fit for any kind of mercantile business ...*
    Dated May 12, 1806—Recorded August 18, 1806

Jacob Miller wrote his will on a single sheet of paper. That paper is now torn, or worn, into three separate pieces, and fragments are broken from its corners. The will was written across the width of the sheet and, when the pieces are placed side by side, it measures about sixteen inches by ten and seven-eighths of an inch. No patching has been attempted; that would be useless because the brittle paper cracks at a touch.

Yet it was a privilege to hold the fragile original document and to visualize the man who wrote it. He was anxious that his two children be trained to take their rightful places in life. He respected education, although his own poorly-written signature might indicate that he himself had not had as much of that as he planned for his son and daughter. Mrs. Miller was instructed

to school and educate my son William Miller in English so that he will be fit for any kind of mercantile business according to the custom of the country.

And, as a special bequest from her father, the executors are further instructed:

to school and educate my daughter Henrietta Miller to read and write English and to cypher through the Rule of Three.

117

Although she would not require as much education as her brother, many a father providing for the welfare of his daughter realized that young men, even on a frontier, did not want unlettered mothers for their children. Education cost money—and money was scarce in most households—but like cows and horses it could mean a richer dowry for a daughter.

JAMES IMBRIE— *. . . dispose of my three youngest daughters into . . . families . . .*
Dated December 20, 1802—Recorded March 4, 1803

James Imbrie, whose holograph will is described earlier, provided that his daughters have a chance to grow up in safe surroundings, where they would learn household arts and the ways of good family life. He took advantage of the opportunities of his day for binding out young people to apprenticeship as a kind of education.

※　※　※　※　※

If a family could afford to give the child a higher education, there were opportunities, even from the earliest days. Private schools taught Latin, surveying, geography, languages, and grammar to both boys and girls if they could pay for it. Needlework, music, and painting were emphasized for girls. Free public schools supported by everyone's taxes were not established until 1840. But there were the Pittsburgh Academy in Pittsburgh, and the Canonsburg Academy in Washington County in the 1780's. Seminaries came early, too: Xenia at Service in Beaver County, 1794; Western Theological Seminary, 1825. As early as 1819, the Academy at Pittsburgh became the Western University of Pittsburgh—with training in the liberal arts, in the law, and in the beginnings of the sciences and humanities which have made Pittsburgh a great industrial and cultural capital for the world.

In the outer settlements, as in the town, there were a motley group: hunters, traders, merchants, lawyers, doctors, ministers, soldiers, and lawless adventurers. Many were men of good taste, good manners, and good morals. These were the ones whose influence led in school and church.

118

The founders of the commonwealth, the Penns, held, remotely, a kind of direction even over these western hills. The Penns gave liberally in Western Pennsylvania for church and burial sites. Some of our oldest churches are built on ground granted them by the Penns; for example, the First Presbyterian, Trinity Cathedral, and Smithfield Street Evangelical Protestant. The first Presbyterian church was situated originally on the corner of Wood and Sixth Street (where Max Azen's store is now) and built of hewn logs. It was established in 1786. Trinity's first church—the "Round Church"—stood on a three-cornered plot at Liberty, Sixth, and Wood. The ground granted to that church was Lots No. 435, No. 436, and half of Lot No. 437, in the plan of the town, ownership of which was confirmed by the State Legislature in March, 1806. Both of these churches have moved up farther on their original land grants, with beautiful and inspiring church edifices. Only Trinity Cathedral, however, retains a part of its burying ground. Smithfield Street Evangelical, which used to be at the corner of Smithfield and Oliver, some years ago gave up that site and erected its building down a little farther on the same side of Smithfield Street, thus gaining revenue from parts of its ground floor.

When the very first churches were founded, denominational differences did not matter much, if indeed they were recognized at all. To substantiate this, read the following *Gazette* editorial of August 26, 1786:

A Clergyman is settled in this town of the Calvinist Church; some of the inhabitants are of the Lutheran or Episcopalian Church, but the distinction is brot little into view, the younger people scarcely knowing that there is a difference in the mode of government of the two churches, for in doctrine there is none, and the more advanced in life not thinking it of sufficient moment to take notice of it. The passions which agitated our fathers are subsided, and the minds of men are gradually clarifying on these subjects, so that in America, or at least in this part of it, there is the most perfect liberality of sentiment.

To understand people it is necessary to know what kind of religion they really have—not doctrines, not tenets—but what they accept to live by daily. The high place that religion had in

119

the lives of people in early Pittsburgh is evident as they set about putting their earthly affairs in order and providing means of enriching the spiritual experiences of people who would benefit by their bequests.

In a chapter presenting early wills favoring religion and education, many more could be presented. On a frontier where the very minimum of necessities were hard to come by, where clearing the land, cultivating crops and livestock, providing an easier and more gracious life for descendants meant hard work and frugal planning, men gave away an estate carefully and prayerfully. The church and the school shared honor with the family as beneficiaries, for in a free land they were the three rocks upon which the will-makers built their own lives and the future of their children.

Women In Wills

Early wills reflect folkways and emphasis on the family—especially wills which refer to women. It is little wonder that a woman still prizes so highly the little things that make up her home—grandmother's silver spoons, heirloom glass, a cherry table, or an old family rocker. After all, for less than a hundred years has she been sure these things were hers to pass on, unless her husband in his will explicitly provided so. Even her clothes, in the early nineteenth century, had to be willed to her at his death. Some husbands recognized that their wives would be more likely to see that the children got their share of the estate, and that the mother was the one most likely to hold together the family treasures, and so some wills reflect the love and trust of the father. But other wills, many of them, bear witness to the prejudice of earlier years that perhaps a second husband would profit from the first husband's estate and so, many wives inherited only "during widowhood."

The will of David Strawbridge illustrates much of this.

DAVID STRAWBRIDGE— *... during her present life ... that is during her state of widowhood.*
Dated April 20, 1792—Recorded August 13, 1794

The will of David Strawbridge is written on unruled paper, 15½ by 7½ inches. He did not write the text—only the signature

is his handwriting. The text is in formal script, painstakingly inscribed; Mr. Strawbridge's signature looks like Str. For a seal
David Strawbridge used a little penciled drawing which resembles
a man's profile with prominent eyemarking. That "seal" is found
in the codicil, as well as in the will itself.

For several reasons this is a most interesting will. One—it
confirms the legal status of women at that time: ". . . to my dear
and loving wife, Ann Strawbridge, all her wearing apparel to use
during her life and dispose of at her death according to her
pleasure." How very inconvenient for Ann, if her own clothes
had been willed away to someone else! Because her husband
remembered to say so, she could do as she pleased with them;
they were really hers to wear.

The next bequest shows definitely that David Strawbridge,
like other husbands of his era, believed in protecting his property
from falling into the hands of another man:

> I also will and bequeath to my said wife during her present life
> in this world, that is during her widowhood, the use of my dwelling
> house, bed, and household furniture, together with one-sixth part of
> the yearly produce and profits of all my real estate for her support and
> maintenance during her life of widowhood and after her death.

Mr. Strawbridge bequeathed "the sum of five shillings and sixpence" to each of his married daughters, Elizabeth Rutherford,
Margaret Bennett, and Ann Kennedy. His grandson was to receive
his treasured gun. As a good husband and father he wished to
insure a comfortable future for his wife and daughters with
legacies of property and money. But to Jean, whom he designated
as "my careful daughter," he left not only "all her wearing apparel"
and "the bed whereon she lies," but he directed that Jean was to
get "all my Tools and Implements for laboring in the woods and
fields." It was not unusual for women to work alongside men in the
wilderness settlement. And Mr. Strawbridge knew well that his
"careful" daughter could be depended upon to keep his plantation in order, that she knew how to use and to appreciate his
precious tools. Above all, he wanted her to have them when, later
on, she came into possession of this other bequest provided for

her: ". . . also 170 acres 64 perches of Patented land, known by the name of 'Castle Shanahan.'"

JAMES McMICHAEL—*The privilege of the house.*
Dated July 16, 1788—Recorded January 20, 1792

James McMichael shows great consideration when he directs that his "dearly beloved wife, Priscilla," is to have

the privilege of the house I now live in and to enjoy it in an unmolested manner with my son John McMichael; but if she, my said wife Priscilla, should think it more convenient to live more retired, in such case my will is that my sons Isaac McMichael and John McMichael do build her, my said wife Priscilla, a convenient dwelling house for her and her girl Mary Hammond, to live in on the same tract of land, or where she may choose.

She might remain in the home she had made, but it would be her son's home, never again the same without her husband. In a little house all her own, with the congenial Mary Hammond to help with the work and to sit with her in front of a cosy fire after the day was done, Priscilla could dream away the twilight years of her life, secure still in her own home. His rare insight had given her security and assured her of independent comfort and enjoyment. Best of all, he had permitted her to make the choice—and surely she would choose her own hearth to sweep. Certainly she would elect to have the new house erected near the old one, dear for associations of a happy life, near enough for grandchildren to run in and out and share their youth and love with her.

Mr. McMichael remembered everything that might contribute to his wife's comfort—he left to her "the bed whereon she now lies, together with household furniture." In addition, he directed that his two sons were "to supply her and her girl with sufficient provisions, together to find her in firewood hauled to her door." The two sons, Isaac and John, would faithfully carry out their father's instructions and, in all probability, would see to it that their mother had many extras in that loving service. For Isaac and John McMichael were good substantial citizens, active in promoting all that was for the welfare of early Pittsburgh and the people in it. James McMichael signed his will four years before it became effective. No doubt, James and Priscilla had gone over it together many times and were in accord as to its provisions— for Priscilla, the two boys, and their daughter Mary. (Mary's legacy was in money, a large sum for that time.) He might have directed his daughter to look after her mother, but he made the wiser choice in having his two sons do it. He made it a man's job. In thus safeguarding their mother's future, he had willed a valuable contribution to his sons' character, also.

The McMichael family lived in Robinson Township, Washington County. Like most of the settlers, they were farmers; another clause in James McMichael's will directs "the said Isaac and John are to keep one horse and one cow and one sheep for my wife Priscilla's use."

JAMES SPEIRS—*Her choice of all my flock.*
        Dated December 17, 1788—Recorded August 1, 1789

James Speirs' will contains the same careful provision for loved ones. He leaves his property to his sons but each year they are ordered "to give to their mother ten bushels of wheat and one hundred pounds of meat." To his wife he bequeaths:

the privilege and benefit of my dwelling house, the new one now raised during her life, together with a feather bed and bedding and a cow, her choice of all my flock to be at her disposal.

Such was *his* way of having his sons allow her all the privileges of the home she had been used to, her own cow (to dispose of as she liked) and the certainty of sufficient bread and meat in the exact quantities of wheat and meat his sons would bring to her during each year, to her home on Moon Run, near the mouth of Chartiers Creek.

JOHN MORGAN—*10 bushels of Indian corn.*
        Dated July 29, 1796—Recorded June 5, 1798

John Morgan gives to his wife:

124

two milk cows, taking her choice of all my stock of horn cattle, also I give two sheep, her choice of my flock, as also I give one feather bed and furniture; her choice of my beds. I likewise give her a small table, one spinning wheel, and half of the pewter now in my possession. And it is my desire that the two cows and two sheep above mentioned have free liberty of pasture and be regularly bedded with hay and the forage as usual.

Mr. Morgan thought of everything—even this bequest to the live stock!

When Mr. Morgan speaks of the pewter in his possession, it might have been his wife's dowry, but he had the right to claim it as his own and to divide it as he wished.

I do devise and it is my will and pleasure that Mary, my beloved wife, have free and undisturbed possession of the dwelling house I now live in during her natural life.

(*Natural life* is a legal term which means her widowhood. If she took a second husband, she would forfeit all legacies under the first husband's will.)

For her maintenance, the widow Morgan need have no fear. The following bequest took care of that:

I give unto my said wife, Mary, and I require that it be strictly observed by my heirs, 20 bushel of good sound grain, viz., 10 bushels of Indian corn, to be delivered on the first day of December yearly, either at the said dwelling house, or at the mill.

There was a gristmill on the Morgan plantation. It is mentioned in the will as a direct bequest to their son, Samuel.

JAMES WOODBURN—*The small stand and her wheel and reel.*
Dated April 29, 1809—Recorded June 7, 1789

Obviously Mr. Woodburn *dated* his will incorrectly, but the recording date is right.

James Woodburn's will lets his wife look out for herself, taking it as a matter of course she will continue to live in her own home. He gives her:

150 pounds specie, bed and bedclothes with the hangans; one horse, saddal, bridle and whip, one cow (her choice of all that I have), the pice of thick cloth about twelve yards and one quarter; the chest of drawers, with her choice of the pots; all the flexstow now in the house; the privilege of sowing half a bushel of flex seed this spring, and to live on the place for one year with a necessary support for herself and the beasts, a part of the tea things, three of the silver spoons, the small stand and her wheel and reel.

Where Mrs. Woodburn is to be at the expiration of that one year the will does not indicate. But if she had to leave the plantation, as the will seems to indicate, the one hundred and fifty pounds specie could establish her in another house. But Mr. Woodburn's will is kindly concerned with his wife's welfare. At any rate, the wheel and the reel would belong to her so that she could continue to spin and weave. Probably she would make more "pieces of thick cloth"—but for *herself*, next time. The flaxseed, if planted right away, would be ready to harvest within the year granted her on the place and, if she had to leave, let's hope she took with her the best of the brass and copper kettles—since she had been bequeathed "her choice of the pots." The Woodburn home, in Moon Township, was about four miles east and across the Ohio River from the mouth of Racoon Creek. It was originally the site of Fort McIntosh.

WILLIAM WITHEROW— . . . *and firewood in sufficiency.*
Dated August 1, 1795—Recorded September, 1795

While William Witherow gave to his wife Rachel "access to remain in my mansion house" and "One-third profits of my real estate," he also said:

if she may think it more eligible that a house be erected for her on some part of my land, that it be done at the expense of the estate and, in lieu of the one-third profits of the real estate, that she be paid annually the sum of ten pounds Pennsylvania currency together with provender for one horse, one cow, and two sheep and firewood in sufficiency made ready for her.

He went on to make it clear that "the above privileges only during such times as she may remain my widow."

126

JOHN WHELEN—*One third of my personal estate absolutely forever.*

Dated April 13, 1807—Recorded May 11, 1807

John Whelen's will is an example of greater generosity and trust than ordinary. His wife got her third of his estate "absolutely forever."

Soon after arriving in Pittsburgh, John Whelen inserted this notice in the *Pittsburgh Gazette,* December 5, 1795:

John Whelan, hairdresser from Dublin, respectfully informs the citizens of Pittsburg that he intends following the hairdressing business in that town. He therefore solicits their favors, and flatters himself that he will give satisfaction to those who may employ him.

N.B.—He lodges at the Widow Irwin's in Second Street.

In the 1790's wigs were out of fashion, and yet, when hair was long enough, it was dressed in imitation of the wig. Often hair was left unpowdered, but it was dressed up in back for a queue. Mr. Whelen, it seems, did give satisfaction to his customers, for when he wrote his will in 1807, he began that document as follows: "As I am not under debt to any person, I have no arrangements to make as to settlement of debts." He had acquired property, too, as the will continues with

I do give and bequeath to my beloved wife Letitia the one third part of all my real and personal estate—the one third of my real estate, viz. of my house and lot situate in the diamond in the Borough of Pittsburg during her natural life, and one third of my personal estate *absolutely forever.*

There were six children in the Whelen family by that time: James, Catherine, Mary Ann, John, Letitia, and Jane. Of the eldest, James, Mr. Whelen stated in his will:

having already given him what I considered reasonable part of my estate with which it pleased God to bless me, I give him one Spanish milled dollar and no more. This I give to him to prevent and put it out of his power to disturb rest of the family as to bequests made to them.

127

That paragraph suggests a rift in family relations—and this notice in the *Commonwealth,* April 16, 1806, lends credence to the idea:

PARTNERSHIP DISSOLVED

The temporary partnership subsisting between John and James G. Whelan of Pittsburgh is this day dissolved, by mutual consent.—All persons indebted to the firm are requested to make immediate payment; and those having any demands are desired to present them, properly authenticated, for payment.

—John Whelan
James G. Whelan

The other five children received equal shares in what remained of the estate. But Catherine, eldest daughter, also got "my brown mare, a saddle and a bridle."

Less than a year after her husband's death, Mrs. Whelen advertised the shop for rent:

Commonwealth, March 12, 1808

TO BE RENTED, and possession given on the first of April. A storeroom, back parlor and cellar. In the Diamond, next door to the Sign of the Buck, now occupied by the subscriber. The stand is well situated for any kind of business and the premises in complete repair. For particulars apply to Letitia Whalen.

Mr. Whelen had selected his wife as one of the executors. The other executor, "of Westmoreland County" was Jeremiah Murray. Witnesses to the will were John Johnston, Joseph McClurg, and James Mountain.

HUGH MURPHY—*To prevent that which is uncomfortable.*
Dated January 21, 1814—Recorded February 17, 1814

To prevent that which is uncomfortable, I order that in dividing the use of my mansion house my wife is to have the exclusive use of the back five rooms and the privilege of cooking and doing such business in the kitchen as to her may appear proper during her natural life.

128

In addition to looking out for his wife's comfort, Hugh Murphy gave her one-third of his personal estate and one-third of his real estate, "together with one horse creature, a milch cow, and seven sheep. In all these, she is to have her choice of my stock, and said personal property is to be hers forever." The third was legally her right, at least for widowhood, but he left her the chattels *forever*—a notable gesture!

And he made another notable gesture:

I give and bequeath to my mother-in-law, Mary Parks, at the expense of my general estate, all that may be necessary to her comfortable support during her life, and all that may be necessary to her being decently buried when dead.

MATTHEW McKINNEY—*A small garden of ten rod.*
Dated March 18, 1809

My beloved wife Ann shall have the right and liberty of my bedroom and fireplace therein, with a small garden of ten rod of land convenient to said rume and free liberty of what frute she may want to make use of each year when their is frute during the time she continues my widow . . . and a 2-gallon pot and liberty of wash kittles when she may want.

ISAAC GREER—*The sole privilege of the fire room.*
Dated February 20, 1809—Recorded July 30, 1809

Isaac Greer, like Matthew McKinney of Elizabeth Township, made his will the same year. He called his wife Martha's partial use of the home she had made for him not her right but her "privilege."

the sole privilege of the fire room in the back part of the brick house . . . and she is to be provided for by my son Jesse in everything necessary to render her life comfortable.

JOHN DUFF—*Food and raiment.*
Dated November 22, 1823—Recorded December 12, 1823

John Duff orders "My son, Alexander Duff, is to provide his mother with food and raiment." There were four other sons, but

Alexander, as the executor of his father's will, was given that important charge to carry out.

Eliezer Meirs—*She shall no longer hold or enjoy . . .*
      Dated February 28, 1790—Recorded March 20, 1790

Over "his mark," Eliezer Meirs was blunt:

that my beloved wife, Elizabeth Meirs, shall have, enjoy, and receive all the benefits, rents, issues, and profits of the Tavern and tract of land whereon I now live and the two other tracts of land devised to my respective sons before mentioned until they respectively arrive at full age. Provided nevertheless that if it so happen that the said Elizabeth Meirs should after my decease intermarry with any person whatsoever then and in such case she shall no longer hold or enjoy the rents, issues, and profits for the lands as before mentioned.

William Butler—*She shall cease to act as an executrux . . .*
      Dated May 12, 1789—Recorded August 1, 1791

William Butler was just as determined that his wife would take nothing to the home of another husband, or deprive his children of their inheritance:

My beloved wife, Jinny Butler, shall have the conduct and management of all my real and personal estate to manage the same as she shall think the most suitable for the mutual advantage of herself and children during her widowhood . . . and it is further my will and I order and direct that in case my beloved wife, Jinny Butler, should intermarry after my decease that then and in such case she shall cease to act as an executrux or have anything to do with the management of the children's estates.

Alexander Ewing— *. . . she is to withdraw from the premises instantly.*
      Dated February 12, 1798—Recorded August 13, 1798

Alexander Ewing states his will in a way to discourage even their son from giving his mother a home if she should marry:

I do give and bequeath unto my beloved wife, Jane Ewing, the full enjoyment of my present possession until my son William arrives at age in law, after which period my above-named son to support his mother in a decent manner agreeable to her rank. But if my wife should marry whilst my son is minor, the executors are to pay her 30£ current money 20 mo. after her marriage, and she is to withdraw from the premises instantly; and if she should marry after my son arrives at age he is to treat his mother in the same manner as recommended to the executors in the state of his minority.

SAMUEL HOLLIDAY—*One-third of all my moveable property inclusive of her bed and bed clothes.*
Dated October 17, 1792—Recorded June 31, 1793

The will of Samuel Holliday, written on a single sheet of legal paper, is grey with age and the ink with which he wrote it himself has become a dull brown. The long *s* runs throughout the writing. The items themselves are quaint and interesting. For instance:

I give to my beloved wife Susannah the one-third of all my moveable property inclusive of her bed and bedclothes . . . also a silk gown which I have sent for with Mr. John Wright and a case of drawers in place of those which I left at Caleb Way's Tavern "at the Sign of the Waggon," when I came out to this country, and to have her maintenance and the maintenance of a horse and cow off the land while she remains my widow. To my daughter Susannah, one bed and bedclothes, and the cow that carrys the bell and four sheep, also a case looking glass. And to my daughter Mary one bed and bedclothes and one cow . . . These articles which have been named to the three girls respectively shall be given them at their marriage, and the sum of forty pounds to be paid in produce at four yearly payments, the first payment to be paid two years after the youngest one comes of age.

It may be that Mr. Holliday remembered Susannah's grief when he had to leave her "case of drawers" behind at an inn on their tedious journey from the east to Pittsburgh. His daughter Jean, his will states, was not to get her legacy until her marriage, when she, too, would get a "case of drawers." Perhaps she would get eventually her mother's, which may have been her grandmother's too.

131

WILLIAM FIFE SR.— *. . . not to be accountable to any one . . . as
long as she remains my widow.*
Dated July 16, 1808—Recorded, 1808

all moveable property, rents, and benefits from place. . . . She is to fortune my daughters as she thinks they deserve, and is not to be accountable to any one for what she does, as long as she remains my widow, but
if she should marry then to give account of everything.

JOHN METZGER—*I utterly disallow . . .*
Dated February 24, 1798—Recorded June 5, 1798

At least one widow was able to find a loophole in her husband's will. John Metzger said in no uncertain language: "I
utterly disallow any of my real estate aforesaid to be sold by any
means during the said Elizabeth's, my wife's, life." Elsewhere in
his will he mentioned "during her natural life" but, because he
failed to say that other property was to be hers only during her
widowhood, his wife Elizabeth, Elizabeth Trough—"late Elizabeth Metzger, widow and relict of John Metzger, deceased,"
found no obstacles in her way when she willed this part of the
estate to her second husband.

JOHN N. ROBB—*At her death she is to have . . .*
Dated April 20, 1804—Recorded April 28, 1804

John N. Robb arranged more explicitly that his estate would
not leave his family. He said that his wife was

to have all personal estate of every kind during life and the use and oc-
cupation of my plantation during her life; and at her death she is to
have the disposal of one bed and bedding, the citching furniture, and
her saddle.

SAMUEL EWING—*At her marriage or at her death . . .*
Dated October 16, 1804—Recorded December 24, 1805

Samuel Ewing of Moon Township prevents a chance of his
wife's leaving anything to her second husband or out of the family.

At her marriage or at her death, the estate is to be put up at public auction and proceeds divided among the children.

CASPER SHEETS—*All my real and personal estate . . . forever.*
    Dated January 31, 1802—Recorded October 3, 1803

Casper Sheets, waiving the precedent of his contemporaries gives his wife

all my real and personal estate to dispose of as she thinks proper during her natural life, and afterwards to her heirs and assigns forever.

How refreshing to find one will which does not limit a wife's right to property to her widowhood!

EPHRAIM HUGHEY—*In case she marry . . .*
    Dated July 31, 1812—Recorded December 18, 1813

Ephraim Hughey is even more blunt than usual where his wife is concerned

the kitchen furniture, beds and bedding, her living and accomodations of the farm I possess, as also a sufficient quantity of wool and flax to make her clothing yearly—that is to say as long as she remains my widow, but in case she marry, my executors shall be exempted from finding her in anything from that period.

I leave my daughter Jane Hays the property I have already given her—that is to say one horse, saddle, and bridle, one bed bedstead and furniture and one bureau, two cows, one breakfast table, four sheep, four chairs, one wash pot, one cook pot, one bake oven, middling size, six knives and forks, six spoons, one tea kettle and tea furniture, three delph dishes and six plates. These I lent to you when married, and now I bequeath them to you as your portion of my property.

This clause makes it impossible for Jane to get any more from the division of the estate beyond her marriage gifts.

✿   ✿   ✿   ✿   ✿

Gruff and austere as most husbands appear in these wills, pioneer men of Allegheny County were gentle and protective toward the women in their families and honestly tried to insure their security when they could no longer look after them. Most of the severity was in the phraseology which was the legal routine of the day.

SINGLE WOMEN

Single women presented the greatest problem for the will-maker. There was little an unmarried woman could do to provide for herself. Often she lived out her days helping a sister-in-law care for her brother's home and children, or she lived alone, an eccentric member of the community. Usually, brothers were instructed to look after their sister's interests. Often their legacy, like the widow's, was only for as long as they did not marry. Sometimes the family home was given to a daughter, who was expected and directed to live in it always.

Such an example is found in the will of Patrick Cavitt, dated August 1, 1820 and recorded January 29, 1835. Mr. Cavitt wanted his daughter Nancy to live with her mother and in her mother's house all her life, and he said so. With that understanding, she was to have $40 and a young mare, a cow, and two sheep. It is "dead hands" controlling another person's destiny—and yet it was an anxious father trying to insure a daughter's future. At Mrs. Cavitt's death, the will says, the homestead was to be Nancy's, and her brothers were ordered to repair the house, at that time.

A unique bequest was made by William McJunkin, of Plum Township: "The privilege of the fire room in which I sleep, to my daughter Ann *while she remains unmarried.*" Mr. McJunkin's will was dated May 14, 1814, and recorded July 30, 1814.

THOMAS MALLARSON—*The privilege of washing in the kitchen.*
Dated July 27, 1812—Recorded December 25, 1813

The daughters of Thomas Mallarson—Thankful, Permela, Phelemia, and Lucinda—were to have

the privilege of washing in the kitchen, the privileges of garden, fire-wood; and each of them one roe of apple trees on the north side of the orchard.

If single women were a problem, surely then Mr. Mallarson's problems were quadrupled! He left the house to their brother Thomas, "with the exception of the south great chamber," which, presumably, was reserved for the four girls' sleeping quarters.

Imagine their sharing the family homestead with Thomas' wife
—after all better than having to leave the home for the uncertainty
of a cold world's destiny—at least no one could ask them to leave.

JOHN FORSYTH—*One large sugar kittle.*
        Dated May 4, 1812—Recorded May 11, 1813

My daughter Polly shall have one chest, one large sugar kittle, one
tea kittle, and one heifer over and above her third part.

Evidently Polly was one of two children, because her mother
would have got one third, and the children would have shared
equally.

JAMES GLENN— . . . *one after another . . . year after year.*
        Dated March 19, 1813—Recorded March 31, 1813

James Glenn—early settler of *Glendale* and for whom it
was named—made a curious will in the pattern of a trust. The
following provisions were made for his single daughters:

   . . . I leave and bequeath unto my three unmarried daughters Peggy
Glenn, Betsy Glenn, and Hannah Glenn, two hundred and fifty dollars,
each to be paid in the following manner viz., one hundred dollars to be
paid to Peggy Glenn one year after my decease and one hundred dollars
to be paid to Betsy Glenn two years after my decease, one hundred dollars to be paid to Hannah Glenn three years after my decease. Four
years after my decease, I order a hundred dollars to be paid to my daughter Peggy, and so on alternately one after another in the manner now
specified, year after year, until the money above mentioned be respectively paid to each and every one of them.

   Furthermore, I leave unto each of my unmarried daughters one
spinning wheel, one bed and bedding, with a comfortable living of the
place, free of expense while they continue in a single or unmarried state.
And in case any or all of these my daughters die unmarried, I allow and
order that her or their portion shall be equally divided among the surviving brothers and sisters unmarried.

Why he made these unusual provisions to delay payment we
cannot know exactly. Perhaps he meant to defer payment of be-

135

quest until each daughter was old enough to use her inheritance wisely. Or perhaps he hoped that by postponing full payment each new installment would be shared by all three daughters.

* * * * *

Struggles for a scant livelihood had possibly narrowed the pioneer's outlook and deepened his possessiveness. There was no actual selfishness or thoughtlessness when he spoke of "*my* bed," "*my* pewter," "*my* mansion house," with never a suggestion of his wife's partnership in household things. Those phrases like "so long as she remains a widow" were just an echo of the law, which in the early nineteenth century neither the man nor his wife questioned very often. Reforms came much later in the century represented by these early wills.

Women's Wills

According to common law, as we have seen in the previous pages, a married woman's identity merged with that of her husband, and so she could not bequeath real estate or dispose of her chattels or even her own clothes without the consent of her husband. In fact, in 1820 a judge of the Supreme Court is quoted as saying, "In no country where the blessings of the common law are felt and acknowledged are the interests and estates of married women so entirely at the mercy of their husbands as in Pennsylvania." Attempts at improvement by laws passed in 1849 were all too often overruled by court decisions. Reforms in 1887 helped somewhat, but not until 1893 did the law give to women sole right over their own property.

Fortunately, however, men in Western Pennsylvania, as shown by their wills, when they had property to leave were careful to see that their wives were provided for. Often they made their wives executrices of the estate, and by special provisions in their wills, protected them against too great dependence on their children. Fathers, too, took whatever precautions the law permitted, to see that their daughters' dowries were protected to their own use—and often secured their wives' dowries "to their own use forever."

Comparatively few wills were made by women in Allegheny County's early days, for pioneer women usually had nothing of

137

their own except what had been bequeathed to them for life or as their men folk directed them how to bequeath family property.

Realizing, then, how unusual it was to get or hold property, and guided by their husbands' wills, women worded their bequests carefully and outlined definitely the disposition of their possessions. Many women were unable to read and write, but they thought nothing of that on a frontier where many were illiterate and under the law their words held as much or as little individual force as the most erudite signature would.

JENNAT FRAIZOR—*One flanning Shift, pair wollen Stockins . . . the bed I ly on.*
Dated September 1, 1790—Recorded October 12, 1790

Jennat Fraizor's will is the first woman's will recorded in Allegheny County. Its principal bequests are religious books—mentioned by their individual titles, as if each were a rich treasure to be prized and handed down to the new owners as something very precious. And yet Mrs. Fraizor's "mark," not her signature, signs her will. Perhaps the writer of her will had pointed to the place for the testator's signature and suggested that she either sign or make her mark and perhaps Mrs. Fraizor preferred to make her own peculiar "mark," even if she could write her name. People sometimes drew pictures or emblems even besides their written signatures; several examples are found in these old wills. Anyhow, Mrs. Fraizor could not have been entirely uneducated; she appreciated her books and, besides, she was businesslike and shrewd in collecting all debts and rents due her, and in making disposition of her scanty possessions. Items of interest are her "cloathes," quaintly described, her household furniture, and grain given to her in lieu of money by her son-in-law Michael Phillips.

In the name of God Amen:

I, Jennat Fraizor, of the township of Mifflin, County of Allegheny and State of Pennsylvania, being weake in body but of sound mind and memory thanks to God but caling to mind the mortality of my body and knowing that It is Appointed for all men once to die, do make and ordain this my last will and testament—Viz. principally and first of all I

138

recommend my soul to Almighty God who gave it and my body to be buried in a decent and Christian manner at ye discretion of my Extrs. nothing doubting but at ye General Resurrection I shall receive the same again by the almighty power of God.

And as tuching such worldly estate wherewith it hath pleased God to bless me with in this life I give demise and dispose of the same in manner and favor following: first that my just and lawfull debts shall be paid by my Extrs. Secondly I will and dequeath to my stepson Samuel Fraizor his father's big Bible. THIRDLY I will and bequeath to my daughter—Elisabeth Craige the following books, viz. Wilson's defence the hind let loose Boston on ye covenants Blackwells Schema Sacrum & Erskins Sermons (two of which I will is to Send to my daughter Sarah McCoy in Kaintuckey) one brown stuff gound one Callico Short gound, one flanning Shift, pair wollen Stockins one Spining Wheele, one pewtar dish, one pewtar quart, one Copper Ladle, flesh fork one gridle One large bucket four pewtar spoons, the bed I ly on, one blue and white kiverlid One pair fier tongs and my Cow and yearling heiffer and one years Rent of Six Pound payable by Michael Phillips the one half to be paid in Spring ninety one in grain And the other In spring ninety two In grain likewise.

FOURTHLY I will and bequeath to my daughter Jennat Phillips the Confession of Faith and the remainder of the books and ye remainder of my Cloathes and Household furniture (And of my part of the Estate unsettled payable by Thos. Crawford suposed to be about one hundred pound) ten pound out of the last payment, And the remainder of Sd. Estate to be Equally divided betwisct Elisabeth Craig and my two grandsons David and Jno. McCoy and their part to be Equally divided betwixt them, and to be put to use untill ye arive to ye years of maturity. Likewise out of four pound Sixteen Shilling due and owing to me by Michael Phillips I will and bequeath to my Cozzin Jennat Stewart Six bushels of Corn Payable In winter & the Remainder for my funeral expences; And Lastly I do Appoint Hugh Sterling and Jno. Findly my whole and Sole Extrs. of this my Last will and testament and I do hereby disallow disanull and Revoke all Wills testaments Legacies and bequests by me heretofore made Ratifying this And none other to be my last will and testament. In witness whereof I Have In these presents this

139

first day of Septr. in the year of our Lord one thousand and Seven hundred and Ninety Set my hand and Seals.

her

Jennat   Fraizor (SEAL)

mark

Decleared published and pronounced
in presence of us
>James Douglass
>William Henry
>John Nisbett

N.B. before Signing, Elisabeth Craig and: Likewise their part to be Equally divided Betwixt them and:—Enterlined before Sining.

The original document is in good physical condition: written on heavy paper, thirteen inches by eight inches, folded crosswise and twice again the same way, and the back of the sheet badly soiled on its center folds.

✻   ✻   ✻   ✻   ✻

Clothes, always important to women, are often in women's wills. Many of the wills made by women of Allegheny County in its early period mention bequests of "body cloathes" but none of them is as specific in distribution as was Hanna McRoberts'.

HANNAH McROBERTS—*Spotted dress, green dress, black silk dress*
...and my Umbrel.
Dated February 12, 1812—Recorded March 5, 1812

. . . spotted dress, green dress, black silk dress, black shall, yellow shall, and all the other shalls, one web of check, one web of flanen and one of linsey to be divided betwixt the two girls; and one piece I will to be taken to the fulling mill to be drest for a riding coat for Hanna McRoberts, and my two coten petticoats I give to the said two girls; all my yarn to my two granddaughters that lives with me . . . and my Umbrel.

The big, clumsy umbrella, which her two granddaughters were to share, was similar to the kind we see in museums, and it

140

was one of the earliest—heavy of frame, very flat, very large, and with but a few ribs.

It is particularly interesting to notice that Mrs. McRoberts' namesake was to receive the material, new-woven and designated for a riding coat. After the fuller had thickened it, it was probably made up in high style—with several small capes over the shoulders, long, and buttoned down the front. For riding coats were styled to look like those worn by stagecoach drivers, only where the revers or lapels left an open space that opening was filled in with a kerchief of gauze, fine linen, or lace—making the wearer resemble a pouter pigeon.

MAREY STEWART—*Four petticoats, three bedgowns, four Shifts . . .
chak aprons.*
Dated December 30, 1795—Recorded June 22, 1796

Marey Stewart lived in "the township of Dicksings, county of Washington"; she signed her will with her "X." On June 22, 1797, it was copied into the Wills of Allegheny County. Later, it was turned over to the Register's Office in Washington County for his permanent records. We do not have convenient access, therefore, to the original document. The provisions are quaint and interesting:

To my son Will a note of hand I have of him of five pounds two shillings.

To his wife a red chak apron.

To his daughter Mary my bed one blanket one quilt one sheete with Bolster and pillow.

To my son John, one Cow, one heifer one stear, four sheep, two petticoats, Spinning wheel and all my household furniture.

That bequest to a man of two *petticoats* sounds peculiar, doesn't it? Remember, though, that pioneer women did not own even their own clothes, that everything in the house belonged to the man. And Mrs. Stewart, in leaving to her unmarried son the livestock, clothes, and all her furniture, planned to equip John comfortably to start his own household, even to petticoats for his wife. She continues with this bequest:

141

I give and bequeath to my dearly beloved John, whom I likewise constitute make and ordain my sole Executor of this my last will and Testament all and Singular wool yearn, flex and ever artical belongs to me except what articals I menchned to my other children or grand-childer.

Her daughter, Mrs. Stewart directed, was to have "four petticoats, three bedgowns, four Shifts" and some "chak aprons"—the number being indistinctly written.

ELIZABETH CUNNINGHAM—*Two-story brick house in Pittsburgh, purchased of Alexander Shaw.*
Dated October 15, 1803—Recorded December 28, 1803

Elizabeth Cunningham, formerly the widow of Conrad Winebiddle, signed with "her mark" a will drawn up for her on October 15, 1803. She leaves to a son, Phillip Winebiddle: "two due bills or notes of hand on Jacob Nigley, one of which is for one hundred dollars and the other for one hundred and eighty dollars."
She further says that, "Catherine and Coonrad Winebiddle are to have whatever may be coming to me on a final settlement of the estate of Coonrad Winebiddle, deceased, my former husband." Here, certainly, she is at fault, for the usual provision was that widows were entitled to legacies *only if they remained widows.* Conrad Winebiddle's will had directed that his wife Elizabeth was to have "two lots of ground with houses and buildings on Market St., Geo. Wallace and Water Street." He mentions "the plantation and tract containing 259 acres which I have already given to my beloved wife *during her natural life or widowhood,*" which are to go to his son and his daughter, Conrad and Catherine. Mrs. Cunningham, of course, in making her own bequests was following out her first husband's wishes. She should, however, have given the property to the children before her death when she remarried. Under the terms by which she came into the Winebiddle legacy, it would be hers only "during her natural life or widowhood," and theirs when she remarried.

To her children, Barbara Negley, Catherine Winebiddle, Conrad Winebiddle, and William Cunningham, she gives her "two-story brick house in Pittsburgh, purchased of Alexander Shaw."

142

JEAN ADDISON—*To Eliza, Ann, Mary, Alex, William and Jane.*
Dated April 21, 1817—Recorded February 19, 1820

Jean Addison, widow of Alexander Addison, signed her will some three years before her death. It is concerned with equitable division of property among her six children:

When my youngest child shall have attained the age of twenty-one the several trustees or survivors of them shall make a fair statement of all my estate real and personal in their hands and divide the same as equal as may be into six shares, each share to consist of real or personal estate or part of both to Eliza, Ann, Mary, Alex, William and Jane.

Mrs. Addison lived for her family, and was proud of them, too. Her husband, the first law judge of Allegheny County, was appointed President Judge of the Courts of Common Pleas in 1790 (under the Constitution of 1790 which required the President Judge to be a regular attorney) and he served until 1803. Judge Addison, a fine, scholarly, Christian gentleman, had incurred the enmity of sympathizers in the Whiskey Rebellion when, as a patriot, he bravely discharged his duties as a judge in that movement. His firm stand against the rebellion led to his being impeached and removed from office in 1803. One historian refers to the impeachment as "a record that will ever be a disgrace to the State."

William Addison, his son, became one of Pittsburgh's most distinguished physicians, and was a member of the staff of its first hospital when the Sisters of Mercy opened it in a building on Penn Avenue near Sixth Street, which had been rented for the purpose. Dr. Addison was a brother-in-law of Dr. Peter Mowry, a famous pioneer physician. He had studied medicine for several years in France, as well as in this country.

RACHEL FLATCHER—*Chest . . . pewter, Spinning Wheel and Reel.*
Dated August 18, 1807—Recorded August 17, 1811

The possessions of most women in the early days were so scanty that we find them eager to pass on the little they have to children and grandchildren. Their bequests are usually personal property, chattels, and clothes, although some few did have real estate. Many of them had to make their wills to carry out the wishes of their husbands—whether the real estate was his property or even their own. The daughters usually inherited household goods or clothes—the sons got the real estate or money.

Rachel Flatcher, for instance, willed "chest, quantity of pewter, Spinning Wheel and Reel, Cupboard, and one small table" to her son, besides her *land*. The land, in all likelihood, had been bequeathed to her during her widowhood and her husband's will had directed that it be given at her death to the son.

MARY WHITMORE— . . . *to take care of my son Petre.*
Dated April 20, 1807—Recorded May 11, 1807

Mary Whitmore, of St. Clair Township, over "her mark," leaves her wearing apparel to her daughters. But, to her son John, she wills all her estate: "to take care of my son Petre until he chuses to go to the learning of some trade."

Other wills made by women are concerned with the education of their children. For instance, the will of Eleanor Elliott.

ELEANOR ELLIOTT—*Priscilla Reed, mother of my grandchildren,*
my sole executrix.
Dated July 11, 1819—Recorded November, 1819

Eleanor Elliott bequeathed everything she owned to her three grandchildren "for the benefit of their educations," appointing "Priscilla Reed, mother of my grandchildren, my sole executrix." It is interesting that here is a woman appointing a woman to administer her estate.

ANN PLUMER—*To keep and have educated my two sons.*
Dated April 25, 1815—Recorded 1815

Ann Plumer, Versailles Township, said that the estate was to be sold and the money used to educate and maintain her children, "Jonathan, John William, Catherine, Thomas, Nancy, and George." She nominates a brother-in-law, George Plumer, "to keep and have educated my two sons Thomas and George, until they are fit to be put to trades—should they choose to learn trades

144

or otherwise as my executors (or their guardians) think best to dispose of them."

Real estate bequests become more frequent in women's wills as the 1800's progress—family lands handed down to a wife by a husband to use during her "natural" life, then to be passed on to the children.

MARTHA HILAND—*All my clothes and Beding and no more.*
Dated February 11, 1812—Recorded December 18, 1817

Martha Hiland gave to her sons, Robert and James, "all my real estate as well as my live stock to be equally divided between them by men whom they are to choose between themselves"; to her daughter Betty—"all my clothes and Beding and no more." "And as to any small moveables," she said, "it is my desire that they remain in the hands of my two sons as their proper wright." This "proper wright" was probably the father's wish.

BARBARA ELLIOTT—*The tract of land called the Bull pens.*
Dated June 2, 1810—Recorded March 8, 1815

Bullock Penns, or "Bull pens," as Mrs. Elliott calls it, was a celebrated hostelry owned by her husband, on the Forbes Road about seven miles from Fort Pitt—near Fifth and Penn, which we now call Point Breeze. It supplied beef to the Fort throughout the Indian Wars.

I order and direct that ye remaining real estate shall be sold by my executor, fiz. a part of the tract of land called the Bull pens containing two hundred acres more or less situated in Allegheny County on the South . . . of the great road leading from Pittsburgh adjoining lots of Col. McNair, Rbt. Elliot and Wm. Wilkins, Esquire."

Money from such sale, she instructed, was to be divided between her son William and her three daughters and their heirs,

namely Mary Noble, Jane and Barbara, share alike, except that my daughter Jane is also to get my negro woman called Nell and her son called John McCowan.

Executors of Mrs. Elliott's will were George Wallace and her son, Arch Elliott.

MARY RICHARDSON—*Small store in Noblesburg.*
Dated December 22, 1805—Recorded August 12, 1806

To Jane Holmes "small store in Noblesburg and the lot in which it stands, also stone house, and out lot." Jane must have been a married daughter to whom her father's will had directed his wife to will the family property, or it might be that she claimed the right of "femme sole" granted to women in trade or business.

✻　✻　✻　✻　✻

Eleanor McDivett, though, does bequeath property to a niece and even a sister in Ireland. She signed with an "X," and her witnesses were Andrew Willard and Harmar Denny.

ELEANOR McDIVETT—*To my beloved sister . . . now living in Ireland.*
Dated October 22, 1818—Recorded June 8, 1820

She gave to her "beloved niece, Mary O'Hara, daughter of Catherine O'Hara":

the third part of my houses and the lot of ground situate on Third Street near to the corner of Redoubt Alley, together with all my personal property of every description whatever. . . .
one other third from said houses and lot of ground I will and bequeath to my beloved sister Mary Ash now living in Ireland, and the remaining one third of said houses and lot I will to my beloved sister Sarah Dougherty also living in Ireland.

MARY FINK—*All my real estate . . . in the state of Maryland.*
Dated September 15, 1821—Recorded October 4, 1824

Mary Fink, over her "X," left to her son Andrew Fink:

all my bedclothes and five yards of flannel for a blanket and my personal property of which I am possessed. To my sons Jacob, Michael, Daniel, Andrew and Abraham Fink, all my real estate lying and being in the

146

state of Maryland, Frederick County, subject however to the payment of one hundred dollars by my said sons to my daughter Barbara Fink.

At first glance, it would appear that Mrs. Fink and most of the women of those early days favored sons, while daughters were left little or nothing. Remember, though, that women could give away at their death only what they could show had been given to them by their husbands as theirs to dispose of at death. Everything else was a part of the family estate, and had to be divided between the children or the nearest relatives of the husband at the widow's death. This explains why mothers bequeathing to a son items of household furniture or her own clothing labeled the gift "his wright." Money was always the rightful inheritance of a son; it had, presumably, been earned by his father and the law held it his as the next male in line for it. Sometimes, however, a mother did use her own judgment as to which son would inherit his father's property. Susanna Miers' will, for example:

SUSANNA MIERS—*To my son Butler Miers, my youngest and now dearest to me.*
Dated May 12, 1817—Recorded December 27, 1817

Having some worldly property and a number of children and wishing to leave what I have to those I believe most deserving of my favours —I give and bequeath to my son Butler Miers, my youngest and now dearest to me, the house and Lotts where I now live, with one thousand dollars out of the last of the money due me by John Irwin—and the feather bed and beding whereon I at present lay . . . Said Butler is not to get possession of the money during his minority but is only to receive from the house etc. to be applied to his education and decent support.

MARIA MILKS— . . . *one bed and bed clothes which she now occupies . . .*
Dated February 2, 1822—Recorded July 22, 1822

Maria Milks, in 1822, willed that her estate was to be "equally divided between my other three children, Jacob Harga, Henry Harga and Elizabeth Chapman," after the executors had

147

taken out "the sum of two dollars, each," for her two sons, and several other bequests. One of these was to her granddaughter Maria Frew—"one bed and bed clothes which she now occupies;" the other:

I do give and bequeath unto my daughter Mary Whitwright one black and white cow together with all the fowls and provision, such as corn, flour, and meat, together with two-fifths of my personal estate.

JANE MONTEETH— . . . *by her not suffering the plantation to be injured by destruction of the Fruit Trees . . .*
Recorded March 26, 1817

The will of Jane Monteeth bears her "X" but it has no date for the signature. It provides for a niece, Jane McMillan, as follows:

the use of my house and farm whereon I now reside with the appurtenances thereunto belonging and the profits arising therefrom during her natural life (except and reserving so much of the profits thereto as may be necessary to keep the plantation in good tenantable repair, and by her not suffering the plantation to be injured by destruction of the Fruit Trees by suffering the timber to be cut unnecessarily or to make sale thereof by her consent or knowledge. Excepting likewise so much of the said plantation as may be surveyed of for the use of my nephew John Gamble (which piece of land will be described hereafter in said will) and after the death of my niece Jane McMillan the plantation to be sold or as much of it as may remain to said John Gamble and out of the amount of said Sale I bequeath to the children of Jane McMillan, should she have any, the sum of six hundred pounds to have and to share alike. But should she not have any, the six hundred pounds shall then be divided between my brothers and sisters.

HANNAH WARD . . . *also the Moiety of one half part of the money . . .*
Dated December 3, 1813—Recorded November 4, 1814

Hannah Ward, whose will was witnessed by Dennis S. Scully and Thomas G. Lea, left her sister, Susannah Connelly, "my wearing apparel, also the Moiety of one half part of the money arising from sale of my personal property."

148

MARGARET ROSS— ... *my red and white Cow ... my oldest black and white Cow ... my other cow ...*
Dated October 5, 1821—Recorded March 27, 1822

Margaret Ross directed that her landed property was to go to "brother John Ross." To her niece Margaret Jane, she left "one feather bed and bedding" and to her niece Eliza G. Ross, she gave "one saddle." To Thomas Ross, the bequest was: "my red and white Cow." To John B. Ross, "my oldest black and white Cow" and, to James Ross, "son of James Ross, my other cow." But to "Nancy Ross, daughter of James Ross," she bequeathed "one bed and beding, lately the property of his Aunt Nancy Ross."

Thus she kept the bed and the bedclothes in the family. Bed *furniture* was a luxury in any bequest. Clothes, too, were expensive, so she hands down "to my sister Jane Henning and sister-in-law Eliza Ross, wife of James Ross, "my wearing apparel—to be equally divided between them." She continues her bequests as follows:

My Beauro and all the remainder of my house and kitchen furniture to my brother John Ross. And to my brothers Joshua and Thomas and to my sister Sally Dunsmore, I wish my executor to pay one dollar."

After several decades in the Pittsburgh settlement, women seemed to own more material possessions. We find many silver spoons and some copperware mentioned in their wills.

MARY GILLAND— ... *unto the poor woman near my former residence ...*
Dated December 16, 1813—Recorded June 18, 1814

Mary Gilland gives to her niece Margaret, "six silver teaspoons" and to niece Rosamond, "One Copper Tea Kettle." (Lucky girl) This will makes the usual bequests, "one feather bed and bedding," legacies to another niece and to a grandniece. But *this* bequest reveals Mrs. Gilland's innate kindness: "unto the poor woman near my former residence, my wearing apparel." It shows kindness not only in the gift itself but in not publicizing the recipient of that gift, although the anonymity suggests that everyone knew who was meant.

149

CATHARINE MOWRY— *. . . to my mother Margaret and her heirs and assigns forever . . .*
Dated January 11, 1815—Recorded June 25, 1819

Catharine Mowry signed her will about four and one-half years previous to her death. It was a short testament, which was not revised in any way later on.

I do hereby will and devise to my mother Margaret and her heirs and assigns forever all my property real, personal and mixed, and I do hereby nominate, constitute and appoint Dr. Peter Mowry executor to this my last will and testament.

Witnessed by Phillip Mowry, Daniel Mowry, and Henry Thomas.

MARGARET HARRAH— *. . . my eight day Clock . . . my largest Looking Glass . . .*
Dated December 2, 1815—Recorded November 21, 1818

Margaret Harrah, to make sure that her personal estate would go to those who would appreciate her treasures, directed that items should be distributed as follows:

To son William, one dollar and fifty cents. To James C. Harrah, two hundred dollars, my large Bible, as also all my farming utensils and all the mecanicle tools I am in possession of, also my eight day Clock during his life and then to his son Charles. To my son Alexander my desk; to son Samuel, my dining table. To my daughter Sarah Howel my Spinning Wheels, Chears and the count reel and cupboard. And to my daughter Margaret Dunn one hundred dollars. To my daughter Mary Long . . . fifty dollars and my largest Looking Glass. To my granddaughter Margaret Long, my second Looking Glass. To my granddaughter, Margaret Baldwin, my silver Tea spoons.

The bed and bedclothes, her pewter, kitchen furniture, etc., were to be divided between the grandchildren. Margaret Harrah was indeed a woman with possessions worth bequeathing. This will is numbered 131 in the County records.

150

ELIZABETH HANNAH— . . . *to Jane Wharey, otherwise Hannah* . . .
Dated March 26, 1807—Recorded August 17, 1808

Elizabeth Hannah, "Otherwise McDowell," made "her mark" to attest the will made for her. She leaves to her "daughter Eliza M——, otherwise Hannah, all and every such property as I shall be found belonging to me after my discease." To her son-in-law Henry M——, she gives two books, "Calvin's institutes and the Psalms of David," while her granddaughter Hannah gets: "twenty pounds, to be paid to her at age eighteen." Another daughter, "Jane Wharey, otherwise Hannah," is to have "my body cloathes and the Confession of Faith, bed and bed cloths."

What an odd way of using a maiden name is this of Mrs. Hannah's, for herself and even for her daughters. It suggests that her will is related to a father's will in the disposal of property.

JANE McCULLOUGH— . . . *to leave . . . all entirely to the discretion of my executors* . . .
Dated November 25, 1820—Recorded January 5, 1821

Jane McCullough's signature is poorly written—the surname hardly recognizable as hers—but the attorney or whoever drew up Mrs. McCullough's will appears to have enjoyed his job. He used a single sheet of paper, twenty-one inches long, sixteen inches wide, and he wrote in small neat letters straight across its width. The heading resembles those often found in old documents, with heavily-shaded capitals, the whole embellished with circles and flourishes of the pen. The thin paper is wrinkled and torn, yet the ink is still black.

The will starts off in an imposing manner:

Imprimis—I give and devise my house situate in Wood Street of the city of Pittsburgh between Diamond Alley and Fifth Street fronting twelve feet and sixteen inches on Wood Street with the privilege of a three foot wide alley, now in the occupancy of F. Pratt, to my dear daughter Sarah Simpson (formerly wife of Joseph McClintock, deceased) to have and to hold the said house and ground belonging (subject however to payments of ground rent and taxes for the same) until such time as her daughter Catherine shall have attained the age of

151

twenty-one years but in case of said Catherine's decease until such time as she would have been twenty-one years of age had she been living. And then my will is that the said house and appurtenances shall be sold to the best advantage by my executor and the proceeds thereof equally divided among such of the four children of my said daughter Sarah and her husband Joseph McClintock as shall be then living, share and share alike.

Secundus—I give and bequeath one bed, bedstead and necessary bedding, one desk and six chairs to each of my dear daughters Mary, Jane and Susan, to be selected by them out of my house furniture, in order of their respective ages, the eldest to choose first.

Tertius—My will is that the residue of my personal property shall be sold and all debts due to me collected to the best advantage in such convenient time and money as my executors shall think just. And after all my debts and funeral expenses are fully paid that the balance remaining in their hands shall be placed out on interest . . . until such time as my youngest daughter Margaret shall (if living) be twenty-one years of age. The proceeds of personal property and debts collected, and the rents of my real estate to form a fund which my executors shall distribute according to their discretion from time to time amongst my children in such proportions as their respective necessities may seem to require.

Quarto—. . . the whole of my real estate (except what is already disposed of) shall be sold to the best advantage and after making a deduction from the proceeds for the amount needed for finishing the said daughter Margaret's education not exceeding three hundred dollars, then the remaining proceeds of the real estate shall be divided into nine equal parts . . . for each of my children my intention being exclusive of the house, etc., above devised to my daughter Sara and the school expenses of my daughter Margaret not exceeding three hundred dollars, all my children shall receive the same sum, share and share alike, excepting only the bequests of the aforesaid house furniture to my daughters Mary, Jane and Susan. And that after making due allowance for such monies as they may have previously received, the amount of each share shall then be disposed of in manner following, Viz., the sum due upon the share of my dear daughter Sarah Simpson shall be paid to her and the same due on the share of my daughter Agnes Darlington shall be paid to her, and to such of my daughters Mary, Jane, Susan and Margaret, as may then be married by and with the written consent of my executor, the sums due on their respective shares shall in like manner be paid. But the sums due upon the shares of each of them as shall at that time be unmarried and single, or shall have married without the written approbation of my executor will be placed out on interest and they shall respectively receive the annual interest of their individual shares, and money, until such time as she shall marry with the written approbation of executor, at which time she shall respectively receive the balance of her share in full, and not before. The sums due upon the shares of my sons John, William and James shall in like manner be placed out on interest and they shall respectively receive the annual interest on their individual shares and nothing more until such time as my executor shall deem it prudent and judicious to pay them the whole, my intention being to leave that all entirely to the discretion of my executors, not doubting but that they will act as they shall find most conducive to the real benefit of my sons. In case any of my children should die single or without issue, previous to the sale of the real estate it is my will that the share or shares of such be equally divided amongst the survivors, subject to the foregoing regulations and in case an advantageous sale of the said real or personal estate cannot be made for cash, such credits shall be given as my executors think proper.

The witnesses to Mrs. McCullough's signing were Francis Herron, W. Blair, and John H. Hopkins.

The executors, who played a prominent part in carrying out the "dead hands" directions of Mrs. McCullough—particularly in granting or in withholding their consent to the girls' marrying—were: Benjamin Darlington, William Woods, and William Hays.

JEAN DONALDSON—. . . *as a just recompense . . . for Supporting me the rest of my life time.*
Dated May 20, 1809—Recorded August 13, 1810

Jean Donaldson, Butler County, made a short will. She bequeathed all her property—"real personal and mixed"—to Francis Hamilton of the same place "as a just recompense to said Francis Hamilton for care over me and maintaining the time past and likeways for Supporting me the rest of my life time."
Mrs. Donaldson signed with a mark which looks like this: U.

153

REBECCA BLAINE— . . . *the estate . . . situate in the counties of*
Cumberland, Center, Indiana, Westmoreland
and Armstrong . . .
Dated March 17, 1820—Recorded June 26, 1820

Rebecca Blaine willed to her brother-in-law, the Reverend
Francis Herron,

in consideration of my having become surety to the said Francis for a
debt of five thousand dollars and upwards for my brother Ephraim A.
Blaine by my share or shares of the estate of my late Father, Alexander
Blaine, deceased, situate in the counties of Cumberland, Center, Indiana, Westmoreland and Armstrong and wherever else situated lying
or being, and my share of the debts due to the said estate of said Alexander or myself of whatsoever nature or kind. . .

The Blaines were important citizens of the County and the
Reverend Francis Herron was the third pastor of the First Presbyterian Church of Pittsburgh.

RACHEL JONES— . . . *all my interest in the Racoon lands.* . . .
Dated August 31, 1823—Recorded November 13, 1823

Rachel Jones, "widow of Fayette Twp.," was the mother of
Ephraim and Thomas Jones, and of Eleanor Jones. To her son
Ephraim and to "Eleoner"—Nelly, as she sometimes called her
daughter—Mrs. Jones bequeathed: "the tract of land whereon I
now live, situated on Chartiers Creek, to be equally divided between them." Later, however, a codicil changed that bequest and
gave the whole tract to Eleanor Jones. "Nelly" was also to receive
"six Silver Table spoons," and three young friends—or relatives?—
were each to get "a set of six Silver teaspoons." To the wife of her
son Thomas Jones, she gave, "all my interest in the Raccoon lands
situate in Beaver County to Sally Jones."

❋   ❋   ❋   ❋   ❋

These are just some of the women who spurred on their men
to achieve success, to preserve for coming generations the things
which are worth while. We owe much to these ambitious, thrifty
women—the helpmates and sisters and mothers of the pioneers.

154

Pittsburgh—Western Frontier
1750-1850

During the western Indian wars which followed the Revolution, Pittsburgh was the base of supplies for ordnance, for Indian trade, and for settlers going ever farther west. Pittsburgh was a recruiting station, too, for the United States Army, and the town benefitted by the money spent in the neighborhood during the Indian wars and the Whiskey Rebellion. Pittsburgh was the theater of action for these wars, and it was their financial center as well.

General Arthur St. Clair's troops, in 1791, spent more than $10,000 in Pittsburgh. General Josiah Harmar's expedition had spent about as much the year before. General Anthony Wayne's large body of troops was quartered in the town for several months, and when the soldiers marched out of Pittsburgh in 1792 for the Indian country they left behind large amounts of money with Pittsburgh storekeepers and farmers for supplies. In 1794, the troops sent to Pittsburgh to quell the Whiskey Rebellion brought another large sum with them.

Through the earliest wills it is possible to trace the growth of trade through barter and currency, when the necessities were the greatest prize, when land became of highest value, until the time when luxuries purchased for large sums of money were handed down in families growing wealthier as businesses grew and expanded with the growing and expanding frontier.

155

In Allegheny County, a century and a half ago, bartering flourished. There was little cash to spend, but plenty of garden produce to trade. Often labor was exchanged for food, clothes, or a place to live.

The nearest bank until 1803 was in Philadelphia, several days' journey away. Money exchanges were made by the merchants with the aid of local brokers. But after the Branch Bank of Pennsylvania was established in Pittsburgh the merchants and manufacturers got a firm foothold and practical experience in loan values. People grew to trust banks and they preferred transferring money by check instead of by the old slow-going stagecoach transfer.

MONEY

The bequests of citizens, high and low, reflect the growing prosperity and the circulation of currency in loans and notes and banking.

Marey Stewart, in 1795, bequeathed her "son Will a note of hand I have of him for 5£2§"; and Elizabeth Cunningham, in 1803, left to her son, Phillip Winebiddle, "two due bills or notes of hand on Jacob Nigley, one of which is for one hundred dollars and the other for one hundred and eighty dollars."

James Speirs in his will of December 17, 1788, left each of his three daughters "one dollar cash from the estate when she comes of age." It was more difficult then to save money for dowry gifts than to accumulate farm stock or produce.

William Witherow, August 1, 1795, left his four daughters "each and severally, Eighty-eight pounds."

John Jones, "Yeoman of Deer Township," September 21, 1809, instructed his executors to see that each of his children—John, Samuel, Edward, Jesse, James, Matthew, Evan, Joseph, Hannah, Rebecca, Mary, Phoeby, and Catherine—have "the sum of sixty-six cents, each." Thus thirteen children received a legacy harder for a farmer to come by than grain or livestock.

A number of foreign coins were in circulation in and around Pittsburgh—the British Pound, the Irish Pound, the Livre Turnois of France, the Florin or Guilder of United Netherlands, the Rix dollar of Denmark, the Rial of Spain, the Milree of Portugal, Tael of China, Crown of France, Rupee of Bengal, and the Pagoda of India. Such foreign coinage, of course, was prized and hoarded, because of the scarcity of gold and silver. So, when on June 2, 1797, Peter Rowleter bequeathed to each of his two daughters "two Spanish milled dollars," the Rowleter girls' legacy was an enviable one.

After the bank came to Pittsburgh, wills more often mention money, and in ever larger sums. James Woodburn, in 1789, left to his wife "one hundred and fifty pounds specie." There is no indication whether the specie was gold or silver.

In his legacy of money, Thomas Jones, January 23, 1824, reveals the strange life of the frontier as it stretched westward into Indian country even so late as the nineteenth century.

To Mary, an Indian woman, who formerly lived with me in Vincennes, daughter of an Indian chief, Fusei, and her two children, named Nancy and Charlotte, $150 each.

Melchior Beltzhoover, whose name lives in a part of Pittsburgh once a prosperous German village and in a fine old Mississippi mansion which is a mecca for garden pilgrims in Natchez, on April 8, 1806, left his son Henry, "One horse, valued at 593 pounds, 15 shillings, money of the commonwealth aforesaid."

Matthew McKinnie, March 18, 1809, left his wife "A hourse creature, to be valued at $40." Could one horse be worth so much more than another in that early day?

James McMichael's will (1788), one of the earliest, left his daughter Mary "ten pounds current money of Pennsylvania . . . to be paid in either horses, cattle, or grain, at a reasonable appraisement, to be paid in two years after my death." He, at least, recognized that grain and livestock might be worth more immediately than money.

But the currency situation for some time was confusing. One could not always be sure of the value of money tendered him. And the wills show the confusion as their makers try to evaluate commodities in terms of currency.

157

WHISKEY

Perhaps the most interesting bequest of these early wills and one of actual value and quick realization was whiskey. When Allegheny County was young whiskey was as good as cash. There was nothing questionable, then, about either drinking it or distilling it.

Crops, too plentiful for local consumption, too costly to send to eastern markets because of their bulk, were converted into whiskey and sent by pack-horse trains over the mountains. In exchange, farmers got sugar, salt, and other needed household articles before they were available in the Pittsburgh markets. Every sixth farmer, it was alleged, was a distiller of the corn and rye which he, or his neighbors, had cultivated. The crops paid good dividends when made into whiskey, for twenty-four bushels of grain converted into whiskey could be carried by one horse whose fair load of actual grain was only four bushels.

And then, just as surplus grain in this form was providing Western Pennsylvania farmers with the necessities of living— and a few luxuries—the new federal government slapped a tax of four pence a gallon on the distilled product. The distillers refused to pay that tax; they resented it as much as we would oppose a tax on food.

The "Whiskey Insurrection," the rebellion of Western Pennsylvania against collection of the tax, was in full force after the *Excise Law of the United States* was passed (in 1791). It was not quelled until 1794, when President George Washington revised the Excise Law to ease the burdens and objections of farmers here.

Meantime, though, blood was spilled and property destroyed, and the President himself came in with troops as far west as Bedford. The distillers who paid the tax did so at the risk of having their houses, barns, and stills burned to the ground by rioters. The first shot in the "Rebellion" was fired when General John Nevill rode up to the Old Stone Manse (a landmark in our South Park) to serve papers on some distillers who would not register for taxation. General Nevill remained loyal to his post as inspector, even after his own house was plundered and destroyed.

But even today, in Western Pennsylvania, descendants of families on opposite sides in the Whiskey Rebellion are known to argue the cause and praise their ancestors' stand on either side, in the year 1794.

Usually, in early wills, the disposal or sale of whiskey is directed for specific purposes. For example, the will of David Magwire, August 27, 1807:

I desire that my still and twenty gallons of whiskey, which is at Mr. Ferrees, together with seven barrels of whiskey, which is in Pittsburgh, be sold to the best advantage.

He directed that the proceeds from the sale were to be held in trust for his father and brother in Ireland. Outside of his still and his liquor, the good Irishman mentioned nothing else except that he wanted a Christian burial and the discharge of debts and collection of monies due him. *Whiskey* represented Mr. Magwire's worldly wealth.

Whiskey is listed in many inventories of intestates and, where it is included in the appraisement of the dead man's estate, whiskey is usually the largest single item represented.

Distilling equipment, no doubt, was costly. It appears in many old wills as a valuable legacy to members of the family. As an example of such a bequest, the will of William McJunkin, May 14, 1814, reads: "I also will to my son William the stills and all my rights and title to the vessels appertaining thereto." Moreover, in outlining some of the "privileges" which his wife was to have, he gives to her "the use of the still house." That bequest gave her a chance to convert her own grain into whiskey for the market.

The will of John Malady, December 8, 1803, is short, and he signed it with a crooked X, but he knew that the grain some of his debtors owed the estate was as important to collect as the money they owed him. And the grain was probably better than the coin, although he was shrewd enough to direct those who drafted his will to interline "in specie," where cash was mentioned as a legacy, before he signed his mark. Grain was tangible wealth,

159

but grain or cash, all debtors were equal as far as John Malady was concerned.

In the name of God Amen; I John Malady being in a low state of health but perfectly in my right senses doth declare that Moses Hopkins doth stand indebted to me fifteen Bushels of Rye and Jackson Lafferty Sr. to me four Dollars and one fourth of a Dollar, and John Anderson one Dollar and Sam McEllily four Bushels and a half of Rye ... Peter Cook owes me a half dollar. And out of what property I own after my Decease I leave Mary Stewart daughter of James Stewart Twenty Dollars in cash, and her brother Jordan one Silver Watch and what I own *in specie* afterward to be divided Equally between Samuel Jordan William Jean and Nancy ... and further I leave my Third of the Grain in the stackyard and also in the ground to be divided Equally between Samuel Jordan and Jean Flemin.

George Wallace, when he made his will December 15, 1803, did not refer to whiskey or distilling equipment, perhaps because his advertisement in the *Pittsburgh Gazette*, April 18, 1795, made the sale he hoped for.

Two Stills, one of 144, the other of 84 gallons. They are almost new, having been run only one season. The copper is of the finest quality, and the arrearages and all demands of government are satisfied. Also, two Slake Stands, 12 Mashing tubs, singling and double barrels, &c. . . . an iron mash-kiln and malt screen. They will be sold reasonable and the payment made convenient.

Enquire of George Wallace, Esq. Braddock's Field.

George Wallace was Allegheny County's first president judge.

Pittsburgh's first mayor, Ebenezer Denny, often advertised in the *Commonwealth* "Stills of the best double Copper" at his "auction store." And even the collector of the hated Excise Tax encouraged payment of the levy in, of all things, whiskey:

Pittsburgh Gazette, June 8, 1794

The Distillers will please to take Notice that this is the month for entering their Stills with the different Collectors who have offices opened for that purpose at the county towns in each county, and that the time of payment for the present year's duty must be paid in the first fifteen days of July next, otherwise suits in general will be commenced. Whiskey will be taken at 1/6 per gallon, if delivered within the time.

> —John Neville, Inspector
> of the Revenue, 4th Survey.

While there is no doubt that payment of the tax in whiskey was most convenient for the distillers, the irony of the situation must have rankled them considerably. Yet it is final proof of the reliability of whiskey as a medium of exchange.

LUXURIES

In some pioneer homes, of course, there were luxuries. Many fine things had been brought from the East and, as circumstances permitted, people sent back for more. Precious possessions were handed down and cherished in families. Early wills show frequent bequests of clocks, mirrors, clothes, and other items of value.

JAMES CARNAGHAM—*The use of the household clock.*
Dated December 12, 1808—Recorded December 28, 1808

James Carnagham, of Deer Township, said his wife was to have "the use of the household clock during her natural lifetime." That meant only *during her widowhood.* Mrs. Carnagham's fidelity was to be measured by the family clock!

JAMES VERNER—*A half share in my clock.*
Dated June 10, 1845—Recorded August 7, 1849

James Verner, of St. Clair Township, in winding up his earthly affairs left "a half share in my clock to each of my daughters, Christiana and Phoebe." It was not unusual to divide the ownership of family heirlooms considered of great value.

MARGARET HARRAH—*My second Looking Glass.*
Dated December 2, 1815—Recorded November 21, 1818

Margaret Harrah bequeathed to one relative "my eight day Clock during his life and then to his son Charles." Mrs. Harrah wanted to make sure that both her mirrors would be duly appreciated, too. She directed that her daughter Mary have "my largest Looking Glass" and "my granddaughter, Margaret Long, my second Looking Glass." (Notice the capitalized words. Here, as in many old wills, the deliberate capitalization sets objects out as if they were personified by their proud owners!)

Clothes figure largely in wills. Often they are bequeathed as a rich legacy, whether or not they fitted the recipients; occasionally, women's clothes were given to a man—probably to distribute to his women-folk or, as in at least one instance, to hold until he had a wife and family.

HANNAH McROBERTS—*The new Black Clock.*
Dated February 12, 1812—Recorded March 5, 1812

Hannah McRoberts certainly considered her "body cloathes" as major items to hand down to her daughters and granddaughters, when she dictated her will. But the most valuable thing in her will was probably "the new Black Clock" which she directed was to go "to the grandson that lives with me."

❊   ❊   ❊   ❊   ❊

We find that men's wills are much more concerned with bequests of clothing than are women's. One reason, of course, is that men always owned their own clothes and could give them away when they were through with them. Women did not often have that privilege. But the conjecture is made that most men prided themselves on their wearing apparel and they enjoyed having as many fine clothes as they could afford.

SAMUEL ROSEBURGH—*My Great Coat, blue straight Coat and Velvet Vest Coat.*
Dated December 19, 1807—Recorded 1808

I allow my wife Agnes Roseburgh to be kept decently—during her natural life. And my whole estate, real or personal, to be divided equally amongst my seven children, John, Jannet. Agnes, Martha, Jane, Thomas, and William, and over and above I bequeath to my son John, my Great Coat, blue straight Coat and Velvet Vest Coat.

162

In the 1800's, men's coats were high-waisted, double-breasted in style, with a deep cut-out just above the waistline in front. From there, the coat fell away in the back to a long-tailed skirt. Mr. Roseburgh's "Velvet Vest Coat" was probably in style with that period—cut high in a straight line across the front so that several inches of it showed under his buttoned-up outer coat, and it probably had the broad lapels which were in favor at the time. The "Great Coat," or overcoat, would be fitted a little more at the waistline, its skirts would be full and long, with small cuffs on the sleeves and perhaps two little capes around the neck.

WILLIAM WARDEN—*The makins of one shift to Elmer McMine.*
Dated September 14, 1789—Recorded October 3, 1789

William Warden of Mifflin Township left to his brothers "all the farming utensils to be equally divided between the above named." Farming equipment was a luxury, too, as well as a necessity—but Mr. Warden seems to have been more interested in the disposal of his clothes. For, he continues:

I do allow and bequeath . . . the blue shute of clothes to Brother James, the other sute to Robert McMine. My good hat and what linen is left I give to Brother James, except the makins of one shift to Elmer McMine.

HENRY HUEY—*My Pantaloons they may divide between them.*
Dated June 25, 1822—Recorded July 31, 1822

Henry Huey, also a resident of Mifflin Township, bequeathed his wearing apparel as follows:

To John McDermott, my blue suit of apparel and hat. I give to James McDermott my brown coat; and my Pantaloons they may divide between them.

Breeches buttoned below the knee or tied with strings were called *pantaloons*. They had been copied from the current French fashion but, to quote an authority (Earle, *Two Centuries of Custumes in America*):

163

They were ugly beyond belief. They were loose, straight in leg, clumsy at the waist, reaching but little below the calf and sometimes slit up several inches at the bottom on the outer side of the leg.

Later knee breeches began to be made longer, with the knee-buckles disappearing altogether. If you think it strange that two brothers should "divide" one pair of pantaloons, remember the fathers and sons who "divide" the best evening suit or overcoat.

But the best descriptions of men's styles, or at least what they had been wearing before such clothing was cast off, are found in the many advertisements for runaway indentured servants. The following notice, for instance, shows some of well-to-do merchant Devereux Smith's castoffs—worn without discrimination as to ensemble:

Pittsburgh Gazette, May 2, 1789

Ran away from the subscriber, on the 12th inst., living near Pittsburgh, a serving lad, named John Murphy, about 18 years of age, 5 ft. 6 inches high, full round face, short black hair; had on when he went away, buckskin breeches, yarn stockings, old shoes, a country linen shirt and a wool hat. He was seen lurking about Pittsburgh from the 12th to the 16th instant. That evening he is supposed to have stolen a canoe and proceeded down the Ohio River. Whoever secures said servant in any jail so that the master may get him again shall receive Two Dollars reward.

—Devereux Smith

N.B.—Said servant boy walks crooked in his knees, and is much given to lying, etc.

✿ ✿ ✿ ✿ ✿

In a number of early wills feather beds are featured as luxury gifts; bedclothes and "hangans"—often referred to as "bed furniture"—were handed down in legacies to family and friends. Iron pots, knives and forks, salt and iron, treasures brought from the East, were luxurious possessions in pioneer homes, and sometimes even willed like the family jewels. For instance,

CONRAD WINEBIDDLE—*A bushel of salt.*
Dated September 3, 1795—Recorded September 17, 1795

Conrad Winebiddle, who had accumulated more wealth than most of his neighbors, left to his wife: "A cask of sugar, a bushel of salt, and six hundred weight of flower." Around the time he made his will, salt—of fair quality—was selling in Pittsburgh at four dollars a bushel. It had been worth many times that amount not so long before, as much as the cost of a cow and a calf. In fact, salt was so precious that no one was permitted to walk across the floor when it was being measured. At the trading posts, the Indians had to be closely watched, because when nobody was looking they stored handfuls of salt in the folds of their blankets, to be used in bartering across the border. Salt was still a luxury in 1795, at $2.40 a bushel, when—through the efforts of General James O'Hara—it was brought to the Pittsburgh market by way of the Lakes from Onandaga. Flour, too, was expensive; it often sold for a dollar a hundred weight.

❖   ❖   ❖   ❖   ❖

In the early 1800's, however, we find a number of bequests of "silver spoons" and jewelry—such as gold watches and gold rings. "Looking Glasses," too, were more plentiful, although still a luxury.

REVOLUTIONARY WAR GRANTS AND BONUSES

Gloomy times followed the Revolution: the soldiers came home weary and bankrupt. The Pennsylvania currency in which they had been paid for their wartime services was practically worthless. The soldiers complained, but there was nothing the state could do about it. It took $75 of state money to buy in 1781 what $3 would have purchased in 1777. An act of the Supreme Council, April 3, 1781, provided a way to adjust and settle payment of debts and other demands or contracts entered into between January 1, 1777, and March 1, 1781. Its object was to reduce the amount of all such obligations to the true value of specie at the time they were incurred. The following was the scale of depreciation set to determine the value of the debts compared with gold and silver:

	1777	1778	1779	1780	1781
January	1.5	4	8	40.5	75
February	1.5	5	10	47.5	75
March	2	5	10.5	61.5	
April	2.5	6	17	61.5	
May	2.5	5	24	59	
June	2.5	5	20	61.5	
July	3	4	19	64.5	
August	3	5	20	70	
September	3	5	24	72	
October	3	5	30	73	
November	3	6	38.5	74	
December	4	6	41.5	75	

The real opening up in Pennsylvania of the "unlocated Western lands" came with the division of these lands by act of March 12, 1783. Depreciation Certificates, redeemable in such lands and in properties confiscated from Tories, were issued to soldiers in amounts representing the estimated difference between the paper currency and hard money. In addition, Donation Lands—bonuses of land—were offered to soldiers and sailors when they completed their war services.

The Assembly divided all of the "unlocated lands" north of the Ohio and west of the Allegheny and Conewango into two sections: those lying south of an imaginary line drawn from near Kittanning to the Ohio line were reserved for redemption of the Depreciation Certificates; those lying north of this line were to be allotted as Donation Lands, from 200 acres for a private up to 2,000 acres for a general officer.

Such was the origin of the Depreciation Lands and the Donation Lands of Western Pennsylvania.

The Assembly appointed commissioners to work with the surveyor-general in laying out the wilderness. To survey the Depreciation Lands to the south was simple and that work was done in short order with no title arguments. But the problem of Donation Lands was a more difficult one. They were Indian Country and claimed by rival states. The land lying north of the Kittanning line was laid out in strips east to west, with a surveyor assigned to each of the ten strips. District No. 1 lay to the south, parallel to the Kittanning line; District No. 10 lay to the extreme north, paralleling the New York line. The other districts were numbered consecutively from south to north.

Allegheny County wills drawn up by Revolutionary War veterans very often bequeath land grants they received for their services, or monies they had received from the new government as soldiers' bonuses. Among these veterans were many Scots and "Scotch-Irish," and Germans from New York state.

FREDERICK SMITH—*One tract of land granted to me . . . for my services in the Late War.*
Dated October 26, 1787—Recorded November 25, 1789

Frederick Smith, "soldier in Captain David Zeigler's First American Regiment," bequeaths:

to my good friend and acquaintance, David Jacobs, soldier in the aforesaid company and regiment, all my pay that is due me from the Regiment aforesaid, and do hereby authorize him to ask and receive it from the paymaster or any other person that may be appointed to settle the books of the Regiment . . . also one tract of land granted to me from the State of Pennsylvania for my services in the Late War. The deed or patent which is now in the hands of Captain David Zeigler—and I do hereby authorize my good friend David Jacobs as aforesaid to ask and receive the above-mentioned deed or patent from the said Captain David Zeigler.

ABLE WAYMAN—*Three hundred acres . . . for my services as Captain in the Jersey Line.*
Dated August 26, 1786—Recorded September 17, 1791

Able Wayman, "late captain in the Jersey Line, and now residing at Pittsburgh," leaves:

to my trusty and well beloved friend, Marmaduke Curtis, hatter, now residing at Pittsburgh, all right, title and claim of, in and to three hundred acres of land given and granted to me for my services as Captain in the Jersey Line during the late war, and whatever other lands or emoluments may be due, owing, and coming to me from Congress or the State of New Jersey, as aforesaid.

JOHN CAMPBELL—*Sundry land Warrants . . . both in Pennsylvania and Virginia.*
Dated July 21, 1786—Recorded April 16, 1802

Colonel John Campbell had some trouble laying claim to the land due him:

As I am possessed of sundry land Warrants issued in consequence of military service, it is my will and desire that my said executors shall take the most effectual measures for locating such Warrants and for obtaining grants for the lands to which I am entitled both in Pennsylvania and Virginia.

Eleven years after the dating of his will certain property was still in dispute, as revealed by this notice in the *Pittsburgh Gazette,* May 6, 1797:

John Campbell enters a caveat against granting a patent to Christian Lisnet, on his warrant dated 3d of September, 1785, for a tract of land in Washington County, alledging that he, the said Campbell, hath an older Virginia certificate for the same. The first Monday in October next is appointed for a hearing of the parties in this caveat, thirty days notice being given.

—David Kennedy, Sec.
John Lukens, Esquire
Survey General

Colonel Campbell, a Virginian working under the direction of the Governor of Virginia, laid out four blocks of streets in Pittsburgh in 1764—on ground which still belonged to the Indians —to give color to Virginia's later claims to this part of the country. The long-standing dispute between Pennsylvania and Virginia was settled, however, soon after the Revolutionary War; the boundary line then was less important to both states than their uniting in a common interest to break away from English despotism. The first practical step to settle state lines was taken in 1779, by appointment of commissioners from both Pennsylvania and Virginia. In their report dated November 18, 1784, the commissioners said:

The underwritten commissioners have continued Mason and Dixon's line to the termination of the said five degrees of longitude, by which work the southern boundary of Pennsylvania is completed. The continuation we have marked by open vistas over the most remarkable heights which lie in its course, and by planting on many of these heights, in the true parallel of latitude, the true boundary, posts marked with the letters P and V, each facing the State of which it is the initial. At the extremity of this line, which is the southwest corner of Pennsylvania, we have planted a squared, unlettered white oak post, around whose base we have raised piles of stones . . . The advanced season of the year and the inclemency of the weather have obliged us to suspend our operations, but we have agreed to meet again at the southwest corner of Pennsylvania on the 16th day of next May, to complete the object of our commission.

In accordance with their agreement, the western boundary of Pennsylvania was established due north from the southwestern corner post to the Ohio River, and the closing report was made by the commissioners on August 23, 1785. It took a long time, however, for Virginia to adjust details on land titles.

Although among the first to apply to the government for the "Western lands," not many of the veterans settled on the lands they were awarded under their service rights. Officers, as well as soldiers, disposed of most of their warrants because of financial need; often they released the warrants for a small percentage of their real value and speculators bought them and held them for years before peddling them out to settlers at high prices. There were various schemes for dividing and selling lands obtained in this way.

On February 5, 1794, John McKee advertised:

A new town is laid out by the subscriber on the spot known for many years by the name of M'Kees ferry. The ground intended for the Town is delightfully situated on a fine level point at the junction of the Monongahela and Youghiogeny Rivers about sixteen miles above Pittsburgh

169

by water or twelve by land. . . . The price of each lot is to be twenty dollars and one dollar ground rent to be paid annually. (Sold by lottery to avoid disputes of lots.)

Because of the frequent disputes of location and ownership of ground bought, the government, too, preferred the idea of selling lots by schemes like McKee's. For example:

Pittsburgh Gazette, August 29, 1789

Agreeable to an act of the General Assembly of the 13th of September, 1787, entitled "An Act for allowing a further time to destribute the donation lands promised to the troops of the Commonwealth." Notice is hereby given, That the drawing of the lottery for, and patenting of the said lots, will commence on the 3d day of November next, to be continued to the 13th of September, 1789.

—Charles Riddle, Secretary.

That newspaper notice was only a reminder, the original having been widely advertised from the Secretary's Office on October 31, 1788.

The farmers, however, usually held on to their warrants; they claimed the lands to which they were entitled and farmed them to improve their value. Some officers of the Revolution came here, liked what they saw of the country, and sent for their families. People settled in Pittsburgh from other lands, opened up places of business, farmed, or became traders. Homesteaders came, because they had heard of the great promise afforded by the Western Country. The Revolutionary War gave the impetus to Pittsburgh to become, in a very real way, the "Gateway to the West."

REAL ESTATE

The land, after all, held the greatest and most lasting value. And those who purchased land around the three rivers early and were able to hold it longest became men of property which some of them, at least, have bequeathed to their children and their children's children. The story of the land is the story of Pittsburgh, for Pittsburgh land represents wealth even beyond the material—

on it citizens build homes and churches and institutions expressing the ideals and hopes of a free people.

In the beginning, and until late in the 1760's, all the land from the mountains to the Mississippi, including territory around the Great Lakes, was a vast Indian reservation. Legally, the white man was forbidden any permanent claim. But in 1768, approximately the southern half of Pennsylvania west of the Allegheny Ridge, plus a large area in the northeast part of the province, was purchased from the Indians by the Penns. From then on, this vast territory was theirs to dispose of, subject only to rival claims pressed by colonial Virginia. This rivalry and the claims of those who settled on land independently acquired from Indians caused great confusion for many years.

Thousands of applications poured into the Pennsylvania Land Office when it was opened up on April 3, 1769, to cover lands in the "New Purchase," as it was called, in the southwestern part of Pennsylvania. Individual buyers of the newly opened lands were limited to three hundred acres, but speculators got around that restriction by taking out applications in their friends' names or by using fictitious names. George Washington, since his first visit in 1753 appreciative of the lands around Pittsburgh, acquired some tracts this way. His friend, Captain William Crawford, was his agent and, as such, filed applications in five different names, each for three hundred acres. The surveys on these five applications returned 1,643 acres and the land so conveyed now comprises the Borough of Perryopolis and part of Perry Township.

"I could have taken more if I had thought they would have been lessened, as it is from half-penny to a penny per acre." So reads a portion of Crawford's letter to Washington, written on January 7, 1769. In 1771, Washington asked Crawford to acquire land for him on Raccoon and Mingo Chartiers Creeks. He wanted tracts in a body of three or four thousand acres. Captain Crawford examined this territory, then reported to Washington:

There was some good land on Raccoon Creek, along the stream, but it was very hilly off from the creek. The hills are of the poorest sort, all piney, where the bottoms are of any goodness. What land is worth anything is already taken by somebody. I have found some good tracts of

171

land on the head of Chartiers Creek. It is good, level, farming land and good meadow, but not that quantity you wanted.

Whether George Washington ever got that particular land is not indicated. His friend, Crawford, was burned at the stake by Indians in 1782. But land owners in Western Pennsylvania, particularly in the farming sections near Uniontown, might be surprised to find, in searching their titles all the way back, that our first President was the original owner of their property. Disposal of his lands in Pennsylvania is a matter of record in the county where they were purchased.

As soon as the Land Law of 1792 confirmed their rights, settlers moved into the section in greater numbers and began to clear off more land. The lawyers and merchants of early Pittsburgh did a profitable business in land warrants which they had acquired from impoverished Revolutionary soldiers; these holders of warrants were able to realize a nice profit in selling them to settlers.

The first sale of land in lots for housing purposes in Pittsburgh was in 1784; the project covered the streets in our Golden Triangle. When the proprietaries, John Penn and John Penn, Jr., decided to sell in the Manor of Pittsburgh, they had George Woods and Thomas Vickroy lay out lots in a regular plan between the two rivers.

Woods continued John Campbell's plan of 1764 from the Point to Grant Street. Liberty and Penn Streets stretched parallel to the Allegheny, crossed at right angles by Marbury, Hay, Pitt, St. Clair, Irwin, Hand, Wayne, and Washington. The other streets, parallel to the Monongahela, ran into Liberty at acute angles, as did the streets which crossed them; they were bounded by Water Street next to the river and Grant Street at right angles to Water on the other leg of the triangle. Not far from Liberty, on Market Street, was a public square, the Diamond, a civic center for the next half century. Thus what began as a fairly orderly scheme, as Pittsburgh spread out farther inland became a problem for traffic planners of the future.

There were other problems, too. The rod used in surveying this plan of Pittsburgh was one-eighth of an inch in every ten feet longer than the United States standard of measurement. That irregularity, which gave Pittsburgh two standards of measurement, has caused from time to time unpleasant results in real estate transactions.

The first "Manor" sales were made to Isaac Craig and Stephen Bayard in 1784; their purchase included the land at the Point which is now the Gateway Center. By the late nineties nothing remained of the old Fort but the brick redoubt, which stands today. Although litigation continued for many years by those who pressed rival claims, the Craig, Bayard purchases were upheld.

David Duncan, whose short but definite will is dated December 30, 1791, was among those who valiantly defended a claim.

Pittsburgh Gazette, March 10, 1787

Whereas Mr. Isaac Craig of this place pretended to have a title to a lot No. 256, on the corner of Short Street, and now in my possession; and as the said Isaac Craig may perhaps sell to some person ignorant of my claim, I hereby inform the public that I conceive myself to have the best title to the said lot, and that I shall hold it until I am put out by course of law.—David Duncan

David Duncan kept a tavern on Water Street, the only paved street in the town. It was a popular gathering place for business conferences as well as for social enjoyment. A notice of such a very important meeting reads:

Pittsburgh Gazette, February 23, 1788

The Trustees of the Pittsburgh Academy are requested to meet at the house of Mr. David Duncan in the Town of Pittsburgh, on Tuesday, the 18th day of March next, at 11 o'clock in the forenoon, to consider some business of importance.

This is one of the first notices of the meetings of trustees for the earliest chartered institution of higher education in Western Pennsylvania, chartered February 28, 1787 and now the University of Pittsburgh.

Duncan was active in all interests of the community, particularly in the town's "meeting house," according to this *Gazette* notice of January 2, 1790:

173

The Trustees recommend to the Congregation of Pittsburgh to meet on Wednesday the 15th of January, at the meeting house for the purpose of giving a call to a minister to said Congregation. All those who have been members thereof, and others who had actually become Members by subscription, shall be eligible to vote.

—David Duncan

The following notice, seven years after the death of David Duncan, appeared in the *Gazette* of March 18, 1799:

NOTICE is hereby given that the subscribers, executors of the estate of David Duncan, deceased, will attend on the lands belonging to the said estate situate on Muddy Creek, now Green County, either to sell or rent on the 25th instant.

—R. Kirkpatrick
Geo. Wallace, Executors

Many early Allegheny County wills specify land in the 1784 *Plan of Pittsburgh,* which the owners bequeath using the Woods' numbering. (See inside Dust Jacket.)

EBENEZER DENNY—*Shares of stock of the Bank of Pittsburgh.*
Dated September 18, 1820—Recorded July 29, 1822

Ebenezer Denny distinguished himself in three totally different fields—Indian warfare, high finance, and political leadership. His crowning achievement was his office as the first mayor of Pittsburgh.

Major Denny, who served in most of the important battles of the Revolution, fought also under George Rogers Clark in the Illinois Country and in two other campaigns against the western Indians. In 1803 he was elected the first treasurer of Allegheny County, and soon afterward was named a director of the Pittsburgh Branch of the Bank of Pennsylvania. He later became a director of the Bank of Pittsburgh, incorporated in 1814. In 1816, under the rules of the new city charter, he was appointed mayor by City Council. He lived in a house at Market and Third Street built of bricks salvaged from the old Fort.

Mr. Denny's will reveals considerable holdings in the Bank of Pittsburgh and in the Allegheny Bridge Company, two very substantial investments. His bequests are to his sons Harmar, William, and Saint Clair—his executors—and to his sister Nancy. He created a trust for his daughter Nancy, one of the earliest set up in Pittsburgh. Each bequest contains property holdings, as well as shares of stock. The reference to "Depreciation land in Cunningham's District" refers to the land which could be bought with soldiers' depreciation certificates, land which stretched from Etna to Tarentum.

1. I do hereby devise to my son Harmar, his heirs and assigns the following described property, to wit: those tracts of Depreciation land in Cunningham's District, numbered 43, 44, and 45, containing together six hundred fifty-three acres situate in Deer Creek and the Allegheny River, about twelve or thirteen miles from Pittsburgh, together with all the tenements belonging, mills, utensils and improvements whatsoever and stock attached to the premises—also twenty-five shares of stock of the Bank of Pittsburgh as standing in his own name on the books of said bank, the certificate of which he now has—and also ten shares of the stock of the Allegheny Bridge Co.

Harmar Denny married Elizabeth O'Hara, the daughter of James O'Hara, whose will closes this book. Their marriage united two very substantial Pittsburgh fortunes and holdings in the Triangle, on the South Side, and along the Allegheny River.

2. I do hereby devise to my son William . . . the following described property, to wit: the two story brick dwelling house and ground situate on the corner of Fifth Street and Kings Alley, being 23½ feet front on Fifth Street and extending along said alley 100 feet and being part of Lot No. 403 in Pittsburgh. Also the vacant lot of 40 feet front on Fifth Street and extending back 100 feet, being part of Lot No. 402 in Pittsburgh.—Also the new two story brick dwelling house (our present residence) and ground attached thereto, being part of Lot No. 327 in Pittsburgh; beginning on Third Street at a private alley where the said new dwelling house stands

175

and extending down Third Street to Chancery Lane 64 feet or there-abouts, thence by said Chancery Lane to Lot No. 326, and by said lot No. 326 towards Market Street about 64 ft. to the line of the aforesaid private alley leading out to Third Street.—Also five shares of stock of the Allegheny Bridge Co., and five shares of stock of the Greensburgh & Pittsburgh Turnpike.—Also twenty-five shares of stock of the Bank of Pittsburg as standing in his own name on the books of said Bank, the certificate of which he now has.—Also twenty-five shares of the stock of the same Bank (completed) being a part of one hundred shares standing in my name.

3. I do hereby devise to my son Saint Clair . . . to wit: One Town Lot No. 13 (unimproved) in the town of Allegheny and one Out Lot No. 29 of said town, containing 7 acres and 94 perches, to-gether with all the improvements thereon.—Also the two story brick house on the corner of Market and Third Street in Pittsburgh with the ground and buildings attached thereto fronting on Market Street about 25 feet and down Third Street about 105 feet to in-clude the two story brick office occupied at present by Richard Biddle, Esq. and bounded by the afore-mentioned private alley back to a line . . . with the outside walls of the necessary wash house and kitchen which are on these premises; being part of the aforesaid Lot No. 327 in Pittsburgh.—Also fifty shares of stock of the Allegheny Bridge Co.—Also twenty-five shares of stock of the Bank of Pittsburg as standing in his own name on the books of said Bank.—Also forty shares of stock of said Bank (completed) being part of one hundred shares standing in my name.

4. In order to create an estate in trust for the support and benefit of my daughter Nancy and the heirs of her body should she marry and have a child or children, I do hereby devise to my sons Harmar Denny, William Denny, and Saint Clair Denny, or the survivor or survivors of them, the following described property, to wit: part of the aforesaid Lot No. 327 in Pittsburgh fronting on Market Street about 32 feet, and extending back (between that portion of the same lot devised to my son Saint Clair and adjoining Lot No. 326) about one hundred and eleven feet including the private alley as afore-mentioned which leads out to Third Street and on which is erected a three story brick dwelling house on the whole front on

Market Street, together with a two story brick back building and kitchen.—Also 25 shares of stock of the Bank of Pittsburg standing on the books of the said Bank in the name of Nancy Denny, the younger.

5. To my sister Nancy for and during her natural life, all that certain lot of ground and buildings situate on the main or High Street in the Borough of Carlisle, which is now in the occupancy of Parker Simmison and which belongs to me. Also the profits and dividends arising from and out of 40 shares of stock of the Bank of Pittsburg —20 shares of which stands on the books of said Bank in her own name, the other shares are part of the hundred shares (completed) standing in my name. The said profits and dividends arising from and out of said 40 shares of bank stock are to be received and enjoyed by my sister Nancy for and during her natural life—and after her death the said lot and ground and buildings are to go to my son Harmar and his heirs and the 40 shares of bank stock are to go to my son Saint Clair or his heirs. In case it should happen that the Bank of Pittsburgh should be discontinued and caused to wind up its affairs before the death of my said sister, then it is my further will that my executors hereinafter named or the survivor or survivors of them invest the proceeds of the said forty shares of bank stock in the stock of some other creditable institution or in Government stocks of the United States, for the use and benefit of my said sister for and during her life.

The will of Captain John Wilkins, a name perpetuated in a town and a Pittsburgh street, is filled with bequests of the numbered lots in the Woods' survey. Captain Wilkins was twice married, had twenty-two children, and his will mentions fourteen by name.

JOHN WILKINS—*Home and lot on what is called Scotch Hill.*
Dated February 6, 1808—Recorded December 14, 1809

Scotch Hill was a section of Pittsburgh below Grants Hill toward the Monongahela where many Scotsmen lived.

Mr. Wilkins was of Welsh descent. As a boy, he had been apprenticed to the saddler business in Lancaster. When his eldest son, John, was two years old, Mr. Wilkins lived in Carlisle. Ten years later, he removed to Bedford. In 1776, when he received a commission from George Washington with instructions to "enlist a company of men and join the Army of the United States," Mr. Wilkins was made *Captain* in the Continental service. After the Revolution, Captain Wilkins opened a store at the northeast corner of Fourth and Wood Streets, again becoming a merchant as he had been both at Carlisle and Bedford.

The mercantile business evidently was profitable for, in the manuscript biography which Captain Wilkins left, he said:

Mark, I never got a shilling of fortune with either of my wives, yet ever since my first marriage to this day I have lived happy with them and God hath blessed me with plenty to keep my children until they were able to provide for themselves.

After Allegheny County was organized Captain Wilkins was appointed one of the Associate Judges of the Court. He served as a member of the Supreme Executive Council in 1790, was chief Burgess of Pittsburgh, Commissioner of Public Buildings, and the County Treasurer from 1794-1803. He was prominent in the town and, because it was customary for men of prominence to be mourned by their immediate family in proper mourning apparel, Captain Wilkins thought it proper to attend to that matter in the very first section of his will—"$50, to purchase mourning."

Captain John Wilkins lived between Second and Third Avenues, on Wood Street. The lot next to his, No. 353, he left to his son, John Wilkins, who built on it a double brick house with a kitchen added. The first insurance policy issued in Pittsburgh was on this mansion.

In later days the old Monongahela House, a hotel, stood on this lot, famous because President Lincoln addressed the assembled citizens from its balcony.

For his daughter, Matilda Denny, he left part of the lot on Diamond near the Markethouse:

my house and lot fronting the public square adjoining to Doctor Mowry's building and on the one side by Joseph Davis being part of

178

Lot No. 394 in the Borough of Pittsburgh and formerly belonging to Wm. Crogen.

To Mary Ann, his own home: "Lot No. 354 in the Plan of Pittsburgh." To his son, William, the adjoining lot, No. 353, between Fourth and Diamond.

To his daughter Jane:

house and lot No. 356 in Plan of Pittsburgh fronting Fourth Street and adjoining Henderson's lot on the one side and Negley's on the other side, and now occupied by Henry Wolf.

To Eluisa, "my youngest":

house and lot on what is called Scotch Hill, No. 202 in the Plan of Pittsburgh adjoining Geo. Robinson's lots to the westward a street to the Eastward and fronting the Monongahela River, now occupied by Peter Eldenhead.

To Mrs. Wilkins:

the land adjoining Alex. Addison's lands and commonly called my pasture lots in equal partnership with my son John Wilkins as may be seen by my books.

His book entries directed that one-half the land was to be conveyed to his son, John Wilkins, Jr., "the other half he is to sell for the benefit of the younger children—or purchase himself for their benefit" after Mrs. Wilkins' decease.

To each of his sons, John, Charles, and Stewart, and to Ebenezer Denny, husband of his daughter Nancy, he left "$50 to purchase mourning." His daughters, Margaret Tannehill and Rachel Hollensworth, each got $200, and his daughter Catherine Earnest, $300.

These two wills keep alive the names of places changed long ago and of people long gone whose descendants still live among us.

The Fabric of Pittsburgh

They shall maintain the fabric of the world ...
For the work of their hands is their prayer.

These wills are woven of the warp and woof of Pittsburgh. They are the wills of a British Indian trader who considered his Bible and prayerbook important legacies for his only son; a German tanner whose descendants have given more than any other Pittsburgh family to the cultural and physical welfare of their neighbors; the grandson of a Swiss, whose family were first citizens of East Liberty, a village which has played an important part in Pittsburgh history; a Scottish immigrant, leader of the "intellectuals" of that early day; a Pittsburgh tavern keeper whose tavern was the setting for much that was important in the social, political, and cultural life on the early western frontier; and an Irish immigrant, Pittsburgh's greatest pioneer industrialist. Many beneficiaries of these wills have followed their way, promoting the growth and prosperity of Pittsburgh.

DEVEREUX SMITH—*Debt and Losses I have sustained by Indians.*
Dated July 13, 1798—Recorded June 21, 1800

Devereux Smith was an important man in early Pittsburgh. He came to this country with the British Army. He presided over a large plantation and carried on a prosperous business with the Indians and with his neighbors. He mentions in his will the famous

180

"Indian Books" which recorded his trade in the late 1700's and which are a part of the William Darlington collection at the University of Pittsburgh.

The will begins with the customary religious preamble and, about halfway down the first of its two pages, continues with bequests to his wife, giving her sole right to his entire estate in a manner unusual at the time when there was a son to inherit, and six daughters. The papers attached to the will show his daughter Sarah and her husband as next in line for inheritance of anything his wife should hold and not dispose of before her death. One cannot help but wonder whether his son, Edward, was still alive, and if so, whether Mr. Smith considered his son-in-law a better business head.

And as touching such Worldly Estate wherewith it has pleased God to bless me in this Life I give demise and dispose of the same in the following manner and form.—First I give and bequeath to my dearly beloved wife Elizabeth all my real estate that I am or may be possessed of at the present date, and at any time thereafter during my natural Life, as also my Personal property of every description whatever, for her only purpose, use, and support with the free Entry, use and possession of all my household goods and furniture of every description whatsoever, the whole and every part thereof for her proper use, and at her disposal during her natural life, and if she should think proper to dispose of any part thereof it is left to her own discretion, excepting the Balance of Debts due to me at this date on my Books, that was due to me on or before the year 1787—or those Ballances that remain due at my Decease, to be applied to the discharge of any Ballances I might have been justly indebted before the above date, as also anything that can be got in my Indian Books, Debt and Losses I have sustained by Indians to be applied as above, as also all notes to be applied as above and excepting all the Ballances of my Book Debts, that may be due to me at my decease That have become due since the 11th of May 1787. Those debts to be applied to the discharge of the Ballances of any just debt I may have contracted since the 11th day of May 1787 for my present use. Also I give and bequeath to my well beloved son Edward Smith all my wearing apparel at my decease, and I recommend to his Mother, at her decease, that she give him my Family Bible and prayer book if

181

he should be the longest liver. And I recommend to my living son Edward and to my living Daughters Mary Amberson, Elizabeth Greenough, Sara Fowler, Margarette Small, Jane Heaney and Hannah Means, to be dutiful and attentive to their aged Mother as Christians ought to be towards their Parents.

And I do hereby Constitute make and appoint my trusty and well beloved friends, Ephraim Douglass, Esqr. of Fayette County, Thomas Greenough late of Allegany County and my dear beloved wife Elizabeth Smith, all or any two of them, my Sole Executors of this my last will and Testament, That all and every part of my property may be disposed of by them, according to the true intent and meaning of this my last Will and Testament Ratifying and Confirming this and no other to be my last Will. In Witness whereof I have hereunto set my hand and Seal this thirteenth day of July One Thousand Seven Hundred and Ninety eight.

DEVEREAU SMITH (SEAL)

Signed Sealed and Published by the said Devereaux Smith to be his last will and Testament, in the presence of us who in his presence, and in the presence of each other have hereunto subscribed our names.

James Kelly
Nathaniel Jones.

Mr. Smith's signature to this will is most interesting. His capital *D* swings out into a big oval to top handsomely that letter. The capital *S* is tall and formal. But the small *h*, ending the name *Smith*, continues with a flourish wide enough to twist around the neck of the *S*, encircle the dot over the *i*, and cross the *t*.

Sixteen months after Devereux Smith signed the foregoing will, he attached the following codicil:

Finding myself dangerously ill, I do hereby for certain considerations, make a Deed of Gift to my daughter Sarah Fowler of my negro girl named *Luck*, on the demise of myself and my beloved wife Elizabeth; as well as any other property she may possess at her demise. In Witness whereof, I have hereunto affixed my hand and seal this 29th of November, 1799.

The difference between the first signature and this later one shows the testator's illness more clearly than anything else could

182

have done. Devereux Smith was evidently having trouble in holding the quill, because the capital *D* is very shaky and crooked, with a splotch of ink obscuring most of the first name. The surname looks almost as bad, an effort having been made to finish it with the usual encircling flourish.

But on the very next day, Mr. Smith's signature on another paper filed with the will shows much improvement; and as he lived another six months after this signing, we can only presume that he had rallied from the weakness so plainly evident in the signing of the codicil. This last paper reads:

I Devereux Smith being convinced of the fidelity and integrity of Alexander Fowler husband of my daughter Sarah, do hereby assign and make over in trust to the said Alexander Fowler all my Day Books, Ledgers, and Dockets, with the Ballances that may be due thereon, for the use and behoof of my beloved wife Elizabeth. The Dockets I desire may be deposited with my friend John Wilkins, Esquire, to recover what may be due thereon.

My Day Books and Ledgers I direct to be tied up, and kept by the said Alexander Fowler, and such Ballances as may appear to be justly due thereon to be put in suit and recovered with as much expedition as possible for the use and purposes aforesaid, and that whatever may be recovered from the executors of William Butler and others may . . . (the paper is torn, here) my said wife Elizabeth's demise be left to Sarah Fowler.

> In Witness whereof I have hereunto set my hand and seal this 30th Nov. 99.

Witnesses to the above were James Kelly and Nathaniel Jones, who had witnessed the original will. On the back of the folded, 7½ by 12½-inch paper appears this notation:

Mr. Devereux Smith's request that on the Demise of Mrs. Smith the Debts and property that they may be possessed of should become the property of Mrs. Fowler.

Son-in-law Alexander Fowler, himself, was an interesting figure in early Pittsburgh. His name is on the charter of the Pittsburgh Academy (University of Pittsburgh) among those of other important people. He had resigned a British commission to take his chances in the Western Country. His daughter married the Register Jones, whose will is on pages 91-92.

How small and how neighborly Pittsburgh seems when you read the familiar names of witnesses, executors, and legal advisors!

In addition to the codicil and notes added to Devereux Smith's will, many interpolations have been made in the text, which is written in wide-spaced lines. The paper bears a very curious watermark—an upright animal and other designs woven in with the head and upper part of a man's body. All of this is fenced in with little pointed pales.

The Indian trading store, run by Devereux Smith and his partner Ephraim Douglass, was a landmark in the first half century of local history. It was patronized by many leading citizens, whose accounts still may be read in the old ledgers mentioned in Mr. Smith's instructions to his executors. It is interesting that at the foot of one page recording debts of the new government, Mr. Smith wrote firmly, "Never paid and never will."

When Dr. John Connally persecuted Pennsylvania's leaders in his zeal for Virginia's land interests, attempts were made to destroy the Smith residence. The home was saved, but a jury of Virginians helped in taking away from Smith, for Connally, a tract of his land.

A Sixth Avenue tract of land was transferred to Trinity Episcopal Church in 1787, by action of its four trustees, one of whom was Devereux Smith. He is probably buried in a Trinity grave, although no record verifies this. A number of old graves were moved and names stricken from the verger's records when the first building was started in 1825. Remains of brick walls were found underground, which were probably the walls of underground vaults. One might have been Devereux Smith's.

The surveyor for the Penns, George Woods, honored Devereux Smith by naming Smithfield Street for him. What a far cry from the fertile valley it used to be is that busy street now—where men and women rush ahead until they are caught at intersections. It is a refreshing experience, while awaiting modern traffic signals, to shut off everything but the vision of Smithfield Street as a broad, green field. Try it! One can almost feel the soft gentle breeze

184

above a summer's day crowd, faintly hear the crinkle of crinoline and the swish of old silk.

CONRAD WINEBIDDLE—*Land which I bought of the sheriff . . . the property of George Croghan.*
Dated September 3, 1795—Recorded September 17, 1795

This is one of the most interesting of the earliest recorded wills. It illustrates almost every topic discussed in this book: slavery and indenture; the legal status of women; real estate; currency. It illustrates, too, the opportunities the frontier offered to gather material wealth and in the freedom of private enterprise to hand down an inheritance which would benefit many generations, not only of a man's family, but of the whole community as well.

Conrad Winebiddle, a German immigrant, was wealthy when he arrived, as wealth was measured in his day. Like Devereux Smith, he came to Pittsburgh attached to the British Army and stayed to settle down and make a home, and like many of the early Germans he brought with him gold, pay for his handiwork, saved against the future on a new continent. During the Revolution he supplied the soldiers with beef and as a tanner made their shoes, too. After the war he continued as a tanner. His wife, Elizabeth Weitzel, was a real partner for him; after his death she proved to be a very good business woman in her own right. Could her father's will be the one on page 49?

Mr. Winebiddle's will includes some of the 500 acres he had bought at the close of the Revolution, of which 300 acres were in the part of Pittsburgh which was first the village of Lawrenceville. All of it was land that during his own lifetime greatly increased in value—and all of it, even by 1795, had a history.

To his wife, Elizabeth Weitzel, he left "two lots of ground with houses and buildings on Market Street, Front Street, Geo. Wallace and Water Street"; to Philip Winebiddle "the home and two lots adjoining John Ormsby, G. Heron on Water Street and Front Street." These were his city property. And so was his bequest to his daughter Barbara, who later married Jacob Negley, Sr.: "the house and lot situate in the Town of Pittsburg, ad-

185

joining Samuel Semple's Kitchen, Front Street and Ferry Street
. . . also my negro girl Poll to hold her during the time of her
servitude." To Catherine and Conrad, daughter and son, "the
plantation and tract containing two hundred fifty nine acres which
I have already given to my beloved wife during her natural life
or widowhood." His two youngest children were to have "the
plantation and tracts of land which I bought of the sheriff of
Westmoreland Co. as the property of George Croghan."

The Croghan land has a romantic history. George Croghan
was perhaps the most exciting and romantic figure of our colonial
period (not to be confused with Col. William Croghan, Sr., or
William Croghan, Jr., grandfather and father, respectively, of
Mary Croghan Schenley, whose name is pronounced without the
g). George Croghan was an Irishman who came into this country
as early as 1745, alert to the possibilities of the Western Country.
He was hated by the French, loved by the Indians, and called in
by England or by Pennsylvania whenever Indians were to be dealt
with. He licensed other traders and he speculated in Pittsburgh
lands on both the Allegheny and Monongahela River. His land
speculations reached far into the western wilderness, over-ex-
tended his means at last, and eventually George Croghan, after
the loss of several great fortunes, died a pensioner of his friends.

A very interesting bequest to Mrs. Winebiddle generously
recognizes her right to her own savings—a gesture necessary if
they were to be hers.

And the money that she has gathered by her own industry, amounting
to between forty and fifty pounds, which I allow her to keep and not
to be counted or returned in the inventory of my estate.

That he was thoughtful for her comfort is illustrated everywhere
in the will:

I also give unto my beloved wife Elizabeth her choice of my cows, one
horse also her bed and furniture and a Bed and furniture for the
youngest children and my desk and Clock Cupboard and two Pewter
dishes six pewter Plates and six spoons, two Iron Potts, a Dutch oven
and two smoothing irons skimming ladle flesh fork, a small iron pot
and skillet and also a negro . . . yearly rents and profits of the planta-

tion a tract of land called Tubs Place at the four mill spring unto my son Phillip Winebiddle when he shall come to be of full age.

The widow survived her husband only eight years; but she meanwhile married William Cunningham, a Scot. Their child, William Cunningham, is mentioned in her own will. Meantime she sold as much of the property as the Winebiddle will permitted —household furniture, slaves, and land—reserving of course the property her husband designated to go at her death to his children.

Will be sold by Public Vendue on Monday the 2nd of November next, at the late dwelling house of Conrad Winebiddle, deceased, about two miles from the town of Pittsburg, on the Allegheny River, Horses, Cattle, Sheep, Hogs, a quantity of Hay, Farming utensils, Tanners tools, togetherwith a quantity of Bark, Household Furniture, a Negro Man, a slave for life, by trade a tanner, and understands farming, also a Negro Woman and child, the woman a slave for life. Nine months credit will be given on giving bond with approved security. Attendance will be given by

Elizabeth Winebiddle, Executrix,
Jacob Negley, Executor.

FOR SALE

The Plantation on which Conrad Winebiddle, deceased, lived situate about two miles from Pittsburgh on the Allegheny River. It contains 113 acres and an allowance; there is on the premises a good dwelling house, a tanyard in good repair, an orchard of 200 trees and sundry other improvements. For terms, apply to

Elizabeth Winebiddle, Executrix
Jacob Nigley, Executor.

N.B.—All persons having accounts with Conrad Winebiddle, deceased, are desired to bring them forward for settlement before the 1st of January next, to the subscribers. Cash and Hides will be taken in exchange for leather.

The will is so soiled it is impossible to read all of it in its original form. The executor, Jacob Negley, Sr., married young Barbara Anna Winebiddle and so united two large estates. Their daughter, Sarah Jane Negley, married a rising young lawyer and banker, Thomas Mellon, founder of the Mellon family and fortune in Pittsburgh, and they lived out their lives on the property she inherited from her father and mother. They started a Pittsburgh family very important to the welfare and culture of Pittsburgh and the nation.

Two streets in East Liberty bear the names Winebiddle and Negley. Old Negleyville became a part of East Liberty and Negley Avenue replaced Negley's Lane.

JACOB NEGLEY, JR.—*Books which have my name written in them.*
Dated January 2, 1830—Recorded February 2, 1830

No will is recorded for Jacob Negley, Sr., in Allegheny County. Jacob Negley, Jr., was the son of Jacob Negley, Sr. and Barbara Winebiddle. The Presbyterian Church in East Liberty, the mother church of Shadyside, Point Breeze, and others, is a monument to their life and generosity. Their descendants have continued its support and made it one of Pittsburgh's most beautiful churches.

And Mr. Negley's appreciation for the future of the city prompted him to lay out Penn Avenue one hundred feet wide where it passed through his property. Would that other property owners on other avenues and streets followed his lead!

Jacob, Jr., married Mary Ann Scott and died only six years later leaving her with two children, the James and Rebecca mentioned in his will. James Negley became a hero of the Mexican War and of the Civil War. Rebecca died at age 19.

Jacob Negley, Jr., ran a large farm and the steam grist mill, the first west of the mountains, which his father had built near the corner of what are now Negley and Collins Avenues in East Liberty. His home was at the head of Negley Avenue, later James Negley's home, "Baywood," and then the home of Alexander King. But because of business depressions, Jacob Negley, Jr., was forced to direct his heirs to sell much of the property he had inherited as his share of his father's and mother's estate. The will emphasizes, though, his interest in a library worth perpetuating, a family interest which has continued in later generations.

The last will and Testament of Jacob Nigley of Pitt Township, Allegheny County. I Jacob Nigley considering the uncertainty of this mortal life and being of sound mind and memory, make & publish this my last will and testament in manner and form following (that is to say) First I Give and bequeath unto my beloved wife Mary Ann Nigley that portion of goods belonging to me individually consisting of beds and bedding, furniture, carpeting, hardware, queensware, household and kitchen furniture generally. And also I give to her the sum of Forty Dollars to be paid annually during her widowhood and no longer.

ITEM. I give and bequeath unto my son James Scott Nigley my surveyor's compass and instruments thereto belonging. My silver watch and all my library of books which have my name written in them, and also my undivided one third part of all the books in the two book cases, and my two files of newspapers.

ITEM. As soon as convenient after my decease it is my will that my Executors hereinafter mentioned make sale of my share of the personal property not yet bequeathed, together with my share of the one eighth part of the property I have held as Agent, such as the contents of furniture throughout my present dwelling not already enumerated, and also the stock of cattle, grain, and farming utensils, and collect what may be of outstanding debts, and with the proceeds thereof, after discharging all my just debts, as shall be by me owing at my death, together with my funeral expenses and all charges touching the proving of or otherwise concerning this my will, shall in the first place, out of my personal effects, be fully paid & satisfied, then my will is, after making ample provision for my children, that the residue be put into some safe ways as to create a yearly income, which with the rents of the two Lots of land to be Deeded in fee simple by James Ross Esqr. to my two children James Scott Nigley and Rebecca Roup Nigley, and the residue if any after their maintenance till they severally arrive at the ages of twenty one to be equally divided between them, share and share alike.

It is my desire that my son James and daughter Rebecca remain in the families in which they are now placed, James with and under the authority and protection of John Roup till he arrives at the age of fourteen years, and Rebecca in like manner with my Mother-in-law Mrs. Boyd till the age of twelve years, afterwards it is supposed they

189

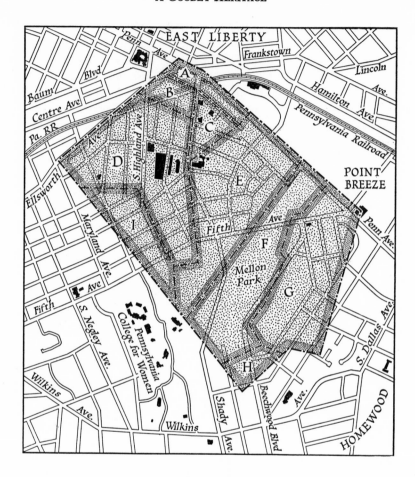

Monticello

*Showing the conveyances thereof made by Alexander
Thomson and the later development of the city*

A—Alex. Thomson's plan

B—to Joseph Sawtell

C - D—to Alex. Thomson Jr.

E—to Thomas G. Thomson

F—to Elizabeth Lafaver

G—to Jacob Roup

H—to Wm. Moor

I—Interference with
Oxford Patent

will be directed by their Guardians. I make and ordain John Roup and Francis G. Bailey & James Ross Esqr. Executors of this my last will and testament. In witness whereof I have hereunto set my hand and seal the second day of January in the year of our Lord one thousand eight hundred and thirty.

Jacob Negley

Signed, sealed, published and declared by the above-named Jacob Nigley to be his last will and testament in the presence of us, who, at his request and in his presence have subscribed our names as witnesses thereunto.

February 2d, 1830. ⎫
Jno Roup sworn as ⎪
Exc. of this will ⎬
the others will appear ⎭

John Beitler
Isaac Peebles

In the body of the will, wherever the testator's name is found, it is spelled with an *i*. This, of course, was inaccurate, although the family name might have been generally pronounced *Nigley*.

After Jacob's death the Negley family regained some of their original holdings through the kind intervention of James Ross, attorney and family friend. Mr. Ross, upon learning that Mrs. Negley was caring for the farm, bought up most of the Negley land on the market. He then sold it back to them for the same price he had paid, gradually and as they became able to afford it.

The children were placed under the authority and protection of relatives on each side of the family: Rebecca with Jacob's mother-in-law and James with John Roup, husband of Kitty Winebiddle, his grandmother's sister.

ALEXANDER THOMSON— . . . *the Lots in East Liberty . . .*
Dated May 29, 1821—Recorded January 12, 1822

Alexander Thomson of Pitt Township bequeathed to his children pieces of land from the East Liberty acreage bought by him from Ephraim Blaine in 1802. "Monticello" (as it was called) was divided by will as follows:

. . . son Alexander so much of Lot No. 2 as marked in the Draught of my Plantation made by Robert Donaldson as shall be included between

191

a straight line running from the southwest corner of Janet Shaw's lot in East Liberty (marked No. 24 in the Draught made by Jacob Negley) until it intersect the line of my said son Alexander Thomson's place and from thence along his bounding line extending northeast until it intersect the Lots in East Liberty, containing fifteen acres more or less, conditionally burdened as shall be hereafter mentioned. . . . ITEM. I give and bequeath to my daughter Elizabeth Lafever and to the heirs of her body No. 3, so marked in Robert Donaldson's Draft, containing sixty-three acres. It is also my will that if the said daughter Elizabeth Lafever shall leave no heirs of her body proceeding at the time of her decease, in that case the above devized property shall revert to my sons Alexander Thomson and Thomas Greer Thomson and their heirs to be equally divided between them. ITEM. I give and bequeath to my son Thomas Greer Thomson and his heirs Lot No. 2 as marked in Robert Donaldson's Draught containing (after the part already devized to my son Alexander Thomson is deducted) about sixty-two acres more or less, together with all the buildings on said Lot . . .

Alexander Thomson was seventeen years old when he came to America from Scotland with eleven of his brothers and sisters. His father (Alexander, Sr.) bought a farm about four miles east of Chambersburg and named the place "Corkerhill" after the homestead in Scotland where his own father had spent his life. Alexander, Jr., whose will we are examining, served his new country at Valley Forge during 1777 and 1778. In addition to the two sons and one daughter mentioned in the above excerpt from his will, there was another daughter—Mary Roup. She was the wife of Jacob Roup, whose land adjoined that bequeathed to her brothers and sister. Instead of real estate, her legacy from her father was in money, but the Roup name still lives in that section of East Liberty.

This will, read in the original, is in good condition. The writing is a neat, clear script, but only the signature is in Mr. Thomson's hand. The text is so nearly like his writing, however, that it was difficult to see the difference—except that Alexander Thomson's *A* is like fancy type and the other *A*'s are in the round script. Witnesses to the Thomson will were Alexander Watson and John

192

Black; the executors were the testator's two sons — Alexander Thomson and Thomas Greer Thomson.

Elizabeth Moorhead, in her book *Whirling Spindle*, includes a letter written by Alexander Thomson, Sr., to friends or relatives in Scotland which gives a clearheaded picture of the economic possibilities at the Forks of the Ohio and a picture of its pleasant climate and gentle living.

ANDREW WATSON—*My farm . . . into lots agreeable to a plan here-unto annexed*
Dated September 17, 1822

Andrew Watson was a Scotsman who had served in a Pennsylvania regiment during the Revolution. He married Alexander Thomson's daughter, Margaret, and acquired property in the town and out of the town east along the banks of the Monongahela. He kept a tavern in his log home on Front Street (now First Avenue) near Market Street, called *The Indian Queen*. It was the center of political conference and the scene of the first courts of Allegheny County and of Pittsburgh's first theater.

Among the Andrew Watson papers in the University Library is the following "account rendered Trustees of Allegheny for rent of Court House—10th March 1794."

The Trustees of Allegheny County
To Andrew Watson—

	Dr		
To furnishing them with a Court house for the purpose of holding Septr Court 1791 — and providing them with Candles	6 – 15.		..
To Do for Decemr Court 1791 and providing Coal & Candles.	7	10.	..
To Do for March Court 1792 and Coal and Candles.......	7	10.	..
To Do for June Court 1792 & Candles....................	6	15	..
To Do for September Co 1792 & Candles................	6	15	..
To Do for December Court 1792 and Coal and Candles....	7	10	..
To Do for March Court 1793—Coal & Candles............	7	10	..
To Do for June Court 1793 & Candles....................	6	15	..
To Do for Septr: Court 1793 & Candles.................	6	15	..
To Do for Decemr Court 1793—Coal & Candles..........	7	10.	..
To retaining providing and repairg Do for their use for March Court 1794.................	3	15.	..
	175	0.	0.

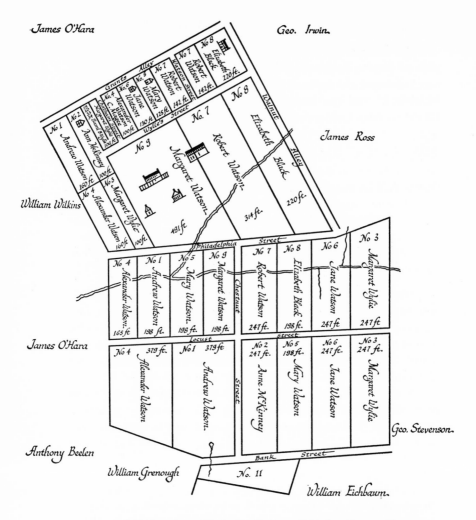

James O'Hara

Geo. Irwin.

James Ross

William Wilkins

James O'Hara

Anthony Beelen

William Grenough

No. 11

William Eichbaum.

Geo. Stevenson.

I, Andrew Watson, of Pittsburgh in the County of Allegheny and State of Pennsylvania do hereby certify and declare the above plan of my farm, mentioned and referred, to in my last will and testament dated the seventeenth day of September, in the year of our Lord one thousand eight hundred and twenty-two and hereunto annexed. Witness my hand and seal this seventeenth day of September one thousand eight hundred and twenty-two.

Attest
Alexander Shields
Nathan McCargo

(Signed) {Seal} And^w Watson.

Andrew Watson Plan

This plan extends Pittsburgh beyond the limits of Grant Street between the "Manor of Pittsburgh" and the present "Oakland"—toward the villages of Lawrenceville, Oakland, Shadyside, Negleyville, East Liberty.

His will is especially interesting because he attached to it a plan of lots he bequeathed to his heirs. This plan extends Pittsburgh beyond the limits of Grant Street, between the "Manor of Pittsburgh" and the present "Oakland"—toward the villages of Lawrenceville, Oakland, Shadyside, Negleyville, East Liberty.

that my farm whereon I now live, containing about eighty acres be divided into lots agreeable to a plan hereto annexed. And that my real estate in the city of Pittsburgh bounded by Market, First and Second Streets shall be leased out . . . rents . . . to be applied to . . .

My wife Margaret the whole of the dwelling house with all buildings on Lot No. 9—garden, fruit trees, annuity of two hundred dollars . . . all my personal property viz. horses, cows, sheep and farming utensils and Library of books, beds and bedding, household and kitchen furniture to have and to hold—absolutely and during her natural life.

His three sons, Alexander, Andrew, and Robert, and his daughters, Margaret, Elisabeth, Jane, Anne, and Mary, inherited as the plan shows. The sons received their property burdened with a sum of money to be divided among the girls. The girls also received money and the unmarried ones the usual bed and bedding, horse and bridle, and milk cows.

Robert, who was one of the executors of this will and a few years later of his brother Alexander's will, managed his father's large estate. "He was a man of wide acquirements, both in classical learning and in natural science." During his travels abroad he collected a library which by his own will came to the Western University of Pennsylvania.

Elisabeth married the John Black who had witnessed Alexander Thomson's will; he became the first professor of the classics at the University. His great-granddaughter, Elizabeth Moorhead, has written a charming account of their courtship in her book *Whirling Spindle.*

The Watson family and their many descendants from the days of Andrew to the present have been very fine and cultured citizens of Pittsburgh.

Another feature of Andrew Watson's city property which is interesting are his dealings with the famous Brackenridge family. Among the Watson papers, along with the copy of Andrew's will and his plan of lots, are several papers covering this transaction, which began with Hugh Henry Brackenridge and continued after his death with Mr. Brackenridge's wife, Sabina, and her sons. These papers illustrate very humanly and realistically the development of Pittsburgh land from cow pasture to industrial metropolis.

JAMES O'HARA—*In order to create an estate in trust . . .*
Dated September 15, 1819—Recorded January 4, 1820

James O'Hara probably made a greater contribution to the development of Pittsburgh industry than any other of its earliest citizens. In every possible way he promoted the growth and prosperity of the city during his lifetime, and through his descendants that active good will continues.

James O'Hara, a native of Ireland, came to this country as a young man, seeking and finding great opportunities. He had served in the British Army under Queen Anne as an ensign (which before 1871 meant a commissioned officer serving as standard bearer).

In 1773, when he came to Fort Pitt, he was an Indian trader. When the Revolution broke out he enlisted as a private, but soon his business qualifications were discovered and he was made assistant to the quartermaster. Later, he became quartermaster general. After the Revolutionary War, General O'Hara filled contracts with the new government for supplies to the Western Armies. His plan of supplying salt from Onondaga to Western Pennsylvania illustrates his great resourcefulness.

He was a man of great vision and a farseeing calculator, for it took a complicated transportation system to get the salt here. So, he packed his provisions for the garrisons in the kind of barrels which were suitable to bring back the salt, and paid in advance for it. He had to have transportation facilities to move the salt from the manufacturers of Onondaga, then to send it by boat to the landing below Niagara Falls. And so, again, Mr. O'Hara built the vessel to get the salt to the landing, procured wagons to take it to Schlosser, a boat to transfer it to Black Rock, and another boat to transfer it to Erie. Then it had to be carried through the swampy road from Erie to the head of French Creek, and loaded on more boats to take it down the creek and the Allegheny River to Pittsburgh—much of the river was navigable only during floods. But O'Hara succeeded in solving every problem; Pittsburgh got the salt and its merchants were able to sell it for $4.00 a bushel, instead of the very much higher price. In fact, just a few years later, salt sold in Pittsburgh at $2.40 a bushel, as others became interested in the trade which General James O'Hara had opened up and put their capital into improved transportation for bringing salt to Pittsburgh. Thus, everything Mr. O'Hara touched brought advantage to the community, and opened up wider opportunities for all.

But James O'Hara was interested in many and various enterprises. He was a merchant, and the following newspaper notice indicates the rich stock in which he dealt:

Pittsburgh Gazette, January 27, 1787
Just opening at the Store of the subscriber in Pittsburgh a complete cargo of West-India Goods, of the first quality, and other Groceries, to which will be shortly added a general assortment of Dry Goods, as usual, all of which will be sold on the most reasonable terms for cash or any kind of country produce at market price.

—James O'Hara

The subscriber wishing to finish the business of James O'Hara & Co. requests that all persons indebted to that firm will make the necessary payments before the first day of May next, as his situation obliges him to put every open account belonging to the company, on that day, into the hands of their attorney. He hopes that his friends and customers will acknowledge the distant period fixed upon for payment, sufficiently generous, and that they will leave him no cause to exclaim or put them to any further trouble. Country produce of all kinds will be received at market prices; all those who have any demands are informed that the necessary arrangement is made for making immediate payments of all the charges that may be brought against them.

—James O'Hara.

He was a glassmaker, too. When O'Hara poured his wealth into buildings and equipment for making glass, it was a hazardous

197

venture. Yet his faith was justified and the success of his glass works marks Pittsburgh's first importance as a real manufacturing center. After the General's death a worn memorandum was found among his papers, proudly proclaiming: "Today we made the first bottle, at a cost of $30,000."

In 1797, when the glass works was established, Major Isaac Greer was in partnership with Mr. O'Hara, but he withdrew from the business within a few years. There was a partnership in the brewing business, also, when James O'Hara started his brewery near the Point around 1802. It was known, at first, by the firm name of O'Hara & Coppings, the junior partner having learned the brewing trade in Europe. Their brewery was the first one to be operated in the borough although a distillery had preceded it. Soon after the brewery was established, this notice appeared:

Commonwealth, November 20, 1805

THE PUBLIC

are respectfully informed that The Pittsburgh Point Brewery is now in complete operation:
Strong Beer and *Porter* in barrels, half barrels, or bottles, delivered anywhere in the borough on being ordered. Porter put up in casks or bottles, for exportation, that will keep in the warmest climate. *Table Beer,* at the low price of two dollars per barrel, will also be furnished during the brewing season. *Grains* may be had every Monday and Thursday afternoons. Orders from town or country, directed to the subscriber, will be carefully executed.

For J. O'HARA, Geo. Shires.

(Sixty cents per bushel given for good Barley)

Unlike most men of his day, James O'Hara had no political aspirations, although he had the distinction as one of the Presidential Electors of helping to elect George Washington first president of the nation.

After the Revolutionary War, when the town of Pittsburgh was laid out, James O'Hara bought up a number of tracts of land for low prices. Also, he bought much real estate in Ohio, Indiana, and Illinois, as well as property in the "Reserve" tract in Allegheny. The sale of this tract is the beginning of old Allegheny City,

Pittsburgh's sister city until 1907, when it became a part of the city of Pittsburgh.

The Act of the General Assembly, dated March 12, 1783, for the purpose of paying off certificates given to Revolutionary War veterans, had also included the provision that a certain tract

containing 3,000 acres in an oblong of not less than one mile in depth from the Allegheny and Ohio Rivers, and extending up and down the rivers from opposite Fort Pitt so far as may be necessary to include the same should be reserved for the State.

This tract included what was known later as Allegheny City, but it was not surveyed until the winter of 1788. On November 19, 1788, the Receiver-General at Philadelphia released a notice that the lots, outlots, and small farms within this reserved tract opposite Pittsburgh would be offered for sale. We find frequent bequests of these lots and outlots in early Allegheny County wills.

The Supreme Executive Council valued the river lots across from Pittsburgh at thirty shillings (or specie equivalent) per acre. Town lots were estimated to be worth, on the average, forty shillings an acre, and farms brought from seven to twenty shillings an acre. A few of the lots had no valuation placed upon them. It was recommended that one outlot be sold with each lot, the remaining outlots to be added together to make farms.

The islands in the river, some of which no longer exist, were also surveyed by direction of the Council. Evaluation of Hamilton's Island—one hundred and thirty-six acres—was twenty shillings an acre. Wilson's Island was valued at ten shillings per acre.

Mr. O'Hara bought much land, here and along both rivers, but he sold very little of it. Land was cheap when these tracts were surveyed and laid out in lots, and even in spite of large tax evaluation, farseeing men must have reaped the reward the land promised when, like James O'Hara, they bought up land and held it until it was worth many times the purchase price. For example, a lot at Fifth and Wood, in downtown Pittsburgh, which the Penns sold for $62.50 in 1785, was worth more than $5,000 in 1819. It was sold, in 1828, for $7,280. In 1941, it was valued at more than $500,000—and now it is valued at about $1,256,760.

199

General O'Hara lived first in a log house east of Stanwix Street—with a beautiful view of the Allegheny and Ohio Rivers—in what was called the "Kings Orchard." When Water Street became the fashionable residential part of town, James O'Hara and his family built a large frame house there, on the Monongahela, and there his will was drawn up, about three months before he died, concluding with a bequest to Mrs. O'Hara of "My Homestead, consisting of Lots Nos. 146, 147, part of Lot No. 145, with the buildings and improvements thereon." These were the homesite on the Monongahela.

The O'Hara will is a long one, copied on many pages of Will Book II and continued in Book III. The original document is now in crumbling strips. It is in such condition that only by spreading out the broken pieces and attempting to match them in some sequence can any of it be read. But photostats of the hand-copied pages from the will books are enclosed in the packet with the scraps. It is difficult to study even these, for the photostats were made from the much-soiled and patched pages of the will books.

The text is carefully worded and neatly written. None of the signature is left in the tattered document but judging from the legal phraseology, the writing must be an attorney's. The will establishes separate trusts for the O'Hara children, starting with one for the son, Richard, who later married Mary Fitzsimmons. Their daughter, Mary Carson O'Hara, became the wife of bibliophile William McCullough Darlington. Richard's inheritance included *Guyasuta*, the Darlington home; part of that estate is now a Boy Scout reservation.

In order to create an estate in trust for the ample support and establishment of my son Richard Butler O'Hara or any child he may have should he hereafter marry, I do hereby devise to my wife, Mary O'Hara, Harmar Denny, Dennis S. Scully, James Ross, and James R. Butler, and the survivor or survivors of them, and to the executor and administrator of such survivor, all lands, tenements, and hereditaments hereinafter mentioned and described with the appurtenances, to wit, all that tract of land containing two hundred and twenty acres or thereabouts situated in Indian Township and county of Alleghany, adjoining lands of James Ross and the estate of the late General Wilkins being tract

No. 10 in Cunningham's District, also those two out lots Nos. 136 and
137 situate lying and being in the reserved tract in Ross township opposite Pittsburgh, and also that two story Brick house situated on
Water Street, Smithfield Street and Cherry Alley with the ground attached to the same extending back to Front Street. Also that two story
Brick house situated on Third Street between Smithfield Street &
Cherry also the ground attached to the same, extending back to Front
Street. Also that two story Brick house situated on Third Street between Smithfield & Cherry also the ground attached to the same, extending through to Fourth street also that two story stone house with
the ground thereto attached situated in West Front and Liberty streets
in Pittsburgh—To have and to hold to the before mentioned lands
tenements hereditaments real estate and every part thereto with the
appurtenances to the said Mary O'Hara, Harmar Denny, Dennis S.
Scully, James Ross, and James R. Butler and to the survivor or survivors
of them. And to the heirs, Executors and Administrators of such survivor UPON TRUST and in special confidence that they will . . . a
lease on same from time to time to such tenants and for such rents as
they approve and on receipt of such rents, issues and profits as may
arise and grow out of said estate that they apply the same in the first
place to the discharge of all public taxes and assessments upon the
said estate . . .

He next provided for his daughter Elizabeth, who married
Harmar Denny, son of the first Ebenezer Denny. Her large holdings were on the Allegheny River and included the original homesite.

In order to create an estate in trust for the ample support of my
daughter Elizabeth and the heirs of her body . . . the two brick houses
at . . . respectively, extending to same width of the respective houses
through from Market Street to O'Hara's Alley and also my Brick house
at the corner of Grant and Second Street on Lot No. 60 in my addition
to Pittsburgh with the ground on which it stands and extending the
width of the house throughout from Second to Grant Street with all
the buildings thereon. Also all my two out lots adjoining and near to
Pittsburgh, being Nos. 1 and 5 in the plan of out lots surveyed for the
proprietors by Col. Woods containing thirty-five arces or thereabouts;
also my Glass works on the south west Side of the Monongahela River

201

opposite Pittsburgh, with all the lots lands tenements, buildings, utensils and improvements belonging thereto and with the same together also with my mills on Sawmill Run and the lands thereto belonging, and all my lands tenements hereditaments in St. Clair township in the county of Alleghany. Also my farm called "Springfield" on the Allegheny River adjoining the Manor line containing about three hundred and nineteen acres with allowances being the same that was formerly held by Thomas Smallman: To have and to hold the aforesaid houses, lots, lands, tenements and hereditaments with the appurtenances to them, (etc.)

Then, a trust, mostly land on the Monongahela, for his daughter Mary, who married William Croghan, Jr., a nephew of George Rogers Clark. Their daughter and only surviving child was Mary Croghan Schenley, whose marriage to British officer Edward W. H. Schenley is still Pittsburgh's most exciting romance. Mrs. Schenley's share of the O'Hara and Croghan estates in Pittsburgh was finally settled in 1951.

In order to create an estate in trust for the ample support of my daughter Mary and the heirs of her body should she marry and have a child or children . . . (several lines here are lost in the original document and tape-covered in the Wills book) Pittsburgh also seventeen lots at the point numbered as follows: Nos. 1, 2, 3, 4, 5, 6, 7, 8, 9, 10, 11, 12, 13, 14, 15, & 17, with the Brewery and all the buildings and improvements thereon together also with Lot No. 144 in the City of Pittsburgh, also eighty-four acres of land adjoining "Springfield" and the Manor land and part of what is called Manor farm, and also the tract of land in Pitt township in the county of Alleghany called Smithfield, containing one hundred and seventy acres, and the tract in the same township called "Mount Airy" containing three hundred and seventy-four acres and a tract of twenty acres situated at the mouth of the four mile run in said township. Also my other Brick house situate on Lot No. 60 in my addition to Pittsburgh together with all the residue of lots Nos. 60, 61, 62, and 63 not hereinbefore devised to my daughter Elizabeth with all the buildings and improvements on the same. Also that portion of my ground beyond Try Street adjoining lands of Andrew Watson, Anthony Beelen and Try Street. Also the two contiguous Brick houses on Market Street in Pittsburgh and the ground on which they stand, extending the same width throughout from Market Street to O'Hara's Alley being the two central houses in my block of Brick buildings standing along Market Street from Second to Third Streets. . . . the net proceeds to be for the benefit and support of my daughter Mary either by direct payment of the whole to her or by advancing what they may think proper and vesting the residue of the nett incomeby loan or otherwise for her future benefit and on her marriage or at any time either before or after that event, as their best judgment may direct, to settle and convey the whole of said estate either in strict settlement or by such other limitations and entailments as may to them appear advisable. And should my said daughter die leaving no issue before such conveyance be made then the whole of said real estate shall be conveyed by the said trustees by such deeds and with such limitations and restrictions and entailments or strict settlement that the issue of my son may enjoy and hold one half of said estate and my daughter Elizabeth and her issue may enjoy and hold the other half of said estate to be divided into two equal portions by the said trustees as nearly as may be before the respective conveyances are to be made and until such continuance and settlements be made as herein directed it is my will and clear intention that the estate and interest of the said Trustees in the premises be deemed and taken as well in equity as at law to be absolute and not in any way to be affected by any act or deed of my daughter Mary or her heirs or by the act of any other person than the said trustees. And it is further my will and direction that the trustees keep their accounts and finally settle the same in the manner hereinbefore directed in relation to the estate of my son.

General O'Hara's death was announced to the community in this manner:

Pittsburgh Gazette, December 21, 1819
Died on the night of 17th instant, General James O'Hara, in the 66th year of his age. Born in Ireland in 1754, emigrated to the United States in 1772, came to Ft. Pitt immediately—engaged in Indian trade as Agent for Simon & Campbell.

None of his large enterprises was mentioned, not so much as a hint given about his valuable services to the town.

203

It takes distance to appreciate a man like James O'Hara. That broken, disintegrating, old document which is his will will disappear into nothingness, eventually. But its maker's personality lives on in his many contributions to Pittsburgh life. Through his descendants, James O'Hara's energies and ambitions for a better Pittsburgh continue: Schenley Park, the Darlington Library, the rooms from the Croghan mansion in the Cathedral of Learning— these are a few of the cultural legacies bearing the names of his children or grandchildren. None of these Pittsburgh gifts bears his name. Perhaps one of his descendants yet will give his name to a memorial symbolizing James O'Hara's daring and common sense and foresight—the personality that is Pittsburgh.

It is especially interesting that James O'Hara's will is a series of trusts which he created for each of his children, for a trust was rare in Allegheny County in his day when wealth was mostly in things, not money.

The idea of trust estates was not new, of course; the origin of them is lost in antiquity. An Egyptian potentate made one back in 2548 B.C., designating his wife as trustee for her children and appointing a guardian for his son. That document is preserved in the British Library, London. And even in the seventeenth century, east of the mountains in the older colonies, American colleges, like the ancient English universities, were receiving endowments in trust funds.

There always have been men farsighted enough to try to leave money for future good. Often their concern has been limited to the welfare of their immediate families. But as time has passed and wealth has come to be looked upon as a public trust, the scope and vision of the testators has widened to include the community and eventually the nation in which the wealth was accumulated. The great foundations created in recent years are an outgrowth and extension of this human impulse to continue and extend an estate, gathered carefully and wisely, for the good of greater numbers of people.

❖ ❖ ❖ ❖ ❖ ❖ ❖

These wills cover a period of nearly half a century, from the earliest struggles on the edge of civilization in the eighteenth cen-

204

tury, to the 1830's in a town abustle with business and cultural opportunities. They show the steady march of homes and churches and businesses from the triangle eastward over the hills through Soho, Lawrenceville, Oakland, Shadyside, and East Liberty. Their bequests made possible the social, industrial, and religious life which steadily and persistently wove itself into one of the greatest cities on the continent or in the world.

In these wills we read the Pittsburgh story—trade, beginning in the log fortress at the forks of the rivers, pushing ever westward over mountains and prairies American homes and churches and schools; homespun ideas and ideals; laws and folkways—honesty, common sense, thrift, friendliness, endurance, imagination, high adventure. These wills are strong men's bequests, expressing the material and spiritual security possible only in a land which is free and brave.

Postscript

In proportion to its size Pittsburgh is the busiest and the wealthiest city in the world. Through the development of steel, glass, and aluminum it is established firmly in commerce and industry. Natural resources and excellent transportation facilities give it leadership in the major industries of western civilization. It is in the front rank of scientific research, for which it has the finest laboratories available. Its life has produced men of distinction. Their great fortunes, through foundations, bequests, and gifts, have dowered schools and churches and hospitals and made the city beautiful. The extent of accomplishments for Pittsburgh is unlimited. The future looks bright.

It is good to look back to get a better understanding of the pioneer past, our proud heritage, for we should face our problems as courageously as the early Allegheny settlers faced theirs. All around us—in the great hospitals, clinics, churches, schools, orphanages, and the various institutions and foundations for the betterment of our citizens—we recognize contributions to the welfare of Pittsburgh and Allegheny County which had their origin in bequests mentioned in the oldest wills. James O'Hara and Devereux Smith began our long tradition of business enterprise. The land on which we have built our most lasting monuments is land they and their heirs bequeathed and donated or sold.

It is good to know that in a world of rapid change and variation, there is a core of stability and security. And that stability,

207

that security—even in the confusion today—can be ours if we keep faith with the past. Such assurance has been confirmed for me by this study of our Allegheny County wills. My certainty grew as I came to know the certainty and faith of the will-makers through their wills.

These wills are our heritage — the hopes they outline, the qualities of independence, thrift, and generosity they witness. Upon the humble acceptance of the responsibilities our forebears have bequeathed, with the opportunity we have of enhancing the values they held, before we, in turn, hand them down to those who will succeed us, rests our anchorage in living. Our alliance with the past becomes our allegiance to the future.

ELLA CHALFANT

Bibliography

BOOKS

ANDREWS, J. CUTLER—*Pittsburgh's Post-Gazette*, "The First Newspaper West of the Alleghanies." Boston, Chapman & Grimes, 1936.

Apocrypha, The Books Called, according to Authorised Version. London, Oxford University Press.

BANCROFT, GEORGE—*History of the United States*, Centenary ed., v.3. Boston, Little, Brown and Company, 1876-79.

BOUCHER, JOHN NEWTON—*A Century and a Half of Pittsburgh and her People.;* genealogical memoirs of the leading families of Pittsburgh and vicinity, compiled under the editorial supervision of John W. Jordan, LL.D., vols. 3-4. New York. The Lewis Publishing Company, 1908

BUCK, SOLON J., AND BUCK, ELIZABETH HAWTHORN—*The Planting of Civilization in Western Pennsylvania.* Pittsburgh, University of Pittsburgh Press, 1939.

CORRELL, H. W.—*Pioneer Pittsburgh Concerns;* thumbnail sketches of some of the city's old organizations. Pittsburgh, Chamber of Commerce, 1929. (Reprinted from *Greater Pittsburgh*, October 12, 1929.)

DAVIS, THOMAS D., M.D.—*Pioneer Physicians of Western Pennsylvania;* the president's address of the Medical Society of the State of Pennsylvania, delivered at Philadelphia, September 24, 1901. (Reprinted from the *Pennsylvania Medical Journal*, October, 1901.)

DILLER, THEODORE, M.D.—*Pioneer Medicine in Western Pennsylvania.* New York, P. B. Hoeber, Inc., 1927.

EARLE, ALICE MORSE—*Two Centuries of Costume in America*, 2 vols. New York, The Macmillan Company, 1903.

EGGLESTON, EDWARD—*A History of the United States and Its People;* for use of schools. New York, D. Appleton & Co., 1899.

FLEMING, GEORGE T.—*Fleming's Views of Old Pittsburgh;* a portfolio of the past. Pittsburgh, The Crescent Press, 1932.

FORT PITT SOCIETY, D.A.R., EDITOR—*Fort Duquesne and Fort Pitt;* early names of Pittsburgh streets, 11th ed. Pittsburgh, Reed and Witting Company, 1946.

HEITMAN, F. B.—*Historical Register of the Officers of the Continental Army During the War of the Revolution; April, 1775, to December, 1783.* Washington, D. C., The National Tribune, 1890.

HERRICK, CHEESMAN ABIAH—*White Servitude in Pennsylvania;* indentured and redemptive labor in colony and commonwealth. Philadelphia, J. J. McVay, 1926.

HOLME, CONSTANCE—*The Wisdom of the Simple.* London, Oxford University Press, 1937.

HUNTER, DARD—*Papermaking through Eighteen Centuries.* New York, William Edwin Rudge, 1930.

JORDAN, JOHN W.—*Colonial and Revolutionary Families of Pennsylvania,* v.2. New York, The Lewis Historical Publishing Company, 1911.

—*Encyclopedia of Pennsylvania Biography,* v.1. New York, The Lewis Historical Publishing Company, 1914.

—*Genealogical and Personal History of the Allegheny Valley, Pa.,* 3 vols. New York, The Lewis Historical Publishing Co., 1913.

—*Genealogical and Personal History of Western Pennsylvania,* 3 vols. New York, The Lewis Historical Publishing Co., 1915.

Laws of the Commonwealth of Pennsylvania; from the fourteenth day of October, one thousand seven hundred, to the twentieth day of March, one thousand eight hundred and ten. Republished, under the authority of the Legislature, in four volumes. Philadelphia, John Bioren, 88 Chestnut Street, 1810.

LINN, JOHN B., and EGLE, WM. H., M.D., EDITORS—*Pennsylvania Archives;* second series, v.3. Harrisburg, B. F. Meyers, State Printer, 1875.

MAIN, SIR HENRY SUMNER, K.C.S.—*Ancient Law;* its connection with the early history of society and its relation to modern ideas, 10th ed. London, John Murray, Albemarle Street, 1885.

MOORHEAD, ELIZABETH—*Whirling Spindle;* the story of a Pittsburgh family. Pittsburgh, University of Pittsburgh Press, 1942.

MULKEARN, LOIS, AND PUGH, EDWIN V.—*A Traveler's Guide to Historic Western Pennsylvania.* Pittsburgh, University of Pittsburgh Press, 1954.

New Funk & Wagnalls Encyclopedia. New York, Unicorn Publishers, Inc., 1949-50.

OSGOOD, HERBERT L., Ph.D.—*American Colonies in the Seventeenth Century,* v.2. New York, Columbia University Press, 1904-07.

SCOTT, EBEN GREENOUGH—*Commentaries upon the Intestate System of Pennsylvania and the Powers of Jurisdiction of the Orphans' Court,* 2nd ed. Philadelphia, Kay and Brothers, 1887.

SPRAGUE, WILLIAM B., D.D.—*Annals of the American Pulpit;* or commemorative notices of distinguished American clergymen of various denominations from the early settlement of the country to the close of the year 1855, with an historical introduction, v.3. New York, Robert Carter and Brothers, 1869.

STARRETT, AGNES L.—*Through One Hundred Fifty Years.* University of Pittsburgh Press, 1937.

STEWART, GEORGE R.—*Names on the Land;* an historical account of place-making in the United States. New York, Random House, 1945.

U.S. Congress, American State Papers, Naval Affairs, v.1, pp. 294-8. Washington, Gales and Seaton, 1834.

WARNER, A.—*History of Allegheny County, Pennsylvania;* including its early settlement and progress, to the present day; a description of historical and interesting localities; its cities, towns and villages; religious, educational, social and military history. Chicago, A. Warner & Co., 1889.

WARWICK, EDWARD, AND PITZ, HENRY C.—*Early American Costume;* with illustrations by the authors. New York, Century Company, 1929.

WHITE, EDWARD—*A Century of Banking in Pittsburgh;* commemorating the one hundredth anniversary of the organization of the first bank west of the Allegheny Mountains. Pittsburgh, Bulletin Index Co., 1903.

WILSON, ERASMUS—*History of Pittsburg, Pennsylvania;* illustrated. Chicago, H. R. Cornell and Company, 1898.

MAGAZINES

BENNETT, ARCHIBALD.—"Rigdon Family History," *Utah Genealogical and Historical Magazine,* v.27, 1936.

DANIEL, WARREN J.—"George Washington: Real Estate Man," *Greater Pittsburgh,* December, 1942.

HISTORICAL SOCIETY OF WESTERN PENNSYLVANIA—*Western Pennsylvania Historical Magazine,* vols. 1-20. 1918-1937.

NEWSPAPERS

Commonwealth, vols. 1-17, 1805-1822.

Daily Pittsburgh Gazette, v. 4, 1837.

Mercury, vols. 1-14, 1812-1826.

Penn Progress, centenniel ed., August 23, 1951.

Pittsburgh Gazette, vols. 1-35, 1786-1820.

Pittsburgh Post, November 6, 1903.

Pittsburgh Post-Gazette, sesquicentennial ed., September 26, 1936.
—165th anniversary ed., August 1, 1951.

Pittsburgh Post-Gazette, PITTSBURGH—Maurice P. Sullivan, Real Estate Editor, Dec. 17, 1951.

Pittsburgh Sun-Telegraph, centennial ed., September 15, 1941.

Tree of Liberty, vols. 1-4, 1800-1804.

JOURNALS

BAYNTON, WHARTON AND MORGAN—*Fort Pitt Day Book;* 1765-1767, with a few entries for 1772. (An account book of Baynton, Wharton and Morgan.)

SMITH, DEVEREUX, AND DOUGLASS, EPHRAIM—*Ledger A, from September 1771 to January 1777, including dealings at Kittanning, &c, &c.*

—*Joseph Douglass' Book, Kept at Pittsburgh in January 1777 after Ephraim Douglass had gone off with the 8th Penn'a Regmt. from Kittanning to join the Revolutionary Army.*

RECORDS

Register's Office, Pittsburgh—*Allegheny County Will Books*, vols. 1-100.

.... *Allegheny County Wills*, originals.

.... *Allegheny County Bond Book*, v. 1.

.... *Allegheny County Proceedings Index*, v. 30, 1854-1855.

.... *Record of Inventory and Appraisement, Allegheny County*, v. 1.

Trinity Cathedral, Pittsburgh—*Verger's records of graves and markers.*

Trinity Churchyard, Pittsburgh—*Monuments and gravestones.*

LETTERS

Brady Publishing Co., Washington, D.C.—William Y. Brady, July 11, 1951.

Genealogical Society of the Church of Jesus Christ of Latter Day Saints, Salt Lake City—Frances Baker, Sec. to L. Garrett Myers, Supt.

The Purse Company, Chattanooga—Spencer Clinton, V.P., Oct. 3, 1951.

The Purse Company, Chicago—Albert Journeay, V.P., Oct. 3, 1951.

Laws of the Commonwealth of Pennsylvania, v.1, p.492-3
Published by John Bioren, Philadelphia, 1810
Chapter 870 (DCCCLXX)

An Act for the Gradual Abolition of Slavery

WHEN we contemplate our abhorrence of that condition, to which the arms and tyranny of Great-Britain were exerted to reduce us, when we look back on the variety of dangers to which we have been exposed, and how miraculously our wants in many instances have been supplied, and our deliverances wrought, when even hope and human fortitude have become unequal to the conflict, we are unavoidably led to a serious and grateful sense of the manifold blessings, which we have undeservedly received from the hand of that Being, from whom every good and perfect gift cometh. Impressed with these ideas, we conceive that it is our duty, and we rejoice that it is in our power, to extend a portion of that freedom to others, which hath been extended to us, and release from that state of thraldom, to which we ourselves were tyrannically doomed, and from which we have now every prospect of being delivered. It is not for us to enquire why in the creation of mankind, the inhabitants of the several parts of the earth were distinguished by a difference in feature or complexion. It is sufficient to know, that all are the work of an Almighty hand. We find, in the distribution of the human species, that the most fertile as well as the most barren parts of the earth are inhabited by men of complexions different from ours, and from each other; from whence we may reasonably, as well as religiously, infer, that He, who placed them in their various situations, hath extended equally his care and protection to all, and that it becometh not us to counteract his mercies. We esteem it a peculiar blessing granted to us, that we are enabled this day to add one more step to universal civilization, by removing, as much as possible, the sorrows of those, who have lived in undeserved bondage, and from which, by the assumed authority of the Kings of Great-Britain, no effectual, legal relief could be obtained. Weaned, by a long course of experience, from those narrow prejudices and partialities we had imbibed, we find our hearts enlarged with kindness and benevolence towards men of all conditions and nations; and we conceive ourselves at this particular period extraordinarily called upon, by the blessings which we have received, to manifest the sincerity of our profession, and to give a substantial proof of our gratitude.

APPENDIX B

How to Look Up a Will

The files in the Office of the Register of Wills, in the City-County Building on Grant Street between Fourth Avenue and Diamond Street, are open to anyone who wants to look up a will. Attendants are on hand to help those who are not familiar with the procedure. On almost any weekday morning the tables next to the stacks of will books are crowded with attorneys and stenographers. Occasionally someone interested in the older documents will make his way among the busy crowd to the balcony, where the early will books are kept. Numbered 1 to 159 inclusively, these are just a fraction of the total number. They are on open rod metal shelves—big canvas-covered volumes, plainly numbered and indexed. Here and there the new white canvas of a rebound volume stands out starkly against the old, dusty volumes. And upon opening one of these early books and seeing the faded, brown paper and the homely, hand-written phrases, who can resist the temptation to tarry a while and turn the pages of a distant age.

While it is interesting to read the accounts of men's lives from the wills copied into these bound volumes, it is even more stimulating to examine some of the original documents. These are kept in metal files in the basement, which is as large as the entire first floor of the Register's Office. About twenty wills are kept in each of the boxes, which are arranged in tiers along the walls from floor to ceiling. To obtain an original will for examination, all one has to do is fill out a card provided for the purpose. It requires the name of the testator, the volume and page number of the will book in which his will was registered, and the year of his death. If only the will is wanted, check the words "Register's Folder"; if other papers in the estate are desired, check "Orphans' Court Folder."

For a complete key to all the wills and Orphans Court proceedings, one should consult the *Russell Index*, reproduced on the opposite page through the courtesy of the Russell Index Company. This ingenious key, based on the consonants *l-m-n-r-t* in the name being investigated, will guide one to the proper Dockets in the Register's Office, where it is an easy matter to trace the name to the will book or Orphans Court proceedings.

TO LOCATE NAMES IN THE INDEX

Determine the first and second Key-letters after the initial letter in the Surname. In the column headed by the Given Name initial of the name for which you are searching, and opposite the Key-letters contained in the Surname, the number of the section is designated where the name will be found. Duplications of the same Key-letter are disregarded. Surnames, not containing a Key-letter, are found in the sections designated by the numbers opposite "Misc." All names other than those of individuals are found in the sections designated by the numbers in the column headed "Corps., Etc.", and opposite the Key-letters contained in the first word of the name, disregarding the article "The."

LETTERS KEY.	GIVEN NAME INITIALS AND SECTION NUMBERS																		LETTERS KEY.
	A	B	C	D	E	F	G	HI	J	KL	M	NO	PQ	R	S	TUV	W X Y Z	Corps. Etc.	
L	110	210	310	410	510	610	710	810	910	1010	1110	1210	1310	1410	1510	1610	1710	1810	L
LM	110	210	310	410	510	610	710	810	910	1010	1110	1210	1310	1410	1510	1610	1710	1810	LM
LN	110	210	310	410	510	610	710	810	910	1010	1110	1210	1310	1410	1510	1610	1710	1810	LN
LR	110	210	310	410	510	610	710	810	910	1010	1110	1210	1310	1410	1510	1610	1710	1810	LR
LT	110	210	310	410	510	610	710	810	910	1010	1110	1210	1310	1410	1510	1610	1710	1810	LT
M	120	220	320	420	520	620	720	820	920	1020	1120	1220	1320	1420	1520	1620	1720	1820	M
ML	120	220	320	420	520	620	720	820	920	1020	1120	1220	1320	1420	1520	1620	1720	1820	ML
MN	120	220	320	420	520	620	720	820	920	1020	1120	1220	1320	1420	1520	1620	1720	1820	MN
MR	120	220	320	420	520	620	720	820	920	1020	1120	1220	1320	1420	1520	1620	1720	1820	MR
MT	120	220	320	420	520	620	720	820	920	1020	1120	1220	1320	1420	1520	1620	1720	1820	MT
N	130	230	330	430	530	630	730	830	930	1030	1130	1230	1330	1430	1530	1630	1730	1830	N
NL	130	230	330	430	530	630	730	830	930	1030	1130	1230	1330	1430	1530	1630	1730	1830	NL
NM	130	230	330	430	530	630	730	830	930	1030	1130	1230	1330	1430	1530	1630	1730	1830	NM
NR	130	230	330	430	530	630	730	830	930	1030	1130	1230	1330	1430	1530	1630	1730	1830	NR
NT	130	230	330	430	530	630	730	830	930	1030	1130	1230	1330	1430	1530	1630	1730	1830	NT
R	140	240	340	440	540	640	740	840	940	1040	1140	1240	1340	1440	1540	1640	1740	1840	R
RL	140	240	340	440	540	640	740	840	940	1040	1140	1240	1340	1440	1540	1640	1740	1840	RL
RM	140	240	340	440	540	640	740	840	940	1040	1140	1240	1340	1440	1540	1640	1740	1840	RM
RN	140	240	340	440	540	640	740	840	940	1040	1140	1240	1340	1440	1540	1640	1740	1840	RN
RT	140	240	340	440	540	640	740	840	940	1040	1140	1240	1340	1440	1540	1640	1740	1840	RT
T	150	250	350	450	550	650	750	850	950	1050	1150	1250	1350	1450	1550	1650	1750	1850	T
TL	150	250	350	450	550	650	750	850	950	1050	1150	1250	1350	1450	1550	1650	1750	1850	TL
TM	150	250	350	450	550	650	750	850	950	1050	1150	1250	1350	1450	1550	1650	1750	1850	TM
TN	150	250	350	450	550	650	750	850	950	1050	1150	1250	1350	1450	1550	1650	1750	1850	TN
TR	150	250	350	450	550	650	750	850	950	1050	1150	1250	1350	1450	1550	1650	1750	1850	TR
Misc.	160	260	360	460	560	660	760	860	960	1060	1160	1260	1360	1460	1560	1660	1760	1860	Misc.
	A	B	C	D	E	F	G	HI	J	KL	M	NO	PQ	R	S	TUV	W X Y Z	Corps. Etc.	

RUSSELL INDEX COMPANY, PITTSBURGH, PA.

Index of Names in the First Three Will Books of Allegheny County

WILL BOOK I

McKnight, William, 165
McLeod, Daniel, 105
McMasters, John, 195
McMichael, James, 56
McMullen, William, 61
McQuiston, John, 167
McRoberts, Hannah, 334
Meirs, Eliezer, 28
Menown, Richard, 336
Metzger, John, 118
Milck, Jacob, 171
Millegan, James, 277
Miller, Gabien, 39
Miller, Jacob, 214
Miller, James, 101
Miller, Robert, 317
Mitchel, Ebenezer, 58
Moirs, James, 282
Montgomery, Robert, 4
Moore, James, 93
Moore, Josiah, 77
Moore, William, 44
Morgan, Charles, 241
Morgan, John, 117
Morrison, Norris, 95
Moyer, George, 349
Murry, John, 305
Neely, Thomas, 354
Neill, Robert, 189
Nevill, John, 178
Nicholass, Joseph, 100
Nisbet, Francis, 177
O'Hara, William, 307
Ormsby, Joseph B., 199
Patterson, Adam, 184
Patterson, Joseph, 153
Patterson, Nathaniel, 84
Pearce, John, 229
Pedin, John, 247
Peirce, Jonathan, 162
Philips, Samuel, 156
Pierce, Joseph, 232
Plumer, Thomas, 315
Porter, William, 258
Ramsey, Anthony, 320
Ramsey, James, 97
Rardon, John, 94
Reddick, William, 315
Reed, James, 90
Reed, James, 130

Richards, Charles, 132
Richardson, Andrew, 288
Richardson, Mary, 225
Rigdon, William, 300
Rippy, Hugh, 33
Ritchey, Jacob, 303
Roach, Richard, 43
Robb, John N., 188
Robertson, John, 271
Robertson, Samuel, 96
Robison, Isaac, 337
Robison, David, 246
Roe, Joseph, 92
Rook, John, 42
Roseburgh, Samuel, 283
Roush, Sebastian, 37
Rowleter, Peter, 136
Rutherford, James, 176
Ryan, James, 350
Sailor, Peter, 102
Sallers, Isaac, 31
Sample, Agnes, 266
Sample, Robert, 265
Sample, Samuel, 263
Sampson, Thomas, 80
Scott, Hugh, 190
Scott, William, 348
Seatin, Thomas, 328
Sheets, Casper, 183
Shoemaker, Bartholomew, 68
Shreader, John, 33
Sloan, John, 166
Smith, Devereux, 134
Smith, Frederick, 25
Smith, Robert, 107
Smith, Robert, 331
South, Daniel, 322
Sparks, Benjamin, 356
Speirs, James, 19
Steel, Thomas, 45
Stevenson, John, 341
Stewart, Marey, 110
Storer, Thomas, 201
Stover, Elizabeth, 359
Stover, Thomas, 358
Strain, Michael, 8
Strawbridge, David, 71
Strochan, George, 194
Stuck, John, 173
Swaney, Thomas, 148

219

WILL BOOK II

Cunningham, Nicholas, 302
Cunningham, Robert, 13
Cuthbertson, Ralph, 276
Darragh, Neal, 330
Davidson, John, 80
Deal, Catherine, 31
Deal, John, 243
Denny, Ebenezer, 281
Dixon, George, 123
Dougherty, James, 164
Duivetter, John, 238
Duncan, Andrew, 212
Eastman, Samuel, 86
Eckles, Andrew, 234
Edwards, David, 141
Edwards, Thomas, 160
Elliott, Barbara, 65
Elliott, Eleanor, 186
Elliott, James, 67
Erwin, Joseph, 306
Ewing, Samuel, 298
Felgentreff, Frederick, 66
Ferguson, Samuel, 228
Ferree, Joel, 9
Fife, John, 50
Fink, Mary, 256
Finney, William, 104
Forsyth, John, 12
Frazier, John, 300
Frew, John, 41
Gilland, Mary, 46
Glenn, James, 2
Graham, Robert, 223
Gray, Thomas, 129
Guy, James, 210
Guy, William, 56
Guyton, Abraham, 95
Hall, John, 114
Hall, Robert, 35
Hall, William, 157
Hamilton, Jesse, 130
Hanna, John, 74
Hannah, John, 291
Harper, John, 250
Harrah, Margaret, 152
Harriott, Ephraim, 125
Harris, Joseph, 167
Hays, Francis, 131
Henning, James, 201
Hiland, Martha, 122

Hooper, Philip, 169
Howell, Lewellen, 328
Huey, Henry, 285
Huey, Samuel, 61
Hughey, Ephraim, 20
Hugoe, Edward, 290
Hutchinson, Joseph, 314
Irish, Nathaniel, 93
Johnston, Robert, 253
Jones, Rachel, 337
Jones, Samuel, 216
Kearns, James, 159
Kees, Philip, 66
Kelly, John, 40
Kennedy, Hugh, 32
Kennedy, William, 287
Kidoo, James, 335
Kimmel, George, 139
Kuykendall, James, 173
Larimer, Samuel, 202
Latta, Deborah, 116
Laughlin, James, 27
Leightenberger, George, 28
Linhart, Michael, 149
Long, William, 118
Loughead, William, 163
Lowderback, Maria, 305
Lowrey, Stephen, 265
Luckey, Joseph, 275
Lyle, Charles, 197
Mackey, William, 297
Magee, Robert, 304
Mahon, James, 70
Mallarson, Thomas, 22
Martin, Richard, 119
Mates, Casper, 272
Mates, John, 241
McCandless, Alexander, 102
McCartney, William, 19
McClelland, John, 14
McCloud, John, 136
McClure, James, 90
McClure, William, 69
McCoy, William, 206
McCullough, Jane, 226
McCullough, William, 73
McCullough, William, 77
McCully, Elizabeth, 60
McCurdy, Alexander, 184
McDivett, Eleanor, 204

WILL BOOK III

McFarlane, Andrew, 386
McFarlane, Magdalene, 342
McFarren, John, 448
McFerron, Nancy, 526
McGee, Mary, 293
McGee, Patrick, 334
McGowen, Samuel, 132
McGregor, Matthew, 488
McHenry, Daniel, 432
McKindley, William, 313
McLaughlen, William, 5
McLaughlin, Edward, 127
McMath, Daniel, 39
McMillin, Mary, 565
McMillin, Thomas, 537
McMun, Alexander, 309
McVicker, William, 213
Meason, John, 509
Meek, John, 178
Megery, Elizabeth, 606
Menoun, John, 457
Menoun, Richard, 22
Merriman, Richard, 564
Miller, Alexander, 477
Miller, Ezekiel, 244
Miller, John, 59
Miller, Robert, 292
Milligan, Ann, 208
Morrow, James, 157
Morrow, Robert, 53
Morton, John, 37
Mullen, William, 204
Murdock, Robert, 589
Murphy, Mary, 115
Murry, David, 321
Neal, Thomas, 349
Neelly, Samuel, 318
Negley, Jacob, Jr., 399
Nelson, Ezra G., 533
Nelson, Matthew, 507
Nelson, William, 439
Newlon, Nathan, 470
Nickel, Timpy, 403
Nickols, Samuel, 378
Nilson, Mathew, 160
O'Brien, James J., 341
O'Connor, Dominick, 494
O'Hara, James, 623
Oliver, Margaret, 95
Patterson, John, 32
Patterson, Joseph, 577

Payne, Joseph, 582
Pearson, Mehatable, 135
Phillips, John, 536
Phillips, Jonathan, 427
Pollock, Robert, 358
Potter, Henry, 22
Pride, Mary, 569
Quick, Moses, 182
Reed, David, 401
Reed, Henry, 518
Reed, Rachel, 124
Reigar, Catherine, 486
Richey, James, 531
Riddell, John, 367
Robinson, Joshua, 529
Rollins, Anthony, 297
Russell, John, 501
Ryley, Barnard, 228
Sample, James, 467
Schade, Charles Henry, 548
Scot, James, 65
Scott, Hance, 144
Scott, Samuel, 373
Seeten, Thomas, 276
Semple, William, 329
Sheldon, John Scott, 235
Shick, Jacob, 24
Shiras, Peter, 108
Short, John, 52
Shrater, William, 273
Shrum, Jacob, 481
Sibbit, James, 361
Silvester, Hugh, 3
Simpson, Robert, 496
Sinclair, Samuel, 450
Smith, John, 187
Smith, Robert, 504
South, Daniel, 242
Steele, Isabella, 482
Stevenson, George, 614
Stevenson, James S., 550
Stewart, Andrew, 415
Stewart, James, 151
Stewart, John, 86
Stonesipher, John, 290
Strackan, Nancy, 247
Sturgeon, Robert, 541
Sullivan, Aaron, 453
Summerville, James, 306
Sutton, William, 411
Swearingen, Nicholas D., 106

Index

Selden, Edward, 90
Semple's, Samuel (Kitchen), 186
Seneca Indians, 7
Sergeant, Thomas, Esq., 56
Shadyside, 205
Shannon, P. C., 21
Share, James, 38
Shaw, Alexander, 142
Shaw, Janet, 192
Shaw, John, 26
Shawnee Indians, 61
Sheets, Casper, 133
Sheriff, John, 46
Shields, Alexander, 194
"Sign of the Buck," 128
"Sign of the Waggon," 131
Simmison, Parker, 177
Simon and Campbell, 103, 203
Simpson, Catherine, 151-152
Simpson, Sarah, 151
Sisters of Mercy, 143
Slavery, 92-105
Small, Margarette, 182
Smallman, Thomas, 202
Smith, Devereux, 164, 180-181, 183-185, 207
Smith & Douglass, 41
Smith, Edward, 181-182
Smith, Elizabeth, 181-183
Smith, Frederick, 167
Smith, Joseph, Prophet, 51
Smith, Peter, 99
Smithfield Street, 184
Smithfield Street Evangelical Protestant, 119
Smittens, Mary, 28-29
Snowden, Isaac, Esq., 114
Snowden, John M., 93
Soho, 205
Soldiers' Bonuses, 167
Speakman, Townsend, 56
Speirs, James, 124, 156
"Springfield", 202
Sprouse, William, 21
St. Clair, Arthur General, 155
St. Clair Street, 64

St. Clair Township, 202
Steele, Robt., 82
Steele, Thos., 21
Sterling, Hugh, 139
Steubenville Gazette, 93
Stevenson, Geo., 194
Stewart, Elizabeth, 33
Stewart, James, 160
Stewart, Jennat, 139
Stewart, Mrs. John, 142
Stewart, John, 106, 141-142
Stewart, Jordan, 160
Stewart, L., 40
Stewart, Marey, 141, 156
Stewart, Mary, 34, 141, 160
Stewart, Nancy, 34, 160
Stewart, Samuel, 160
Stewart, Thomas, 80
Stewart, Will, 141, 156
Stewart, William, 160
Stills, 160
Story of Pittsburgh, 170
Straight Coat, 162
Strawbridge, Ann, 122
Strawbridge, David, 120-121
Strawbridge, Jean, 122
Strochan, George, 25, 26
Supreme Council, 165
Susquehanna Division of the Pennsylvania Canal, 107
Swazey, Mary, 20

Tael of China, 157
Tannehill, Margaret, 179
Tannehill, Adamson, 11, 86-88
Tannehill, Agness M., 87
Tarascon Brothers, James Berthoud Company, 97
Taylor, 105
Taylor, John, 65, 82
Taylor, Archibald, 82
Tettrington, Adam, 105
Tettrington, John, 105
Tettrington, Joseph, 105
Tettrington, Matthew, 105

This book was composed in linotype Caledonian text with Ludlow Bodoni modern heads and printed on 60 lb. White Warren's Olde Style by the Herbick and Held Printing Company of Pittsburgh, Pennsylvania. Russell Rutter Company, Inc., New York, bound the book in Novelex cloth.

DATE DUE

GAYLORD   PRINTED IN U.S.A.